ORNAMENT OF
SHERWOOD FOREST

For Dorothy
With best wishes
John Fletcher
January 2006

THIS BOOK IS DEDICATED TO SANDRA,
MY BELOVED WIFE AND BEST FRIEND

ORNAMENT OF SHERWOOD FOREST

FROM DUCAL ESTATE
TO PUBLIC PARK

JOHN FLETCHER

Published by:
Country Books
Courtyard Cottage, Little Longstone, Bakewell, Derbyshire DE45 1NN

ISBN 1 898941 95 5

By the same author:
WHERE TRUTH ABIDES:
THE DIARIES OF THE 4TH DUKE OF NEWCASTLE-UNDER-LYME (1822-1850)

Printed and bound in England by:
Antony Rowe Ltd, Chippenham, Wiltshire

CONTENTS

INTRODUCTION   Pages   i - ii
BACKGROUND   Pages   iii - v
NEWCASTLE FAMILY CENTRAL TO THIS STORY   Page   vi
LIST OF ILLUSTRATIONS   Pages   viii - x
MAPS   Pages   xi - xii

***

CHAPTER ONE – 1878 to 1880   Pages   1 - 22
A new forester arrives – The absentee duke and his problems – The forester settles in for a long haul – Death of the 6th Duke – Fire at Clumber House – The 'Little' duke – The forester consolidates his position – Rebuilding a mansion and a reputation.

CHAPTER TWO – 1881 to 1887   Pages 23 - 37
It was not all work – The new duke made his second visit – The heir to the throne called – Clumber's new atrium opened for worship – Miscellaneous happenings – The duke came of age – Something in the air – A Proper Party – The New Chapel – Outings, champagne and a Golden Jubilee – More financial matters.

CHAPTER THREE – 1888 to 1898   Pages 38 - 81
Rumour, romance and roving – Improvements in the Park – Clumber's new school – 'Convert', Pervert or neither? – Still on duty with the forester – Marriage of youngest duke and duchess in England – Clumber Chapel (completed and dedicated) – Clumber's Cedar Avenue and rhododendrons – The duchess 'cared about doggies' – 'The open road, the dusty highway' – Financial matters – More public visits to Clumber Park – Grand Ball in Clumber's Hall – Paternal care – Rudolph Schmidt – Clumber cricket – Royal visitors – Our guide's activities and other happenings – Lord Francis Hope (heir to the dukedom) – St Cuthbert's College, Worksop – A new chaplain-in-waiting – More about the duke – A new hymnal, a marriage and a Diamond Jubilee.

CHAPTER FOUR – 1898 to 1907   Pages 82 - 114
Clumber's finest hours? – 'Economies, economies, economies' – A dead statesman and lively royalty – The nineteenth century closes – Motor cars arrive in Clumber Park – The forester was still travelling – Clumber Shows – Fire at neighbouring Welbeck – Queen Victoria died – Life goes on for the estate workers – Lord Francis v the Hope diamond – Duke robbed by his lawyer – Routine, yet changing times – A new Post Office – Joel Haslam takes ill-health retirement – Royalty motor in Clumber – Estate staffing – Electricity introduced – The duchess was not amused – The daily round – A loss and some gains for the Pelham-Clintons.

CHAPTER FIVE – 1908 to 1918   Pages 115 - 160

A Liberal Budget & other irritants – Minerals, Cars & Investments – The Gardeners & the Inland Revenue Inspector – Clumber's 'Normanton Gates' – The Alcock Family – National publicity for Clumber's glories – The Forester's Activities – Demands of Royalty – Clumber Troop of Sherwood Rangers – Leased & Tied Cottages – Leisure Pursuits – A Funeral & a Wedding – Coronation 1911 – Estate events and family matters – National Insurance – The fire of 1912 – Terrace Ornaments – The London and Fort George Land Company Ltd. – Village School – Duke's Clumber Choir School – The Dowager Duchess died – Army Training in Clumber Park – Garden Parties – Silver Wedding celebrations – Royals visit Nottinghamshire again – The realities of War – Belgiums, Canadians and Others arrive – Yet more Financial Adjustments – Wartime effects on Schooling at Clumber – There was always the Timber – The duke's and duchess's London interests – Our first Guide retires.

CHAPTER SIX – 1919 to 1928   Pages 161 - 180

Several new Guides – The aftermath of War – Comings, Goings and Pensions – Financial Matters - Home Farm – Duke and Duchess – More changes in School arrangements – Sales and Other Money matters – London and Fort George Land Company – The Duke's Last Will and Testament – The death of the 7th Duke.

CHAPTER SEVEN – 1929 to 1936   Pages 181 - 202

The 8th Duke of Newcastle – Probate – '... the Park will have to be broken up' – 'Utmost Economy' – Chapel, Choir School & Worksop College – Lord Lincoln & his sisters – An American influence – More leisure activities in the Park – Well-foundered rumours & a new interest – Clumber Chapel, a casualty of the mid-1930's – Some miscellaneous happenings – Moving towards the final decades as a ducal estate..

CHAPTER EIGHT – 1937 to 1946   Pages 203 - 240

A smaller Clumber House to be built? – Coronation 1937 – Clumber Sales – The 'Chantry' – Preparations for War – Clumber House came tumbling down – Lord Lincoln's Tenancy Agreement – Plans for a new sawmill and workshops – The sale of the Nottingham Park estate – War declared, access to Clumber Park restricted – The arrival of the Military – 'Colonel Warden' meets 'Nellie' – Lord Lincoln became the last Duke to live at Clumber – Clumber residents join the war effort – A few of the duke's exploits – Clumber Park saw action from the air – The Crucial Decision.

CHAPTER NINE – POSTSCRIPT   Pages 241 - 252

The Dukedom headed towards extinction – A New Life: Clumber Park's Third Creation – Clumber Chapel – Army Out, Public In – Clumber Gardens – Clumber's Stableyard and other buildings – Goodbye to the 'Lincoln' frigate – The first of two Duchesses returned to Clumber – A duke (and later a duchess) revisited.

APPENDIX ONE	- CLUMBER SPANIELS	Pages 254 - 255
APPENDIX TWO	- 7TH DUKE'S WAR SPEECH	Pages 256 - 257
APPENDIX THREE	- 'NELLIE', THE EVACUATING MACHINE	Pages 258 - 259
APPENDIX FOUR	- NEWCASTLE TENANTS [1885]- FAMILY NAMES	Page 260
ACKNOWLEDGEMENTS & BIBLIOGRAPHY		Pages 261 - 262
INDEXING		Pages 263 - 270

> 'Rode over Thoresby yesterday ... Clumber is full as capable of as many bounties at the least, the park in general I should think is as good, if not better, and plantations would thrive to be just equally as well. The River might be made anything of, and the variety of the Hills and Vales are much more considerable and bolder, – indeed greater variety of Ground can not be seen any where.'
>
> Henry Fiennes Clinton, 9th Earl of Lincoln, 27th September 1760

INTRODUCTION

THIS IS THE TALE OF THE FINAL DECADES of a ducal estate, mainly based in the Sherwood Forest county of Nottinghamshire. The decision to write the story was prompted by a keen desire to pass on the results of many years of research. Numerous enquirers who have attended the illustrated talks I have presented on behalf of The National Trust also encouraged it. But – there is a certain complication in this matter.

Various titles and content of my presentations have been based on the 'History of Clumber Park and the Dukes of Newcastle' theme. What was only a slight problem in the early days of those public offerings has subsequently grown into a major dilemma as my understanding of the magnitude of available research material has grown. There is undoubtedly too much of it to offer in any one presentation, or indeed, in any digestible size of narrative.

The 'Newcastle Manuscripts' that are held at the University of Nottingham and the British Library, also as part of the Glynn-Gladstone papers at St. Deiniol's Library in Harwarden, constitute a monster of an archive. There is much supplementary information in other repositories. The core period covered is roughly between 1700 and 1946, the latter year being when Clumber Park was sold to The National Trust.

Better, perhaps, to present the material in 'bite-size' batches? My first offering: "*Where Truth Abides, Diaries of the 4th Duke of Newcastle-under-Lyme 1822 to 1850*" was published in 2001. The central and significant position that generation of the Newcastle dynasty held in the overall tale, and the neat package of material offered by the fourth duke's journals and associated manuscripts lent themselves to a relatively straightforward presentation.

The volume before you now covers the final sixty-plus years of a tale about the fall, rise and fall again of this ducal estate. Two generations are involved in this present work – although three dukes are included. Two brothers and a son took centre stage during the eventful years unfolded here – they were to become the seventh, eighth and ninth dukes of this title.

The period covered in this book is arguably one of the most interesting in the life of the Newcastle estates. This era began with the desperate struggles of a seriously distressed dynasty to regain financial control of their impoverished estate, also to transform the duchy's tarnished reputation. It was also a time when the untimely death of the duke was promptly followed by severe fire damage to the ducal mansion. The story ends happily, as Clumber Park (albeit minus the mansion) was transferred to the hands of the National Trust soon after the end of the Second World War and is now a public amenity of national and international appeal.

In addition to the research material available in the official archives, much has been gleaned from the offerings of descendents of families who lived and worked on the Newcastle Estates. There is the evidence of one of the last of Clumber's parlour maids, plus that of so many other generous people – including the relatives of a Clerk of Works, a Clumber House Joiner, two Postmistress's, a school master (who was a keen photographer of all things 'Clumber') and many more. Particularly useful have been the diaries of a Head Forester, Wilson Tomlinson. Through these it has been possible to glimpse deeper into the social lives of the family of this 'head of department' in a way that the official papers cannot hope to reveal. We owe them all much gratitude and I hope that the inclusion of their memories and photographs in the body of this work, together with the acknowledgements contained in the appropriate appendix, will mark that debt.

After much deliberation it was decided not to place footnotes or referencing throughout this publication, it must therefore be a matter of faith that there is a record of the source of the item in question – I trust that a substantial index will go some way to compensate for this decision. The sources are legion and this is not intended to be a learned piece – merely an enjoyable one – for those who share my fascination with the local history of the 'Dukeries' area of Nottinghamshire.

The narrative involves tales of numerous estate residents, employees, aristocrats and others – hopefully they will combine to give the flavour of an age now gone but not to be forgotten.

John Fletcher
Edwinstowe
December 2004

BACKGROUND

CLUMBER PARK, NOTTINGHAMSHIRE, has been in the safekeeping of The National Trust since July 1946. The property is visited by many hundreds of thousands every year. Lime Tree Avenue; Clumber Bridge and extensive Lake; the superb Chapel; Pleasure Grounds; Temples and Walled Gardens are especial delights.

Members of the Clinton dynasty made their home at Clumber from the second half of the eighteenth century. Clintons had been granted the 'Earls of Lincoln' title in the sixteenth century and it became the secondary title of the Newcastle dukedom from 1768. In that year, the incumbent Lord Lincoln (Henry Fiennes Clinton) inherited the ducal title as second Duke of Newcastle-under-Lyme on the death of his uncle, Thomas Pelham-Holles. This Clinton added 'Pelham' to his surname in recognition of his uncle's generosity to him. Lord Lieutenancy of Nottinghamshire was just one of the new duke's offices, a carry-over from his late uncle's appointments, now awarded to the new man by King George III. Clinton also inherited land in Newark, Nottingham (including the famous Castle) and in many other towns and villages. At different times, the landholdings totalled some 34,000 acres of the county, with more in other areas of England and Wales during subsequent generations. These properties included freehold and leasehold purchases. Sizeable mortgages were involved at all times.

The Earl of Lincoln's move north from his home at Oatlands Park, Weybridge, Surrey, and the eventual development of Clumber Park as his main country seat, were actions that provided a substantial boost to employment prospects in the 'Dukeries' area of North Nottinghamshire. Apart from the need for many foresters, other 'woodmen' were required to serve in the estate workshops; such as sawmills workers, carpenters and joiners. Additionally, blacksmiths and other tradesmen and professionals (e.g. drainers, engineers, glaziers, roofers, accountants, surveyors and clerks) were employed there and in the estate offices. The numerous indoor staff of the mansion (steward, butler, housekeeper, valets, footmen, maids and cooks) was supplemented by grooms, carters, odd-job men, night-watchmen, dairy and laundry maids – plus many more.

An enormous financial outlay produced a magnificent park of almost four thousand acres, containing a farming project with: "the largest farm buildings in the county". Highland cattle and various breeds of sheep were introduced. Rotation arable farming was also soon in evidence, with the duke taking advice (e.g. from the likes of the notable agriculturist, Arthur Young) on the profitable use of manures and other farming innovations.

In addition to the much-admired Clumber House, numerous outbuildings, cottages and lodges were constructed. Pleasure Grounds, Summerhouses and a Walled Garden were formed. A substantial lake of almost ninety acres was developed from the previously meandering River Poulter. Many thousands of trees were planted throughout the Park; with both decorative and commercial intent. Stables and Kennels were established, and the famous 'Clumber Spaniels' bred at nearby Haughton.

By the time of the second duke's death in 1794, his personal and estate finances were severely diminished. The only remaining son (at loggerheads with his father due to debts and choice of bride) inherited the title as third duke but little else - he then died the following year. His eldest son, to whom most of his grandfather's legacy had been willed, succeeded as fourth Duke of Newcastle-under-Lyme who - mainly through a fortunate marriage - found that he had the finances to re-establish the estate. It was during this fourth duke's incumbency of almost fifty years that features such as terracing, rock gardens and formal lakeside walks were added to Clumber splendours. Money went through the fourth duke's fingers like water, for example he recklessly added to his landed estates with the purchases of over 60,000 acres at Hafod, in central Wales, as well as the 6,000 acres that comprised the Worksop Manor estate, the latter previously owned by the Duke of Norfolk.

During the 1850's, the fifth duke (who had achieved high political office) attempted to consolidate the situation but eventually, he too was persuaded to spend on improvements at Clumber and a further extensive land purchase – the Morton estate – adjoining the Ranby lands previously purchased by his grandmother. On that duke's untimely demise – and after he had left clear instructions that his own heir's spendthrift ways should be carefully trimmed – Trustees were appointed to take control: "as though they were the owners". The senior Trustee was no less than the fifth duke's friend, the famous William Ewart Gladstone, later to be four times Prime Minister.

A clear sign of the estate's reduced influence in the county (where the Newcastle's had long filled the post of Lord Lieutenant and were senior benefactors) was the position regarding

Nottingham Castle. After well over two centuries in the ownership of various 'Newcastles' – the building was now in the hands of the Nottingham town council. In October 1875, the: "useless, graceless hulk" had been signed over to the town's Mayor on a 500-year lease by the Trustees. It was just under three years later that the Prince of Wales opened the newly renovated building as the Midlands Counties Art Museum.

Rents, mineral royalties, investment interest and timber sales had always produced the main income for the estates to function. The expenses on maintenance, replacements, wages, a multitude of tax demands and the incautious spending of a succession of patrons outstripped this income.

***

We are to pick up the story in the late 1870's, with Clumber Park and the whole landed estate of the Newcastle duchy in a state of uncertainty. There was no duke or duchess in residence at Clumber, the financial situation was still very fragile and no one was even remotely confident as to where it was all going to end.

NEWCASTLE FAMILY CENTRAL TO THIS STORY

6th duke (born 1834 – died 1879)
Married Henrietta Adele Hope in 1861 (she died in 1913)
2 sons – Henry (7th duke) and Francis (8th duke);
3 daughters – Beatrice, Emily and Florence

***

7th duke (born 1864 – died 1928)
Married [Frances] Kathleen Candy in 1889
[*No children of this marriage*]

***

8th duke (born 1866 – died 1941)
Married Mary Augusta Yohé in 1894 – divorced in 1902
[*No children of this marriage*]
Married Olive Muriel Owen in 1904 (she died in 1912)
1 son – Hugh (9th duke); 2 daughters – Doria and Mary

***

9th duke (born 1907 – died November 1988)
Married Jean in 1931 – divorced in 1940
[*No children of this marriage*]
Married Diana in 1946 – they divorced in 1959
[2 daughters of this marriage – Patricia and Kathleen]
Married Sally in 1959 – divorced
[*No children of this marriage*]

***

10th duke (born 1920 – died December 1988)
[*Cousin of the 9th duke*] Unmarried

***

The ducal title became extinct on the death of the 10th duke

LIST OF ILLUSTRATIONS

FRONT COVER – Painting by E.W. Haslehust [by courtesy of Robin Murray-Walker]
TITLE PAGE   – Clumber House west front [National Trust Collection – 'NT']
REAR COVER   – Coloured print of a sketch from the 'Illustrated London News' [John & Sybil Weth]
MAPS   – Nottinghamshire locations (page xi)
                – Clumber Park [outline by 'Rich Designs'] (page xii)
                – Sketch map [by Barrie Webster] (pages 54/55)

CHAPTER ONE
Fig   1 – Wilson Tomlinson and some of his men [John Alcock - 'JA']   – Page   1
Fig   2 – 6th Duke [University of Nottingham Manuscripts & Special Collections - 'NUMD']   – Page   2
Fig   3 – 6th Duchess [NUMD]   – Page   3
Fig   4 – Dining Room [NT]   – Page   7
Fig   5 – Markham-Clinton Mausoleum   – Page   8
Fig   6 – 1879 Fire at Clumber House [NT]   – Page   10
Fig   7 – 7th Duke (aged 14) [NT]   – Page   11
Fig   8 – Copy of Duke's letter to Gladstone [Sir William Gladstone]   – Page   13
Fig   9 – Hine's unfinished Chapel [NT]   – Page   15
Fig 10 – 'After the Fire' – 1879 [Barraud & Jerrard]   – Page   18
Fig 11 – West Front of the mansion [NT]   – Page   19
Fig 12 – Lincoln Terrace [Country Life Picture Gallery – 'CLPG]   – Page   22

CHAPTER TWO
Fig 13 – Grand Hall [NT] –   Page   25
Fig 14 – Repairs Dept 'Rules' [Charles J. Stableforth – 'CJS']   – Page   27
Fig 15 – Clumber House & Chapel [NT]   – Page   28
Fig 16 – Joel Haslam, Agent ['Worksop Guardian']   – Page   29
Fig 16a – A prize catch from Clumber Lake [Bassetlaw Museum – 'BM']   – Page   30
Fig 17 – Duke's drive through Worksop [Copyright reserved, collection unknown – 'CR']   – Page   31
Fig 18 – Lady Charlotte Pelham-Clinton [CJS]   – Page   32
Fig 19 – Presentation of a Casket – 1885 [David Marshall]   Page   33
Fig 20 – Laying the foundation stone of the Bodley Chapel [NT]   – Page   35
Fig 21 – Normanton Inn [NT]   – Page   37

CHAPTER THREE
Fig 22 – Organist's House at Hardwick [NT]   – Page   40
Fig 23 – Duke and Duchess [BM]   – Page   42
Fig 24 – Choir, Clergy and Chapel [NT]   – Page   45
Fig 25 – 1889 Choir [JA] –   Page   47
Fig 26 – 7th Duchess [Frances Soubry]   – Page   48
Fig 27 – Hardwick Kennels [NT]   – Page   49
Fig 28 – Budby Corner [David A. Chapman]   – Page   49
Fig 29 – 'The Bohemian' ['Book of the Caravan']   – Page   52
Fig 30 – Caravan profile   [ditto]   – Page   52
Fig 31 – Interior of the caravan   [ditto]   – Page   53
Fig 32 – Sketch map by Barrie Webster   – Pages 54/55
Fig 33 – Crimson Drawing Room [CLPG]   – Page   57
Fig 34 – Greyhound Hotel advert ['Sissons Penny Illustrated Guide to the Dukeries']   – Page   59
Fig 35 – Walled Gardens [NT]   – Page   60
Fig 36 – South face of Clumber House   – Page   61
Fig 37 – Truman's Lodge and arrivals [CR]   – Page   62
Fig 38 – 'Dolph' Schmidt [JA]   – Page   65
Fig 39 – George Anderson and his wife [NT]   – Page   66
Fig 40 – 'Cricket' extract from the Church Magazine [NT]   – Page   68

Fig 41 – Ice breakers [NT]   – Page   71
Fig 42 – Worksop Priory Gatehouse ['Worksop Guardian']   – Page   71
Fig 43 – Fire Instructions for Clumber House [CJS]   – Page   72
Fig 44 – Mary Yohé [CR]   – Page   74
Fig 45 – Egmanton Church [BM]   – Page   77
Fig 46 – Clumber medal – 1897 [JA]   – Page   78
Fig 47 – Tomlinsons at Cabin Hill [Diana Bakel – 'DB']   – Page   80
Fig 48 – Yellow Drawing Room [CLPG]   – Page   81

CHAPTER FOUR
Fig 49 – South face of Clumber House [NT]   – Page 82/83
Fig 50 – 11 Hill Street, London   – Page   86
Fig 51 – William Ewart Gladstone [CR]   – Page   88
Fig 52 – Western Corridor [CLPG]   – Page   90
Fig 53 – Eastern Corridor [CLPG]   – Page   91
Fig 54 – Car and Chauffeur   [Doris Smith]   – Page   94
Fig 55 – Coachmen playing cards   [ditto]   – Page   95
Fig 56 – Clumber Show Ground sketch plan ['Worksop Guardian']   – Page   96
Fig 57 – Luncheon Tent [NT]   – Page   97
Fig 58 – House party at the Show [NT]   – Page   98
Fig 59 – Lord Edward Pelham–Clinton [CJS]–   Page   98
Fig 60 – 'Pall Mall Magazine' cover [NT]   – Page   99
Fig 61 – George Marshall, solicitor ['Worksop Guardian']   – Page 103
Fig 62 – Mary Alcock, Hardwick's first postmistress [JA]   – Page 105
Fig 63 – Hardwick Post Office [NT]   – Page 106
Fig 64 – Hardwick postal stamp impression   – Page 106
Fig 65 – Arthur Elliott, Agent [JA]   – Page 107
Fig 66 – Grand Drawing Room [CLPG]   – Page 109
Fig 67 – Cricket Ground Cottages [NT]   – Page 113

CHAPTER FIVE
Fig 68 – Gardeners [Elizabeth Davy]   – Page 117
Fig 69 – Gates at Shireoaks Hall Farm [Peter Brammer}   – Page 119
Fig 70 – Normanton Gates – 1934 [JA]   – Page 119
Fig 71 – Richard George Alcock [JA]   – page 120
Fig 72 – Richard Alcock junior [JA]   – Page 120
Fig 73 – Sammy Barker, Head Gardener [NUMD]   – Page 122
Fig 74 – Herbert Tomlinson on the 'Lincoln' [JA]   – Page 123
Fig 75a – Sherwood Rangers at Training Camp [JA]   – Page 125
Fig 75b –   [ditto]   – Page 126
Fig 75c –   [ditto]   – Page 126
Fig 76 – Cricket Team [Hilda Favill –'HA']   – Page 128
Fig 77 – Football Team [Frank R. Smith]   – Page 129
Fig 78 – 'Lincoln' frigate under repair [NT]   – Page 130
Fig 79 – Billiards Room [NT]   – Page 131
Fig 80 – Duke's Study [NT]   – Page 132
Fig 81 – Brownies & Guides [Margo Lovegrove – 'ML']   – Page 132
Fig 82 – Adeline Genée [National Portrait Gallery, London – 'NPG']   – Page 132
Fig 83 – Olive Muriel, wife of Lord Francis [Roxanna Van Oss]   – Page 134
Fig 84 – Lord Frances, with his son and eldest daughter [JA]   – Page 135
Fig 85– 7th Duke & nephew [Roxanna Van Oss]   – Page 135
Fig 86 – Duke's nieces   [ditto]   – Page 135
Fig 87 – 1912 Fire [NT]   – Page 136
Fig 88 – 1912 Fire [NT]   – Page 136
Fig 89 – 1912 Fire [NT]   – Page 137
Fig 90 – Lakeside view [NT]   – Page 139

Fig 91 – Choir Hostel [NT]   – Page 141
Fig 92 – Hardwick Village School [NT]]   – Page 142
Fig 93 – Henrietta, Dowager duchess [CJS]   – Page 142
Fig 94 – Sherwood Foresters [Paul North & 'Reflections of a Bygone Age']   – Page 143
Fig 95 – Duke, Duchess & army officers [Paul North & 'Reflections of a Bygone Age']   – Page 143
Fig 96 – Enlargement of Figure 95 (part)   [ditto]   – Page 143
Fig 97 – Mr & Mrs George Thompson [NT]   – Page 146
Fig 98 – Huntsmen & hounds [NT]   – Page 147
Fig 99 – House Party [NT]   – Page 147
Fig 100 – Richard Alcock and fellow officers [JA]   – Page 149
Fig 101 –Army Officers at Clumber [JA]   – Page 151
Fig 102 –Hostel & Schoolmaster's house [NT]   – Page 151
Fig 103 –Welsh Ponies [NUMD]   – Page 153
Fig 104 –Wilson Tomlinson [DB]   – Page 158
Fig 105 –'Thetis' statue in the Grand Hall [CLPG]   – Page 160

CHAPTER SIX
Fig 106 – 'Calvary' memorial [NT]   – Page 163
Fig 107 – William Stanhope, Clerk of Works [JA]   – Page 164
Fig 108 – Hile family at Cabin Hill [Constance Hile – 'CH']   – Page 165
Fig 109 – Bill Salmon, blacksmith [NT]   – Page 166
Fig 110 – Sydney Stanhope, joiner [NT]   – Page 166
Fig 111 – Ranby Hall [Frank W. Stevenson]   – Page 167
Fig 112 – Ploughing team [Ron Sissons]   – Page 169
Fig 113 – Staff of Clumber House [NT]   – Page 171
Fig 114 – John Adcock, blacksmith [Graham Adcock – 'GA']   – Page 172
Fig 115 – Kathleen, Duchess riding 'Kitty' [ML]   – Page 172
Fig 116 – Forest Farm, Winkfield [Ruth Timbrell]   – Page 176
Fig 117 – Lord Arthur Pelham–Clinton [CJS]   – Page 177
Fig 118 – 7th duke's grave at Eton   – Page 178
Fig 119 – Memorial Services card [NT]   – Page 179
Fig 120 – Clumber House [Richard Alcock]   – Page 180

CHAPTER SEVEN
Fig 121 – 8th duke [NPG]   – Page 181
Fig 122 – Olive Muriel [Lady Kate Pelham–Clinton–Hope]   – Page 182
Fig 123 – Car & chauffeur [Doris Smith]   – Page 184
Fig 124 – Dowager duchess & borzois [Doris Smith]   – Page 184
Fig 125 – Billy Milton at the Nursery [JA]   – Page 186
Fig 126 – Eton cricket picture 1926 [Mike Spurrier]   – Page 188
Fig 127 – Clumber Cottage [Sybil Weth]   – Page 189
Fig 128 – Lady Doria Lois [Roxanna Van Oss]   – Page 190
Fig 129a – Lady Lincoln & 'Nero' ['Nottinghamshire Magazine']   – Page 192
Fig 129b – Lord Lincoln [NT]   – Page 192
Fig 130 – Lord Lincoln & the Clumber cricket team [NT]   – Page 193
Fig 131 – Parsonage & Chaplain [NT]   – Page 195
Fig 132 – Burnt–out Village School [NT]   – Page 197
Fig 133 – Pringle family [Ailsa Pringle]   – Page 200
Fig 134a – Charles Read & 'Rita' [Margaret Hallam]   – Page 201
Fig 134b – The 'Lincoln's' outside the Parsonage [NT]   – Page 201
Fig 135 – Aerial photo of Clumber House [Unit for Landscape Modelling, Cambridge University]   – Page 202

CHAPTER EIGHT
Fig 136 – Search for a new House site [CH]   – Page 204
Fig 137 – 1937 Coronation [Royal Photograph Collection]   – Page 205
Fig 138 – Presenting the Coronation Glove [CR]   – Page 205

Fig 139 – Charlie Favill [GA]   – Page 206
Fig 140 – Christie's Catalogue [NT]   – Page 208
Fig 141 – Oak Fireplace [NT]   – Page 209
Fig 142 – 4–poster bed [NTs]   – Page 210
Fig 143 – 'Napoleon' Statue [ditto]   – Page 210
Fig 144 – Major Murray–Walker [Susan Garratt]   – Page 211
Fig 145 – Sketch of House Ground Floor [Barratt Stanhope]   – Page 213
Fig 146 – Grand Hall standing empty [CJS]   – Page 214
Fig 147 – Library cupboard standing bare [CJS]   – Page 214
Fig 148 – Demolition, viewed from South Lawns [JA]   – Page 216
Fig 149 – Demolition, Great Drawing Room [Philip Hile]   – Page 217
Fig 150 – Demolition, viewed from the east   [ditto]   – Page 217
Fig 151 – Piles of house material awaiting sales [NT]   – Page 218
Fig 152 – Spencer's sale catalogue [NT]   – Page 218
Fig 153 – 'Ned & Flo' [R. F. Barrowcliffe]   – Page 223
Fig 154 – Sketch of troops unloading ammunition [JA]   – Page 224
Fig 155 – 'Nellie' & 'Col. Warden' [Trustees of the Imperial War Museum]   – Page 227
Fig 156 – 'Nellie' & the trench   [ditto]   – Page 227
Fig 157 – Royal Engineers [Ron Turner]   – Page 228
Fig 158 – 9th duke, in RAF dress uniform [Lady Kate Pelham–Clinton–Hope]   – Page 229
Fig 159 – Norman & Cyril Tideswell [Nancy Hibbs]   – Page 231
Fig 160 – Ron Sissons   [Ron & Veronica Sissons]   – Page 232
Fig 161 – Veronica Sissons [ditto]   – Page 232
Fig 162 – 'Cissy' & friends [Hilda Favill]   – Page 233
Fig 163 – Lady Diana Montagu–Stuart–Wortley [NPG]   – Page 234
Fig 164 – Wing Commander, 9th duke [NT]   – Page 234
Fig 165 – Estate Office, Worksop   – Page 239

CHAPTER NINE [243–254]
Fig 166 – 10th duke [Trustees of the National Museums of Scotland]   – Page 242
Fig 167 – 'Fire' headline – ['Worksop Guardian']   – Page 245
Fig 168 – Three boys on the 'Lincoln' frigate [CH]   – Page 248
Fig 169 – Georgiana memorial   – Page 250
Fig 170 – Georgiana being moved to Clumber ['Newark Advertiser']   – Page 250
Fig 171 – Clumber Bridge [CLPG]   – Page 252

COLOUR PLATES
Plate Number 1   – Clumber House Fire   [John & Sybil Weth]
Plate Number 2   – Grand Hall – sketch by Charles Barry   [RIBA Library Drawings Collection]
Plate Numer   3   – Clumber Chapel   [Cecil Brown Collection]
Plate Number 4 (a) and (b) – 'Newcastle-under-Lyme ducal Coat of Arms   [Manorial Society]
Plate Number 5   – Hope Diamond   [Smithsonian Institution, Washington]
Plate Number 6 (a) and (b) – Silver Wedding Casket (1914)   [N.U.M.D.]
Plate Number 7   – Clumber Spaniels   [Bill Ironside]
Plate Number 8   – Clumber House Library & Reading Room   [C.J.S. *also* A.C. Cooper (Colour) Lyd.]

The author and publisher offer grateful thanks to all those individuals and organisations by whose courtesy these depictions are displayed. Every effort has been made to ensure that all credits are correct: we have acted in good faith and on the best information available to us at the time of publication. Any omissions are inadvertent, and will be corrected in future editions if notification is given to the publisher in writing,

AN OUTLINE MAP OF NOTTINGHAMSHIRE, INDICATING A FEW OF THE LOCATIONS MENTIONED IN THIS BOOK

KEY:

A – Martin, near Bawtry.
B – Shireoaks; Steetley; Whitwell;
    Worksop (including Manton).
C – Clumber (including Hardwick).
D – Nottingham (including
    Bagthorpe; Basford; Beeston,
    Bulwell, Carlton, Hucknall, Wollaton).
E – Newark
F – Retford (including Ordsall).
G – Brinsley, Heanor.
H – Bevercotes; East Markham;
    Egmanton; Gamston; Milton;
    Tuxford; West Drayton;
    West Markham.
 I – Bothamsall: Elkesley;
    Haughton; Lound Hall;
    Normanton.
 J – Welbeck.
K – Thoresby.
L – Ranby.
M – Osberton.
N – Rufford.

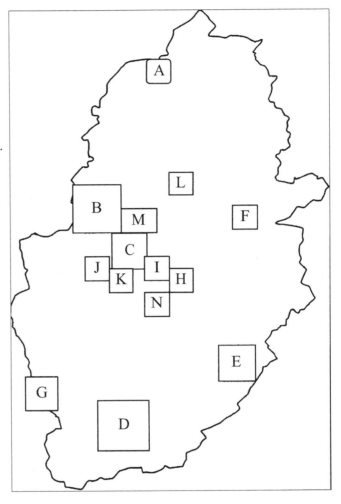

Also mentioned are Annesley Grange, Arnold, Babbington, Babworth, Bagthorpe, Balderton, Barlborough, Barnby Moor, Belph, Besthorpe, Boughton, Budby, Carburton, Car Colston, Carlton–in–Lindrick, Checker House, Claypole, Clowne, Cromwell, Crookford, Cropwell Bishop, East Stoke, Edwinstowe, Everton, Farndon, Firbeck, Flawborough, Flintham, Gateford, Girton, Gunthorpe, Hodsock, Harworth, Holme, Kelham, Kilton, Kilvington, Kirton, Laneham, Langold, Langwith, Laughton–en–le–Morthern, Lound Hall, Ollerton, Orston Peverell, Ossington, Mansfield, Markham Moor, Milton, Morton, Nether Headon, Newthorpe, North Muskham, Shelton, Shirebrook, South Clifton, South Scarle, Southwell, Stockwith, Sutton–in–Ashfield, Walesby, Warsop, Wellow, West Bridgford, Westerfield, West Stockworth, Willoughby, Winthorpe.

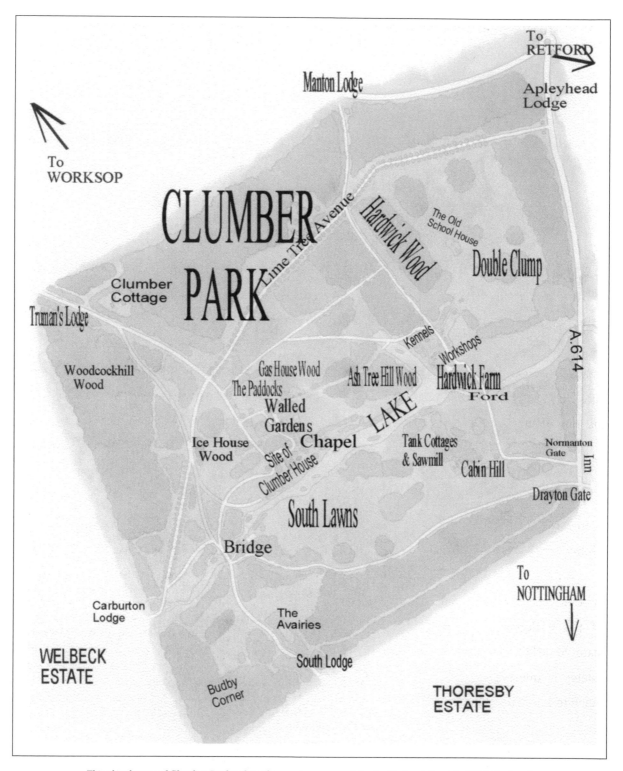

To
RETFORD

Manton Lodge

Apleyhead
Lodge

To
WORKSOP

The Old
School House

CLUMBER

Lime Tree Avenue

Hardwick Wood

Double Clump

Clumber
Cottage

PARK

Truman's Lodge

A.614

Kennels

Woodcockhill
Wood

Gas House Wood

Ash Tree Hill Wood

Workshops

Hardwick Farm

The Paddocks

Ford

LAKE

Walled
Gardens

Ice House
Wood

Site of
Clumber House

Chapel

Tank Cottages
& Sawmill

Normanton
Gate

Cabin Hill

Inn

Drayton Gate

South Lawns

To
NOTTINGHAM

Bridge

Carburton
Lodge

The
Avairies

WELBECK
ESTATE

South Lodge

Budby
Corner

THORESBY
ESTATE

This sketch map of Clumber Park is based on a plan prepared for the National Trust by 'Rich Designs'.

CHAPTER ONE

1878 to 1880

A new forester arrived – An absentee duke and his problems – The forester settled in for a long haul – Death of the 6th duke – Fire at Clumber House – The 'Little' duke – The forester consolidated his position – Rebuilding a mansion and a reputation.

A NEW FORESTER ARRIVED AT CLUMBER

WILSON TOMLINSON WAS THE LATEST in a sturdy line of Head Foresters (or 'Woodsmen') to arrive at Clumber Park, and he could not have arrived at a worse moment. It was now late spring in 1878 and the consequences of a fierce storm that had torn through the district in the previous October were only too plain to see. Over the previous two decades, much timber had been felled, as the income from its sale was a vital component in the estate's financial standing. A thousand or so deer were currently present in this almost four thousand acre enclosed park, and they were feeding well on the bounty of the owners. The Pleasure Ground to the east of the one hundred-year-old mansion and the Pinetum to the west were unkempt, lacking proper control and sorely requiring a dose of tender loving care. These formerly delightful aspects of the Park were destined to come under the control of the new Forester.

As he stood amongst this scene of storm desolation, it is highly probably that Wilson had mixed feelings about his recent appointment. How much he knew of the background to the gloomy state of affairs on the Newcastle's estates is questionable. There was much to know of.

Figure 1 –
Wilson Tomlinson and a few of his foresters at work in Clumber Park

AN ABSENTEE DUKE AND HIS PROBLEMS

Figure 2 –
The 6th Duke of Newcastle-under-Lyme

Henry Pelham Alexander Pelham-Clinton, 6th Duke of Newcastle, had been declared insolvent in 1869. Perhaps it could have been worse for him – as that was the year when imprisonment for debt was abolished! In that same year (and to discharge the bankruptcy) the duke's mother-in-law, Anne Adele Hope, had taken control of certain estate matters not appropriate to the fifth duke's Trustees. Mrs Hope reluctantly financed him during these troubles to the reported sum of £60,000, but this was principally directed to the support she gave her daughter and grandchildren. Henrietta, the duchess, received around £8,000 per year from her mother and she in turn used much of this towards the settlement of her husband's debts.

Almost ten years on from those dramatic days in the Insolvency Court, the disgraced nobleman (whose situation of: "pecuniary embarrassment" and "humiliation" was still the subject of unsympathetic press comment) was currently living in a London hotel, permanently separated from Henrietta. She and their five children initially lived with her wealthy widowed mother in London, also at the Hope's Deepdene property, near Dorking in Surrey and Castle Blaney, Co. Monaghan, Ireland.

Figure 3
Henrietta, Duchess,
wife of the 6th duke.

There were many management problems at the tip of the Newcastle estate pyramid. Mrs Hope was in lonely competition with an impressive team of Trustees who had been nominated in 1864 on the death of the fifth duke (father of the current unfortunate), to take control of all substantial matters. Trustees included the eminent statesman, William Ewart Gladstone, and Lord de Tabley (George Warren). For fifteen years these worthies had: "worked with vigorous hands to straighten the tortuous complications the late duke had left". These were the problems that had caused the sixth duke to consider himself to be an unlucky man.

It was a fact that he had been very, very unlucky – especially in connection with his compulsive gambling! For years prior to his father's death, the reckless nobleman's youthful enthusiasm for throwing away money on his favoured pastime had been the tittle-tattle of his social set. Horseracing had proved to be his ruin, most directly attributable to his debts in connection with the purchase of a racing stud. Queen Victoria had already confided to her diary that he appeared to be: "very worthless". The estate solicitor, Mr Ouvry, showed little respect for the duke in his correspondence to Mr Gladstone, scornfully describing this young man as: "our Henry".

The Reverend Cornelius Thompson of Kirton Rectory, Ollerton, wrote a letter to Gladstone, explaining that:

> When the unfortunate reality of the Duke's imprudence reached Clumber every thing there was, in a measure, paralyzed: and the servants and labourers and other necessary appendages to the Estate had to be given up, which occasioned suffering and hardship on all sides.

THE FORESTER SETTLED IN FOR A LONG HAUL

In all probability the new Forester was much more concerned about the future than events of a decade past, and was keen to find out where he would live and work, and what his staff would be like. He had been born at Manton Bar, Worksop in 1849 and baptised in the nearby Augustinian Priory. On his appointment at Clumber, he and his family were firstly housed in one of the Newcastle estate's Sparken Farm properties at Worksop. They were later to move into a more substantial dwelling known as Cabin Hill, close by Clumber's south-eastern boundary with the Thoresby estate. This old Shooting Lodge was and is adjacent to the Sawmill and just across the Lake from the Hardwick village Workshops, where the men of the Joinery Shop and other skilled tradesmen were based. Hardwick is the estate village for the Park.

Wilson was to find that many of his men (designated as Woodsmen or Woodsman Labourers) were much older than he was, and some had been on the Newcastle estate for many years. In addition to man-management, he was accountable for the selection and harvesting of suitable timber, estimating likely profits, attending timber sales, planning the establishment of suitable ground for new plantings, including burning, draining and fencing as required. He was then to plan the purchase and planting of new trees, ensuring an orderly programme for the weeding, thinning and other maintenance needs of the plantations. His expertise was frequently called upon for counsel on the wider aspects of timber matters, and he was expected to undertake various representative duties away from the Estate. His overall purpose was to restore some order and profitability to a department of the duchy that should have provided regular and substantial income for the estate.

During his first few months in his new post, and using the counterpart of a modern day company car – in this case a horse and trap, plus the luxury of his own groom (the diminutive John Thompson of Tank Cottage) – this young 'Head of Department' had visited many regions of his new empire, both inside the Park boundaries and far beyond them. Travelling around Ranby and Martin (north-west of Bawtry) in the north, Bothamsall, Elkesley, Haughton, Normanton and Tuxford in the east, and the Worksop Manor lands to the west, he would soon have come to realise the extent of his new responsibilities. And, as yet, he had still to see the Newark and Nottingham areas that were under the Newcastle ownership. He most likely felt that control of the plantations within Clumber Park alone was worth somewhat more than the £170 annual salary he had accepted – notwithstanding his rent-free status and the additional benefit of two rabbits per week!

His October trip to the Handsworth Nurseries, near Sheffield, is a reminder that this company had been a main supplier to the Dukeries estates for well over a century. Saplings and plants of all descriptions had been ordered from there since the first formal plantings at Clumber in the 1760's. The firm was now set to receive much more cash from the ducal coffers! Controllers of those monies were amongst those with whom the Forester dined during those early months. Joel Haslam, accountant at Clumber for around twenty years, was soon to replace Mr A.G. Williams as Estate Agent, the senior and highest paid employee. Mr Haslam operated from his residence at Sparken House, the earlier home of Worksop Manor Estate Agents since the time of the Duke of Norfolk's ownership. Mr Williams continued to live at the impressive Park House, Worksop and the estate administration was centred next door at the purpose-built Newcastle Estate Office. Clerical, financial, rent collections, surveying and record keeping were among the duties controlled from there by Thomas Hutton, who was chief clerk for many years. Wilson's other dining companions included fellow Heads of Departments, such as John Miller, Head Gardener and Isaac Sweeting, Clerk of Works (soon to be replaced by William Stanhope, recruited from the Duke of Rutland's Belvoir estate).

The Forester must also have made the acquaintance of the remaining department heads, such as those of the Game-keeping and Stables commands, and especially William Wilkinson, Bailiff of the Hardwick Farm.

The Clumber mansion – developed between 1760 and 1768 as a ducal residence around the frame of a previous house – had undergone much modification in the years since. It had now been in mothballs for almost a decade and indoor staffing was thin on the ground. The estate's plentiful staff numbers of previous years were no more. Most had been made redundant at the time of the bankruptcy of 1869. An exception to this rule was Mrs Eliza Condon, the Housekeeper, supported by two general domestics who undertook cleaning duties. The House had been opened for public visits on occasions during the past few years, but there was a heavy gloom over this once splendid and previously well-populated ducal dwelling. The 'Newark Advertiser' newspaper described it as: "a desolate, dreary unfrequented mansion ... swallowed up by the turf". No one knew how long this unsatisfactory condition would continue, or what was to happen to the stately home, nor indeed, to the entire duchy.

'Rent Audits' were held at the Normanton Inn on the eastern edge of the Park and close by the villages of Bothamsall and Elkesley. Wilson Tomlinson attended these events, as it was necessary for him to be known to those farmers who had tree plantations on or alongside their properties. Many of them belonged to families who had been on the estate farms for several generations (reputably over three hundred years in some cases). They, no doubt, gave him choice words of wisdom at the dinners that followed the formalities of these occasions.

The fourth duke's impetuous purchase of the Duke of Norfolk's Worksop Manor estate in the late 1830's had belatedly proved to be quite shrewd! Lord Foley (a cousin of the Clumber duke) had leased the property from the late 1850's and, since 1874, Mr William Isaac Cuckson – together with his family and twenty servants – had rented it from the Newcastle Trustees. The surrounding woods had continued to be a profitable source of timber monies for the Newcastles. Land sales in and around the town of Worksop had been well supported and, in addition, coal was successfully mined at nearby Shireoaks and Steetley.

At Worksop, Wilson attended the training grounds known as Plain Piece, and witnessed the colourful sight of (amongst others) the Clumber Troop of Sherwood Rangers Yeomanry, undertaking their volunteer army manoeuvres. He also visited Ranby Hall, where sixty-six year-old Lady Charlotte Pelham-Clinton, spinster daughter of the fourth duke, still lived. He dined there with the Lathams, whose service had spanned three generations of Newcastles. Welbeck (home of the Duke of Portland), Thoresby (Lord Manvers' residence) and Sandbeck Park (Lord Scarbrough's) completed this list of 'familiarisation' outings.

To bring to an end what must have been a fascinating first year for this new recruit to the duchy, the forester and his wife, Jeanette (known as Janet), were invited to a New Year's Eve celebration at Worksop Manor. The following year was to be even more interesting. A death and a fire were to lead to a new reign and a very busy time for Wilson Tomlinson and his colleagues.

DEATH OF THE 6ᵀᴴ DUKE

The New Year began quietly enough for estate staff with the novelty of a game of curling on Thoresby Lake. This helped Wilson to cement new friendships with senior staff of the neighbouring 'Dukeries' estates. Then – the Forester noted:

22 February 1879

His Grace 6th Duke of Newcastle died in London.

This nine-word diary entry was full of significance for the whole estate. It indicated that the death of the 45 year-old duke: "after suffering from gout for some time", would bring exciting prospects of a new regime at Clumber.

From the scene of his death in the Park Hotel, Park Lane, St. James', London, the duke's remains were brought to Clumber and laid out in the Grand Dining Room that had stood empty for so long. Here sumptuous celebratory meals had been served to mark both his birth and coming-of-age. Many tenants and members of the general public now filed past his coffin, whether through respect or morbid curiosity no one can now judge.

Figure 4 – The Dining Room at Clumber House, where the 6ᵗʰ Duke's body was laid out.

As the 'Retford Times' reported: "the living stream moved slowly round the coffin almost continuously for several hours". Some of those present probably remembered the former dazzling and festive occasions.

Figure 5 –
Markham-Clinton Mausoleum.

The funeral service was held at the family mausoleum in the Markham-Clinton parish. As with the two previous dukes, the hearse – accompanied by many estate workers, tenants and local dignitaries – travelled the eight miles from Clumber to the church, which stands on the hill between Milton and West Markham. The chief mourners were the late duke's sons (the new duke – full name Henry Pelham Archibald Douglas Pelham-Clinton – and his brother Lord Francis). Other close family members included two of the late duke's brothers, Edward and Albert; his twin uncles, Charles and Thomas; also his aunt, Lady Charlotte Pelham-Clinton of Ranby Hall.

The Forester must have made an impressive mounted figure at the head of the lengthy column of mourners, leading the slow procession along the elm-lined avenue known as 'the Duke's Last Drive', from Clumber Park to the mausoleum. He was directly followed by the Clerk of Works, Mr Sweeting, then by other servants including Mr Prentice, ex-House Steward, and Mr Latham, steward to Lady Charlotte. Ten private carriages of local dignitaries followed the eight official mourning coaches. Pall bearers comprised estate employees, including woodsman George Thompson of Tank Cottage, born at Clumber in 1831. Despite nasty drizzling rain a large number attended the funeral, which was conducted by several of the clergy who were present from 'Newcastle' parishes. These included the Rev. H. F. Clinton, Rector of Cromwell; Rev. E. Hawley, Vicar of Worksop and Rev. Seymour Bentley, Vicar of Markham-Clinton. Clergy and parishioners from East Markham, Egmanton, Elkesley, Kirton and Shireoaks were also represented.

There were many other notables who were: "regrettably unable to attend". Those with family connections included the Duke of Hamilton and the Marquis of Londonderry. Also absent were William Ewart Gladstone, Trustee/Executor (the one-time Guardian of the late duke) and his fellow Trustee, Lord de Tabley. One friend who did attend was Sir Robert Peel – son of the famed politician who had been such a guiding light in the life of the fifth duke. After the service, central members of the funeral party rode to the Newcastle Arms at Tuxford for luncheon, from whence many of them departed for London or beyond.

The 'Retford, Worksop and Gainsborough Times' commented that, during the 1870's, the duke had been an absentee from Nottinghamshire:

An exile from his home, through reasons for which he alone was responsible ...
the ducal residence has been desolate for some time past ... no sounds of revelry,
no merry voices, no bounteous hospitality had been within these walls for years.
Its owner had seldom resided there whilst alive ... [this] magnificent Estate ...
visited only by large numbers of sightseers.

Obituary notices and letters to the press included the following careful comments:

'His honesty greatly exceeded his shrewdness' ...
'His impulses easily overcame his common sense'.
'... easy of approach ... considerate of the feelings of others – ever ready and willing
to help whenever he could see his way'.
'... a frank and affable manner and a kindness of heart'.

In a poignant touch to the reporting of the event, a denial statement was issued in the 'Pall Mall Gazette'. It was regarding a report that there had been a certain floral display sent from Paris by the estranged duchess. This was strongly refuted. It is unlikely that she – and certainly not her mother – would have anything to do with the funeral, other than to permit the late duke's sons to attend. Mrs Hope had declined an invitation to give financial assistance with funeral costs.

Meanwhile, the fourteen years-old heir to the Newcastle estates returned to his studies in the house of Walter Durnford at Eton College. It would be six years before the young duke could claim his inheritance. The dual control of the fifth duke's Trustees and that of Mrs Hope would now be gradually wound down, with the aim of providing a secure future for the young nobleman and his estate.

FIRE AT CLUMBER HOUSE

26 March 1879
Great Fire at Clumber House, £50,000 damage done.

Figure 6 – This striking sketch of the Clumber House fire appeared in the 'Illustrated London News'.

On this fateful Wednesday morning, just four weeks after the death of the sixth duke, another body blow was dealt to the structure of Clumber, surely amongst premier division leaders in the league of disaster-prone dynastic estates.

The fire had started above the housekeeper's room in the north-west area of the House. A strong north-westerly wind whipped-up the flames, engulfing the central labyrinthine block of rooms, plus the entrance lobby and staircase: "noble – rising to the top of the building and ending in a dome". Some twenty of the one hundred and five rooms were affected, with sitting rooms and bedrooms being badly damaged or completely gutted.

Unsurprisingly, the financially-straightened Clumber estate was devoid of substantial fire-fighting appliances and so other outside assistance was urgently required. The availability of telephones being more than four years ahead, servants and telegrams were hurriedly despatched to the brigades at Worksop, Retford and Sheffield, as well as to alert the Trustees. Estate employees were also sent to request aid from the neighbouring 'Dukeries' estates, Thoresby and Welbeck – both of which did possess fire engines. The Worksop machine was the first to arrive, just forty minutes after the outbreak occurred.

Without waiting for the arrival of such help, Clumber's housekeeper, fifty-seven-year-old Eliza Condon, mustered the available staff and estate tenants, directing them in removing valuables from the House to the safety of the terraces and lawns. Many paintings, art treasures and the contents of the Library were saved. This praiseworthy action in moving precious items away from the flames was somewhat negated by the snow which then began to fall upon them! At this stage: "hundreds of people" are said to have arrived from all the neighbouring villages. They assisted in moving the treasures to relative safety in the Chapel or the Lincoln Stables. Whilst doing so, many of the helpers were startled by the sound of the stained-glass dome of the House's main staircase crashing to the floor.

Lord Albert Pelham-Clinton (uncle of the new duke) and Mr Williams, the Agent, were the first representatives of the family to arrive on the scene. Soon, telegrams were being sent to all interested parties, and plans made for new designs and repairs. In the event, 328 of the House's 500 pictures had been saved from the blaze. Amongst these were four Snyders (of game, fruit and two of fish), valued at around £25,000. Fortunately, a valuable Gainsborough was away at the new Nottingham Castle Museum, on display with several other pictures. Also amongst the pieces rescued, were those by Van Dyck, Reynolds, Lely, Kneller, Murillo, Teniers, Poussin, Rubens, Guido, Correggio, Vandermeulen, Van Vos, Titian, Holbein, Ruysdael, Durer and many others. Two sarcophagi plus several vases and urns – treasures taken from the ruins of Pompeii – were amongst the most expensive casualties. Other major losses were two cabinets and their contents of rare old china, one containing Sevres and the other, Worcester, Dresden and Indian ware.

Another alleged effect of the destruction was the loss of much documentation relating to the recent activities of the duchy. Although Mr Gladstone had transferred some papers relevant to the 1860's from Clumber to his home at Harwarden Castle, Flintshire, many of those relating to the period from the time of the bankruptcy to the mid-1880's arrival of the seventh duke seem to have disappeared – possibly into some solicitor's archive? The duke's uncle, Lord Edward Pelham-

Clinton, was to later declare his belief that they had perished in the flames of this recent conflagration.

Decisions on rebuilding the mansion had now to be taken, there were urgent insurance claims to make and the Trustees needed to redouble their efforts to establish a viable inheritance for the heir to this seriously injured estate.

THE 'LITTLE' DUKE

On the 7th April, 1879, the schoolboy duke wrote from Eton to his guardian, William Ewart Gladstone:

> I thank you very much for your kind and sympathising note, which I have been unable to answer before. I thought it very merciful that the fire at Clumber did comparatively so little harm, and I am exceedingly obliged to every-one for [their] exertions in saving the valuables.
>
> I think it is a good opportunity to rebuild the hall on a grander scale, and it would be very nice, if there was enough money, to build it on the plan of Sir Charles Barry. I hope too that the chapel will be seen to, for I should like the Hardwick people to have their service again. As to your good wishes about myself, I do earnestly hope to grow up a good man, and gain the affections of my people and friends, and it is a great deal to receive encouragement from you.
>
> I am thankful that I had my leg off, for I am able to do a great deal I could not do before.
>
> With kind regard,
>
> Yrs very sincerely – Newcastle.

Figure 7 – 7ᵗʰ Duke of Newcastle-under-Lyme

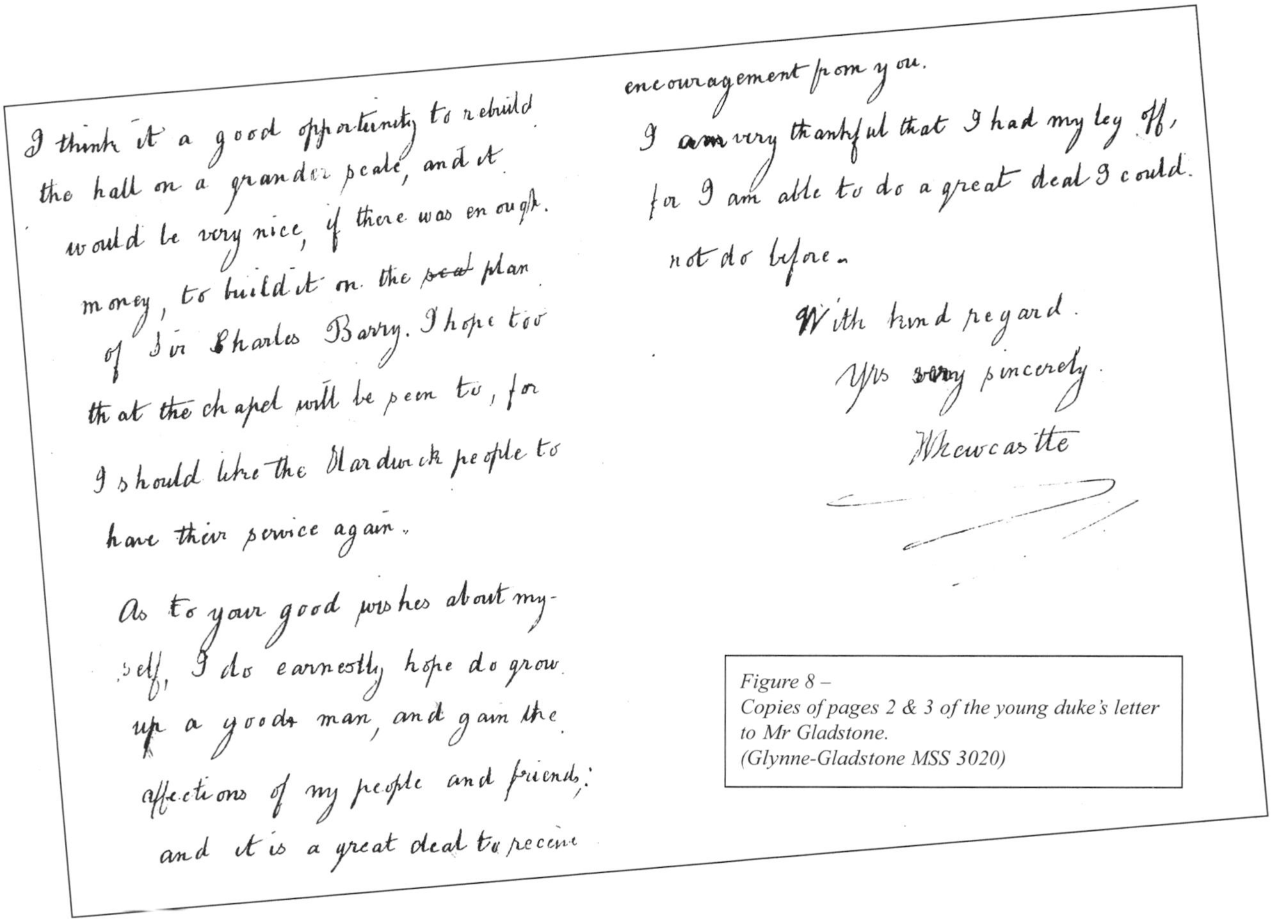

> I think it a good opportunity to rebuild the hall on a grander scale, and it would be very nice, if there was enough money, to build it on the best plan of Sir Charles Barry. I hope too that the chapel will be seen to, for I should like the Hardwick people to have their service again.
>
> As to your good wishes about myself, I do earnestly hope do grow up a goods man, and gain the affections of my people and friends; and it is a great deal to receive encouragement from you.
>
> I am very thankful that I had my leg off, for I am able to do a great deal I could not do before.
>
> With kind regard.
>
> Yrs very sincerely.
>
> Newcastle

Figure 8 –
Copies of pages 2 & 3 of the young duke's letter
to Mr Gladstone.
(Glynne-Gladstone MSS 3020)

The mention of the new duke's amputated leg is a reminder that this young man's early life had not been as 'silver spooned' as he might have hoped.

Henry Pelham Archibald Douglas Pelham-Clinton, fourteenth Earl of Lincoln and seventh duke of the 'Newcastle-under-Lyme' title had already spent most of his young life surrounded by difficulties which were not of his own making. One of his earliest misfortunes led to a lifetime of health difficulties. Born on 28 September 1864 into the fading years of aristocratic rule, it was also the year that his father inherited the distressed dukedom as the sixth holder of the title. As a baby, the young Henry suffered from a leg disablement. Published reports are confused as to the cause. One states that he was born with a bone deformity; another account is that he fell from a table and suffered the injury. More recently a further explanation has been offered, this from a family with a long connection with the Clumber estate (one of whom was a maid in the mansion in late-Victorian times). This version being that a major accident occurred when his nurse dropped him whilst she took the child a stroll along the Lincoln Terrace. Having reached the higher of the semi-circular seats, the baby is said to have fallen from her arms and crashed to the mosaic flooring, damaging his head and left leg. Medical attention was delayed, allegedly because the nurse was too frightened to inform anyone of the accident.

Inevitably, the injuries were discovered and doctors belatedly called in. The long road to possible recovery then began, but was to lead to an artificial leg being fitted some twelve years after the accident. The duke's damaged leg was re-broken in order to be re-set, but the operation was unsuccessful. Although treatment was sought over the years, in France as well as England, the young nobleman was greatly handicapped by the injury. At the age of thirteen, he informed his maternal grandmother, Mrs Hope that he wished to be rid of his: "useless foot". In November 1877, at her home in Belgrave Square, London, the operation was successfully completed and he was subsequently fitted with an artificial leg.

The extent of the head wound is unrecorded, but the consequences are said to have led to the duke having a skull that was disproportionately large, although his mental qualities not adversely affected. Another outcome (which may not be relevant to the accident) was that he never grew anywhere near to average height for a male of his times. Many photographs in later life indicate that he was probably several inches less than the claimed height of five feet (four feet six inches is the least generous guess). This schoolboy, who had become one of Britain's youngest peers, was to become hurtfully known as: "the Dwarf", or "Pelican Pelham", by some of his colleagues in the House of Lords.

***

The Chapel mentioned by the duke as needing to be: "seen to", was an impressive edifice, built close to the east of the mansion, but it was neither completed nor used. Begun by his late father in 1867, the building's designer (Thomas Chambers Hine), and the owners of the construction firm, had been casualties of the 1869 bankruptcy. The unfortunate creditors received only 5/6d [27p] in the pound of their contracted monies. It was to be some ten more years before the young duke's hopes for a Chapel would be realised.

Figure 9 – The "fine and costly structure"..."unfinished within and desolate and the birds fly about at their will" [William E. Gladstone]

THE FORESTER CONSOLIDATED HIS POSITION

Whilst his employers and their advisers wrestled with the problems of restoring the Mansion and Park to a satisfactory state for the new duke, Wilson continued to settle into his new post. A pattern was being established, as our senior woodsman established his credentials throughout the district. He was often to be found at Mr Garside's splendid 'Carlton House' in Worksop. Joseph Garside was a timber merchant and owner of the Prior Well Brewery. He was one of the most eminent and wealthiest men in the area and held shooting rights on Newcastle land. In the aftermath of the late-duke's bankruptcy, Mr Garside had purchased several of the disgraced nobleman's personal effects (e.g. cups, wines, guns, aviary birds) from the sales held at Clumber House. It is not known whether Garside enjoyed any of the six thousand bottles of wine that were sold at that time. It was at Carlton House that, in April 1879, the Forester met William Ewart Gladstone, although he did not record whether this senior Liberal politician impressed him, being himself of staunch Conservative views. He was probably more stirred by Gladstone's warranted reputation as an axe-man of some proficiency.

In May, Wilson made his first appearance in Worksop Court, where he was giving evidence in a case of theft of timber from Tranker Wood (east of Shireoaks). One George Holden was fined 22/6d (around £60 today) for the offence. In July, Wilson escorted Charles Blagg to be the new Woodsman at the 1,500 acre Martin estate, near Bawtry. The retiring employee was George Harwood, who had served there for fifty years, and in his earliest days must have been very aware of the archaeological finds connected with a Roman camp on that site.

Throughout the year Wilson continued to visit neighbouring estates. He enjoyed riding with hunting parties throughout the county and beyond, both with the hounds at Belvoir, Patmore and the Worksop estate, and also in the rook-shooting events on Manor Hills. He attended the Doncaster St. Ledger and other race meetings and, with his wife, went on outings to the Doncaster, Gainsborough, and the Penistone Shows. They also travelled to the Retford Fair and to Sheffield. In July they attended a royal event at Brocklesby Park, where the Prince and Princess of Wales reviewed the Lincolnshire Yeomanry – Wilson's brother, Joseph, worked in the Nursery at Brocklesby. His father and mother came over from Shafton (north of Barnsley) and stayed for a few days.

Towards the end of an eventful year, he noted that the 5th Duke of Portland – the "underground man" of Welbeck – had died in London, aged 79 years. Wilson would not have known it, but 'Scott Portland' had (from his London home and despite poor health) contacted William Gladstone directly after the Clumber House fire, regretting that he had only been able to organize the supply of one single fire engine to aid the dramatic rescue operation. He expressed satisfaction that he had been instrumental in assisting the: "saving of the most beautiful rooms", but mentioned: "the terrible misfortunes that have befallen Clumber and my dear young friends, the Duke & his brother". Portland had then repeated an earlier offer to store any pictures and furniture at Welbeck, whilst Clumber House was being restored to its previous magnificence.

1879 ended with many people skating on Clumber Lake and with very heavy snowfalls and thirty-one degrees of frost.

***

REBUILDING A MANSION AND A REPUTATION

Clumber Park residents must have quickly realised that a new dawn was breaking. It was not long before insurance assessors were studying the causes and consequences of the mansion fire. A settlement was agreed, based on a combined house and contents insurance of £110,000, of which four fifths was payable. The Newcastle Trustees, together with Mrs Hope, also the Solicitor and the Agent, were now considering their next moves. They needed a solid recovery plan for the arrival of the new duke as patron of the Newcastle duchy. Rebuilding the fire-damaged mansion (see Figure 10 below) was the first priority, and the duke's preference to use the plans of the late Sir Charles Barry's was high on the agenda. These designs had been drawn up almost twenty-five years earlier, and would have required levels of expenditure that were just not available – and never had been during that time. However, the elder architect's son (also named Charles) was both ready and willing to provide plans for a less expensive new mansion.

Figure 10 – Sketch of the fire-damaged mansion

The latest designs supplied by the younger Barry made use of some of his father's ideas, but considerably modified those for the central portion of the House, which had contained: "many and inconvenient stairs and tortuous passages" In the event, the first estimate for re-building – £59,000 – was turned down as too costly. The next was then reduced to around £37,000 by the exclusion of the dome and towers, which would have topped the central hall and the four wings. A report was circulated that Mr Barry's full plans would be eventually implemented, when finances allowed. This may have been a pacifier to the young duke, who was probably more attracted by the splendid towers and high-domed roof than most other aspects!

Mrs Hope and the new Trustees (Lord Edward Pelham-Clinton and Lord Lyttleton, Mr Gladstone having retired and Lord de Tabley died) accepted Barry's designs and work began almost immediately. Delays then ensued when a main contractor died but, in June 1880, Messrs. Lucas of London undertook to complete the work. Prior to doing so, the firm had been working on neighbouring Osberton Hall and later was to undertake the renovation of the beautiful Norman chapel at Steetley, in the parish of Whitwell.

Clumber House's reconstruction was well advanced by the following year, and a much-admired stately home was to be the result. As part of the rebuilding, the two indoor courtyards had been replaced by the east-end of the Grand Hall and the enlargement of the main dining room. The latter measured some 60 feet long, 34 feet wide, 30 feet high, and was reportedly large enough to seat 150 diners. Several fine statues and busts were soon in position along the ground floor corridors, notably one of Napoleon as Emperor, placed in the east corridor. Five ebony cabinets and four pedestals surmounted with crystal chandeliers graced the State Drawing Room – these had been purchased at a sale of items from the Doge's Palace in Venice. Numerous valuable pieces of furniture were to be found in other rooms; some obtained by an earlier duke from the King's Palace in Bermuda.

As pride and joy of the House, the rich mahogany Library and Reading Room still claimed attention. Having only narrowly escaped devastation by the fire, they contained a magnificent collection of books, built up by the second, fourth and fifth dukes. Numbering in excess of 60,000 items, the Library boasted three notable Caxtons – 'The History of Reynard the Fox' (1481), 'The Chronicles of England' (1482), and 'The Golden Legend' (1493). A similarly aged manuscript of Gower's 'Confessio Amantis', first and second folios of Shakespeare, and vellum printing of 'Froissart's Chronicles' also enhanced this fine room. The Smoking Room, Oak Room, Yellow and Red Drawing Rooms, Billiard Room, and the previously mentioned chambers, displayed many paintings by old masters. Holbein, Van Dyke, Lely and Hogarth were among them. A grand staircase, positioned midway along the north side of the Hall, led to ballustraded galleries and the first floor bedrooms.

Figure 11 – The repaired west face of Clumber House. The central door was the main entrance to the mansion.

The Stableblock structure (constructed in the 1760's) lay slightly north of the Kitchen Wing of the House. With its distinguishing Clock Tower it had little changed from those early days. Stables, coach-houses and storerooms surrounded the cobbled square, with accommodation for grooms and others (including a billiard room for the staff). A Blacksmith's shop – to be close on hand near the 'Lincoln Stables', which housed the duchess's favourite horses – and a single-storied cottage, were a few feet away from the Housekeeper's rooms.

The high-status Walled Gardens to the north of the House site were again the centre of much interest. With no ducal presence in the Park, these had been uncared for during the 1870's, and the need for upgrading, renovating and re-stocking was now high on the list of priorities. It was to be several years before the duke would come of age and be ready to move into Clumber House. Then (as in the days of the fifth duke and his forebears) the Gardeners would again be tested to the full. The extensive Glasshouses (for fruit and flowers), the Walled Gardens and vegetable plots would once more be required to be full to overflowing with fine produce.

Pleasure Ground, 'Lincoln Terrace' walk area and the Pinetum, also the House Terraces and Parterres were made spick and span. The adequacy of the water supply from the lake was under scrutiny – it had long been a problem and a new reservoir was required and provided. Additionally, a gasometer was now available and the need for increasing its supply was soon apparent. Neglected paddocks and kennels were spruced up, roads repaired, lawns and verges close-cut, lodges redecorated and park fencing replaced and painted white. Boats and the boathouse were made ready for the use of the new owner, family and friends.

Reconstruction work at the mansion had been matched by similar efforts in the estate village, less than a mile to the east of the noble residence. In Hardwick, the ancient Grange Farm buildings and outhouses were modernised to be in keeping with the ducal status of the Estate. Farm servants (domestics, farm-labourers, cow men and horsemen, dairymaids etc.) found that their needs were being more carefully considered than of late. Cottages and single men's 'Bothies' (such buildings as that at the west-end of the Hardwick Grange, and the property currently used as the National Trust Estate Office) were also enhanced, particularly with plumbing and damp-proofing needs. The Clerk of Works' house was prepared on the south-west corner of the Hardwick Grange property.

Hardwick's Workshops were improved. These factory shops of the Newcastle domain provided services for all its Nottinghamshire properties. The Clerk of Works had some forty-plus men in his charge. Their skills involved those of Stonemasons, Carpenters, Blacksmiths,

Wheelwrights, Painters and Drainers. Other tradesmen had working accommodation there. Joiner's Shops, storerooms, machinery rooms, creosote rooms, cottages and mess rooms were included. Some of the Forestry and Gamekeeping staff had workrooms in the complex. The Sawmill at Cabin Hill was also renovated.

***

All in all, there was an eager anticipation of the new lease of life offered to the Estate by recent tragic events. Further afield, in the county towns and villages with direct 'Newcastle' interests, the ripples of change must have been felt. One upshot of the planned arrival of this new regime was that some twenty-five or more tenants gave notice that they would be quitting. It undoubtedly was a time of severe agricultural depression but whether this was the cause (or if it was just a 'cunning plan') is not clear, nevertheless the consequence of their action was that in most instances rents were reduced by up to twenty per cent!

Figure 12 –
The 'Lincoln Terrace' in the Pleasure Ground at Clumber Park – one of these semi-circular seats reputedly being the scene of the childhood accident that led to the 7th duke's leg amputation.

[Country Life Picture Library]

CHAPTER TWO

1881 to 1887

It was not all work – The new duke made his second visit – The heir to the throne called – Clumber's new atrium opened for Worship – Miscellaneous happenings – The duke came of age – Something in the air – A Proper Party – A New Chapel & other Church Matters – Outings, champagne and a Golden Jubilee – More financial matters.

IT WAS NOT ALL WORK

AS WE HAVE ALREADY NOTED, despite the traumas of those first years it was not all work at Clumber. The Forester's diary highlights some 1880 leisure-time events, such as attendance at the Sheffield Pantomime "Puss in Boots", a County Ball at Worksop and a Dance at the Manor. At this time, Wilson was connected with the Worksop Priory choir, evidenced by his going with them on a summer trip to Scarborough. Working duties continued to develop, as did the sporting life for the estate's top brass. Shooting jackdaws and rabbits around the site of the Major Oak, in Birklands, near Edwinstowe, featured alongside their hunting with hounds, and shooting parties at various locations, for hares, pheasants, woodcock and pigeon.

In March, Wilson proudly noted that his own estimate on the value of Newcastle estate timber (£6,000) to be sold in a sale at the Royal Hotel, Worksop had proved to be out by only £20! Other wood sales were held at Morton Hill Farm and Lound Hall. Fire had damaged the plantations at Manton Wood and he was involved with the local militia commander and Joseph Garside over this matter. Contacts with other leading timber merchants at this time are recorded – John Oates's firm (and that of Godley and Goulding) were among those who were to rival Mr Garside for ducal estate contracts.

Word had now reached Clumber that the young duke was a keen angler and the next task was to obtain fish to restock the Lake in readiness for his arrival. This was done by netting the river at Elkesley and also at Beard's Dam in Worksop.

THE NEW DUKE MADE HIS SECOND VISIT

30 July 1880
The Duke came to Clumber, and Lord Francis.

This diary entry indicates the local residents' first sighting of their new Master for some months. The duke was now fifteen years old, his brother Francis was fourteen. Their widowed mother had recently married Thomas Theobald Hohler and had also become a convert to Roman Catholicism. Both boys were on vacation from their studies at Eton. The youthful noblemen would have seen much activity at the mansion site, with the debris of the great fire having been cleared, and rebuilding work moving on apace.

THE HEIR TO THE THRONE CALLED – AGAIN

In 1881 Edward, Prince of Wales, travelled through the Park en route from Welbeck Abbey to Retford railway station. He stopped for an hour or so to inspect the progress of rebuilding at Clumber House, expressing approval for the on-going work and reminiscing on the subject of his previous visit some twenty years before. It would be interesting to know whether the Prince gave a thought to the memory of Lady Susan (sister of the sixth duke), a favourite mistress of his in the late-1860s.

Lord Edward Pelham-Clinton, youngest brother of the late duke, was also well known to the Prince, and during this same year was appointed as a royal Groom-in-Waiting (at £334 for six weeks attendance each year). Thirteen years later he was to become the Queen's 'Master of Household' for the rest of her life. As mentioned earlier, Lord Edward had replaced William Ewart Gladstone as the Newcastle estate's Senior Trustee. Gladstone's duties as Prime Minister, together with the fact that he had been engaged on the estate's financial affairs for around eighteen years made it a suitable time for change; – and, besides which, Mrs Hope wished it so!

In February 1883, Lord Edward met the Forester to discuss improvements to Clumber's Pleasure Ground. This was a well-protected wonderland of fine shrubs, trees, peaceful glades, winding paths and sheltered seating, stretching from the Chapel site to the boathouse. Shortly after this meeting, trees were felled adjacent to the Chapel as part of the agreed plan of action to rearrange the area between the Pleasure Ground and the Walled Gardens.

CLUMBER'S NEW ATRIUM – OPEN FOR WORSHIP

8 April 1883
At service in the Grand Hall, Clumber, the first held there.

The service in the 'Grand Hall' mentioned here indicates how far the rebuilding of the mansion had progressed since the fire. This great white-marbled atrium of a central room was a wholly new feature at Clumber, and had replaced the fire-damaged smaller rooms of the House which earlier visitors had described as a: "labyrinth". The new room was 92 feet long, 45 feet wide and 50 feet high and included corridors and vestibules. [See Colour Plate 2]

Figure 13 – The east end of the Grand Hall at Clumber House.

This impressive Hall was obviously the most fitting location for the service to be held and the preacher at this first service was the Rev Henry T. Slodden, newly-installed Vicar of Worksop Priory, who received fifty pounds per annum for his duties as Chaplain at Clumber Park. The Chapel that had been built close to the east of the House was an unfinished victim of the 1869 bankruptcy and could not have been used. It had never been available for worship and during this current decade was to be replaced by another, built to the wishes of a young nobleman (now pursuing his first year studies at Magdalen College, Oxford) who was developing into an ultra High-Churchman.

MISCELLANEOUS HAPPENINGS 1883-1885

An epidemic of diphtheria caused gloom at Clumber in August 1883. This may or may not have been brightened by an archery meeting and the knowledge that the new-fangled telephone service had reached the Park. The Forester's men were much occupied in the planning and setting-up of the necessary poles for the cabling. Wilson then proudly recorded:

22 November 1883
The telephone finished to Clumber – the first time I ever spoke through one.

Soon after this excitement, he wrote of: "a terrific gale - thousands of trees blown down – half the cedars in the centre of Apleyhead and two large ones at Clumber". Despite this setback, the telephone work continued after Christmas, extending the facility to Hardwick village.

There is then another gap in the forester's diary entries. When they resumed in late 1885, it was at a time when the new duke had come of age, but due to the rebuilding work being unfinished (as were the duke's university studies), it had been decided to reschedule any 'formal' celebrations until the following year.

NEWCASTLE ESTATE.

RULES

For Workmen employed in the "Repairs" Department.

1. The working time to be 55½ hours per week from the 20th day of February to the 9th day of November, commencing at 6 a.m., and leaving at 5-30 p.m. The working time from the 9th day of November to the 20th day of February (winter season) to be 51 hours per week, commencing at 7 a.m., and leaving at 5 p.m. Work to commence on Monday mornings at 7 a.m., and leave off on Saturdays at 1 p.m. the year round.

2. During the winter season breakfast to be had before commencing work—excepting men who work by gas-light in the shops—who will work 55½ hours per week as during the rest of the year.

3. Walking time is allowed one way at the rate of 3 miles per hour. Any distance over 3½ miles to be allowed each way after the 3½ miles are walked.

4. No smoking or intoxicating drink allowed during working hours.

5. No materials of any kind whatever—old or new—to be taken off the Estate by any workman.

6. Wages will be paid according to ability, and in case of any workman leaving, 3 days' notice to be given on either side, excepting under conditions laid down in rule 7.

7. Any man found idle, neglecting his work, using foul or abusive language, breaking these rules, or committing himself in any way, shall be discharged at a moment's notice.

8. Every man employed to keep his own time in a proper form, on a sheet supplied by the foreman, to be given up to him the Friday before each pay, or upon leaving.

NEWCASTLE ESTATE OFFICE,
WORKSOP,
May, 1883.

H. P. SISSONS & SON, Steam Printers, Bookbinders, &c., Potter Street, Worksop.

Figure 14 – 'Rules' at the Hardwick workshops in 1883

Figure 15 – circa 1886 –
The rebuilt Clumber House and the soon-to-be-demolished Chapel.

THE DUKE CAME OF AGE – KEEP IT QUIET!

28 September 1885
His Grace came of age, no rejoicings until the following Easter.

Whilst down from his first year of study at Magdalene College, Oxford, the duke had arrived at Clumber Park for his twenty-first birthday 'muted' revelry. He was probably surprised by the extent of the arrangements that had been made.

The chief Forester and other senior staff were on hand to welcome him. These included Joel Haslam, Clumber's accountant, now promoted to Estate Agent (at an annual salary of around eight hundred pounds), also William Stanhope, the new Clerk of Works and Fred Stokes, Farm Bailiff. The west entrance to the House had been decorated to a magnificent degree; this camouflaged some parts of the unfinished building work, in addition to providing the appropriate festive appearance. The Worksop Brass Band provided musical entertainment, under the leadership of Henry Pressley.

Figure 16 – Joel Haslam, Estate Agent – depicted by the press as 'much-put-upon'.

These celebrations continued on the following day and included the (6 a.m.) firing of Clumber's lakeside cannon. This was echoed by that of a twenty-one gun salute in the area of the Buslings in Worksop, close by the premises of Rueben Shaw and Sons, near to where crossroads currently control foot and vehicular traffic along Bridge Street and Newcastle Street. During the late afternoon, the duke, with his eldest sister, Lady Beatrice Adeline Lister-Kaye, drove through Worksop in an open carriage, acknowledging the good wishes of the crowds. Mrs Anne Adele Hope, the duke's wealthy grandmother, had died the previous year but his mother, Henrietta, Dowager Duchess, and his uncle, Lord Edward, accompanied them around the town.

The Union Jack was flown from the 175 feet high chimney at Shireoaks Colliery, and throughout the day the local church bells pealed. Shops and streets of the town were dressed with bunting and garlands for the occasion. The bell-ringers of the Worksop Priory church, had been at their labours from early morning until nine in the evening. They then hastened to the Royal Hotel on Bridge Street to enjoy a meal financed by the duke. House parties, shooting parties and trips to the Doncaster Races had also been prearranged. Then the duke returned to his studies at Oxford.

As Christmas 1885 approached, the duke arranged for a gift of evergreens to be sent from Clumber Park to St. Paul's Cathedral, London. This instance of festive decorations being sent to St. Paul's was the first in what became an annual offering – a tradition that was still being practised almost fifty years later.

SOMETHING IN THE AIR

The malodorous condition of the Lake had been noted for many years. Waters to the west of the boathouse were severely affected by discharge from Clumber's sewerage outlets, ensuring that at certain times the Pleasure Grounds did not live up to their name!

New piping was being laid on the lakebed. This meant that waters had to be drained and all fish being taken to the ponds at Hardwick, to be returned when the lake was refilled. The fish (wrote Wilson) were: "mostly pike, dace, tench, carp, perch, eels etc, about 45 tons. We had several watercarts going – some of the largest pike were over 30 lbs."

Figure 16a – A fine speciman of Clumber Park's pike!

A large amount of mud was cleared from the Lake and the locals (principally those who lived on the south side of the lake) enjoyed the novelty of: "walking across the Lake to Clumber on planks".

NOW FOR A PROPER PARTY!

All preparations completed, the biggest celebratory event to have occurred at Clumber Park for many years was all set to begin.

29/30 April 1886
Clumber all day and night.
Grand Banquet, Fireworks etc. A full week's festivities.

An outside caterer was there to help ensure that these festivities were glittering occasions. Nothing in the duchy had remotely matched them for over thirty years, when the sixth duke's majority was celebrated on a similarly lavish scale. The duke arrived home on the Tuesday, 26th April 1886. With him were his mother, his brother Francis and sister Florence. The folk of Worksop greeted him with a twenty-one gun salute and the guns on the Battery at Clumber answered this as he approached the House. Venetian masts with their colourful flags decorated the lanes through the Park, along with numerous lights. Arc burners of 2000-candle power lit the House, Terraces and Lake. Temporary stables, to house 3000 extra horses, were lit by electricity.

Figure 17 –
The duke's drive
through Worksop

Here the duke is seen being driven past the shop of David Winks (butcher) and – across the street – William Straw's (grocer).

31

By Wednesday a large marquee had been erected in the courtyard. It measured 170 by 50 feet and was hung with giant crystal candelabra. The marquee pavilion was the biggest of its kind, being without any interior support. Mirrors supplied extra lighting for the revellers as they enjoyed the feast and the dancing which followed – the latter being on a raised stage-cum-dance floor. Floodlights and searchlights, of 6,000 nominal candlepower, enhanced the whole scene. 600 guests enjoyed the banquet, with the top-table guests eating from a gold plate dinner service. A minor scare occurred as a small fire started in the hangings of the Grand Ballroom, when an electric incandescent light cover broke.

Earl Manvers of Thoresby, Lord Galway of Serlby and Lord Edward, the duke's uncle, were chief guests, together with principal tenants from the Clumber, Newark and Nottingham estates. However, one special person was missing – the duke's great aunt, Lady Charlotte, who was very ill and was to die during the following week. A seventy-four year-old spinster, she was the second of the fourth duke's daughters, and had personally observed the duchy through so many distressing decades.

Figure 18 –
Lady Charlotte Pelham-Clinton

As a young girl, she had become acquainted with the young Princess Victoria, and as a result had attended several functions in the Queen's presence over the years. Charlotte's father had been over-protective with all four of his daughters – never finding any men good enough for them – and she was well into her thirties before he died. After his death, she lived at Ranby with her elder sister, Georgiana, until the latter's death in 1874 – they were widely known as 'The Ladies Clinton'. She must have had a wealth of recollections of the Clumber estate prior to the building of the House parterres and terraces, the 'Lincoln Terrace' or the planting of the Lime Tree Avenue. She would have seen the expansion of those embellishments, also the Lady Garden, the Aviaries (close by South Lodge and on the site of the 'Little Farm', designed by her mother), the Gun Battery and so much more.

Thursday and Friday of this week also saw other big events – dinners for the dignitaries of East Retford and Worksop – and another grand ball. Amongst the many gifts presented to the young duke was a beautiful volume of eighteen illuminated pages, prepared by Messrs. Sissons and Sons of Worksop. Gold mounted, it was enclosed in a substantial casket of carved oak.

Figure 19 –
Presentation of a casket and a 'Loyal Address'
– See Appendix Four

On the Saturday, a Ball was held for 500 servants of the Estate and 600 children were invited to tea and entertainment. Each guest was given a gift, with a commemorative silk bannerette for each child Amongst the recipients was young Florence Winks, daughter of David, the Worksop butcher. Mr Winks supplied meat to the House and estate at Clumber as well as for the Welbeck estate and many of Worksop's townsfolk. Daughter Florence was later to marry William Straw, now famous far beyond his hometown, for the prominence afforded his semi-detached suburban house at Blyth Grove, Worksop since its purchase by The National Trust.

As though these celebratory parties were not sufficient, the 'smaller tenants' (with rents of less than £80 per annum), together with local tradesmen, were entertained at the Newcastle Arms Hotel, Tuxford, with music again provided by the Worksop Brass Band. The speeches offered during the week contained these mature comments of a young and privileged man on taking up his inheritance:

> 'Impressed as I am with the responsibility of my position, I hope that I may rise to
> the level of its requirements, and discharge the duties of an English landlord in such
> a manner as to promote the happiness of all whom Providence has in a certain
> degree committed to my charge.'
> '... It has pleased God in His providence to place me in a position of great
> responsibility, at an early period of life. Wherever there are rights there are duties.
> Wealth, power and influence are so many important gifts, and just in proportion as
> these are possessed by anyone, whether patrician or otherwise, so is his
> responsibility. Men are too prone to imagine that such a station in life is one of
> unmingled happiness, quite forgetting the numerous cares and harassing anxieties,

which always accompany it. The old adage reminds us that 'every rose has its thorn', and there is no position in life of pleasure unalloyed. You have most touchingly and affectionately alluded to my sufferings in days gone by; and I hardly need assure you that he who has suffered can the more readily sympathise with sufferers. I hope ... to interest myself in your affairs, to support the charities of the town and neighbourhood, to promote education in every department, and to foster true morality, irrespective of creed. ... I shall never allow any political difference to influence my conduct in relation to you all ... Inexperienced as I am, it would be presumptuous on my part to tender such advice as that given by my grandfather in 1851, but this much I know – that landlord and tenant are dependent on each other, and that so far from being antagonistic, they will succeed best by mutual co-operation. It will therefore be my interest to promote your interests, as it will be my pleasure to contribute to your welfare by every means in my power ...'.

The duke's comment on 'political difference' indicated an understanding that an alliance to the Conservative cause (he had already become a member of the Carlton Club) was not shared by all who heard him speak. The radical causes of those times were well-supported in the county and there was smouldering hostility by many towards the landed interests that he represented.

The special events of these two years, together with the financing by the estate of a variety of teas or dinners in the outlying parts of the Newcastle duchy, ensured that the announcement of the new duke's arrival at Clumber was heard. Other symbols of his presence were the donations he made to various good causes. One of the earliest of these was a gift of five-hundred guineas to the Newark Hospital.

A NEW CHAPEL & OTHER CHURCH MATTERS
29 July 1886 – At the laying of the foundation stone of new Church at Clumber ...

Another venture began its existence during 1886, when the foundation stone was laid for a new chapel. The Bishop of Southwell (whose newly-formed diocese was just two years old at this time) officiated and the duke was insistent that this major undertaking should reflect his 'High-Church' preferences. The previous unfinished and financially reckless edifice was demolished, with much of the material recycled into the new building. The duke had plans drawn up by George Frederick Bodley, R.A. (of Bodley and Garner), and contractors Messrs. Franklin and Sons of Oxford were employed to transform these designs into reality. Planned to be resplendently impressive, full of ritual, colour and splendour, this was to be a miniature cathedral to Anglo-Catholicism. Work proceeded gradually and it was to be almost three years before the dream came to fruition.

Away from Nottinghamshire, the duke was certainly finding his financial feet. Whilst still at university he decided to offer charitable gifts to two religious concerns in the London area. They were the Church of the Holy Redeemer at Clerkenwell and the Old Palace School at Croydon. At the latter, the duke had bought the Old Palace of the Archbishops of Canterbury and presented it to Mother Emily, of the 'Sisters of the Church' an Anglican community. These were significant endowments and set a pattern of philanthropic offerings that was to be repeated throughout his life.

OUTINGS, CHAMPAGNE AND A GOLDEN JUBILEE

October 1886 saw a visit to London by the Forester's men, where they attended the Colonial Exhibition. This 'works outing' also provided a well-packed day for Wilson. He himself visited Westminster Abbey, the Houses of Parliament, the Natural History Museum and the Albert Hall, where he heard the Great Organ being played.

Then it was back to normal activities, with visits to Belvoir Castle's timber sale and to Cromwell, where, after inspecting the glebe land there, Wilson lunched with the Vicar, the Rev. H. F. Clinton, a cousin of the duke. A few weeks later, a poaching affray at Normanton Bridge led to a court case at Retford. The defendant, one James Charlesworth, was accused of setting five nets and bagging ninety-nine rabbits. The New Year started with planting at Little Morton and Morton Grange, followed by a timber sale at Worksop.

In late April, a champagne breakfast was enjoyed at the Normanton Inn, after Wilson and his friend John King, Head Keeper, had put two thousand trout into the River Idle near the Normanton Bridge. This was just the beginning of a period of great excitement and celebrations for the Tomlinsons. Having now moved from their Sparken Hill home at Worksop, improvements and extensions (required as a result of the increased family numbers) commenced at their new dwelling on Cabin Hill.

***

MORE FINANCIAL MATTERS

Re-adjustments of Newcastle's land and property possessions were now moving on apace. Central to the well-being of the duchy's survival were incomes from rents. Around £33,500 per annum was received from some 28,000 acres of the land controlled – these were spread over some thirty parishes/locations. The death of Lady Charlotte Pelham-Clinton had presented the opportunity for the Ranby and Barnby Moor tenancies to be transferred to the duke's holdings. Conversely, advertisements were now regularly appearing for the sale of various land packages, such as the Worksop Manor Park.

During his first three years in command, the seventh duke had disposed of all his licensed premises in Newark, including the Clinton Arms and the Trent Brewery, as well as hotels and at least seven public houses, plus a beer shop. Those sales raised £34,970 for the ducal coffers, and may have been linked to his well-known support of the temperance cause. If this was the case, a more pragmatic decision was taken in not closing the Normanton Inn (now known as the 'Clumber Park Hotel' – on the 'Great West Road', a route currently numbered as A614). In that instance it is perhaps significant that it was the nearest public house for the duke's employees and tenants who lived in and around the Hardwick village!

Figure 21 — The 'Normanton Inn' – opposite to the Clumber Park entrance that leads to Hardwick village [photograph circa 1900]
[Note the Duke of Newcastle's coat of arms – the Inn has also been known as the 'Newcastle Arms']

CHAPTER THREE

1888 to 1898

Rumour, romance and roving – Improvements in the Park – Clumber's very new school – 'Convert', 'Pervert' or neither? – Still on duty with the forester – The youngest duke and duchess in England – Clumber Chapel (completed and dedicated) – Clumber's cedar avenue and rhododendrons – The duchess 'cared about doggies' – 'The open road, the dusty highway' – Financial matters – More public visits to Clumber Park – Grand ball in Clumber's hall – Paternal care – Rudolph Schmidt – Clumber cricket – Royal visitors – Our guide's activities and other happenings – Lord Francis Hope (heir to the dukedom) – St Cuthbert's College, Worksop – A new chaplain-in-waiting – More about the duke – A new hymnal, a marriage and a Diamond Jubilee.

RUMOUR, ROMANCE AND ROVING

IN 1886, THE DUKE, having completed his studies at Magdalene College, Oxford, took 'two years out' to roam around Europe and America, indulging his enthusiasm for church architecture and the classical style in everything. When combined with his expertise with the newest cameras, this must have led to a fine series of photographs from these visits to so many cities of the old and new worlds. A certificate authorising him to take photographs in Paris (the home city of his grandmother's family) is preserved in the Manuscripts Department at the University of Nottingham, and magazines and newspapers mentioning his prowess in that activity have also been noted. But – despite isolated examples – no substantial archive of his work has been tracked down to display here or elsewhere. It has been inferred that the pictures were intentionally destroyed following his death. Hopefully, this premise will one day prove to be incorrect.

Soon after his return to Clumber, the 'shy and reserved' duke became attached to a beautiful young lady, whom he was to marry during the following year. This duchess-elect was Kathleen Candy, fifteen years old at the time of their first meeting. One unsubstantiated report states that the couple met in Lincolnshire, on the platform at Louth railway station. It seems even more likely that they had become acquainted in Ireland, as both families had homes in County Monaghan – the duke's mother's family owning Castle Blayney and Kathleen's being from Rossmore Park. Wherever their first meeting, there will be more about the consequences presently.

IMPROVEMENTS IN THE PARK

Estate tenants and their families probably knew little of this romantic development at the time. What they undoubtedly knew was that the state of Clumber House and terraces, the pleasure grounds, lake, boats and fishing facilities had just about reached peak condition as a result of the years of preparation. The verges of approach roads through the Park were immaculately manicured, and there was much fresh paint on the boundary fencing. Cottages at Hardwick; the Grange Farmhouse and Workshops had been put in good order to complement the improvement work on the mansion. Developments on the tree plantations and in the gardens had moved on apace. Staffing numbers in Clumber House were being built up to better serve the occupier and his visitors. A new vessel was now sailing the waters of Clumber Lake. The yacht 'Salamanca' was noted alongside the forty-ton 'Lincoln' frigate and there were other smaller boats available for the indulgence of the duke and his friends. Many picnics or fishing outings were to be enjoyed in the idyllic setting offered here. 'Simply messing about in boats' again became a favoured pastime. The ducal portion of the estate was vibrant once more after its disastrous fall from grace during the eighteen-seventies.

CLUMBER PARK'S NEW VILLAGE SCHOOL

23 July 1888
Helping to set out for the new School at Hardwick

Wilson's diary mention of the 'new school' is a reminder that the provision of this '100 pupil' co-educational establishment was an honouring of one of the duke's undertakings at his coming-of-age festivities just two years earlier.

The thirty-year-old schoolhouse in Hardwick village, attended by the children of Clumber Park families, was now to be replaced by a new two-roomed building lined with pitched pine: "planned in accordance with the Regulations of the Educational Department, and provision is made for the accommodation of One Hundred Children". These children lived as far away as Apley Head Farm, Cottages and Lodge. Later, others also attended from the Lincoln Waterworks cottages near Elkesley. Schoolmistress Mrs Elizabeth Salmon (with the help of Miss Leaver and various visiting clergy) kept firm control of the pupils until her retirement in 1892.

On Mrs Salmon's departure, George J. Tredaway arrived to take over as headmaster. Originating from Somerset, he was an experienced organist-choirmaster and had previously been employed at the Church of St Mary Magdalene at Chewton Mendip. One of the most substantial cottages at Hardwick was put aside for the use of Mr Tredaway and his family.

Figure 22 – The Organist's cottage at Hardwick

'CONVERT', 'PERVERT' OR NEITHER?

The press had heard of the forthcoming attraction of the Clumber's new 'High Church' Chapel. It was now almost finished, some one hundred and fifty yards from duke's purpose-built Billiard Room (later known as the 'Duke's Study'). Many of the building materials for this place of worship had been recycled from its sad and uncompleted predecessor. Newspapers produced strangely worded articles and comment began to flow relating to the duke's intention.

These reports indicated that the duke was about to become a: "Pervert"! It was claimed that such a seemingly abusive term was the common currency in those days to denote a 'convert' to the

Church of Rome. Whether or not this was the true intent of the story, the duke's response consisted of an unequivocal rejection of the assertion – and he must have spent much money on letting the world know for his vigorous denials appeared in many publications. This led one newspaper to a comment that: "Sceptical persons declare that it is the invariable practice of intending perverts to deny that they have any such intentions".

Whilst not following his mother's example and converting to Roman Catholicism, what he was doing, clearly announced by his chosen fourteenth century style for the Chapel at Clumber, was emphasising his preferences for the High Church traditions available within the Church of England. The Chapel has been rightly described as a: 'remarkable example of aristocratic patronage'.

STILL ON DUTY WITH THE FORESTER

Wilson Tomlinson's diary entries for 1888 indicate a pattern of activity that is now becoming comfortably familiar to us, with attendance at timber sales in Worksop and his other duties throughout the duchy. During the period from January to April he mentions planting lime trees at Lound Hall Avenue; beech at the Cocked Hat Plantation, Elkesley Forest; poplars at Milton and an unspecified species at the Hardwick Wood Round. Other working visits were made to the duke's lands at Tuxford, Newark, Holme and Sutton-on-Trent.

Wilson records at this stage that His Grace had instructed him not to take any timber down within the Park boundaries. It is interesting to note from this that the twenty-four-year-old successor to the ducal title was now taking firm decisions on long-term projects. In respect of financial well-being, timber production was obviously a mainstay of the estate, and the duke's instruction to the Head Forester regarding the conserving of stocks within the Park was a distinct identification of its importance.

The Forester's leisure pursuits included rook shooting and hunting with the Rufford Hounds, also with Lord Galway's party at Serlby Park. In July he attended the Royal Show at Nottingham and, in August, the Chesterfield and Clay Cross Show.

THE YOUNGEST DUKE AND DUCHESS IN ENGLAND

Figure 23 – Duke and Duchess of Newcastle

20 February 1889
His Grace married Miss Candy.

On this wet and wintry Wednesday morning, the ship's guns were fired on board the 'Lincoln' frigate, as were those on the Battery at Clumber, matching similar discharges in the towns of Retford and Worksop. The Sherwood Rangers Yeomanry troop (which included the Head Forester) was in attendance to carry out mounted escort duties on the occasion of the marriage of the little duke and Miss Kathleen Florence May Candy. Their engagement had been announced just two months earlier – according to the newspapers: "a love match ... not one of convenience" (perhaps a barbed reference to the rumour that had spread about the late duke's marriage back in 1861). Kathleen's family homes were reported as being at 'The Grove', Somerby, and 'The Barn' at Winkfield, near Windsor. Her father, Major Henry Augustus Candy, was a Justice of the Peace for Rutlandshire. From a family of silk merchants who had made their reputation in the City, he was known to his intimates as 'Sugar Candy'. Her mother was the Hon. Frances Kathleen Candy – from an Irish sporting family, the Westenras; and sister of Baron Rossmore of Castle Blayney, County Monaghan.

The marriage service was held at All Saints, Margaret Street, London – not (as the duke had originally wished) at St. Alban's, Holborn, where he had usually attended Sunday worship when in London as a single man. All Saint's was a regular place of worship for the Prince and Princess of Wales, and arguably the most ornate church of the day – scene of colourful (and very lengthy) High Church ceremonies. Land for the site of the church had, in the 1850's, been gifted by a great-uncle of the duke's – one Beresford-Hope.

The church was packed for the wedding and many of the invited guests could not be seated. The duke's brother, Lord Francis, was appointed as the best man. National newspapers reported that the two-hour ceremony began at the early time of nine thirty – noting that it was probably the earliest that any of the eight bridesmaids or the two young pages had ever got up! The bride: "tall, with a fair complexion, brown wavy hair and bright grey eyes, and as with all Irish girls, inclined to laughter", was only seventeen at the time of her wedding – the bridegroom was twenty-four. This made them the youngest duke and duchess in the country.

Clumber's Head Gardener, Michael Gleeson, had prepared the bride's bouquet of eucharis lilies, lily of the valley and orange blossoms. These blooms enhanced her dress, which was described as: "white and silver Louis XV brocade, with a very long train, front edged with a fringe of orange blossoms and Pont d'Alecon lace, opening over a skirt of plain white satin. The bodice at the throat was slightly pointed, and trimmed round with a cascade of filmy lace."

The large congregation included a certain Oscar Wilde and his wife – they bought the happy pair a 'Japanese box' as a wedding present. The infamous playwright (although ten years older than the duke) was a fellow student of the duke's Alma Mater – Magdalen College, Oxford. Amongst numerous splendid gifts from their many friends, wedding presents from Clumber Park included a fluted silver writing set from the House staff, a crocodile blotting-book from the employees at Hardwick Farm and the Clumber estate, plus a silver-mounted stationery case from members of the Clerk of Works Department.

The Bishop of Lincoln officiated at the service, using his sermon to remind the duke and duchess of their duty:

> We beg you to remember your great responsibilities.... Remember that your household is to
> be a Christian household; take into your service only such as is godly... [Your household] ...
> must be hallowed by daily prayer in your own private Chapel; you must have a faithful priest
> as your Chaplain ... You must take care that the young on your estates are given a Christian

and not merely a secular education; and see to it too in the great council of the nation in which you are called to take your part...'

After the service, the couple left the church flanked by spectators of the event reported to be five or six deep all the way to Regent Street. The wedding breakfast was held at 7, South Audley Street, Mayfair, London.

CLUMBER CHAPEL – COMPLETED AND DEDICATED

Following their honeymoon at Pau in the Pyrenees, the newly-weds moved into Clumber House at the end of May. The next big event was to be the long-awaited opening of the new Clumber Chapel. This impressive edifice was dedicated to the Blessed Trinity (later re-dedicated to St. Mary the Virgin). Built with warm red Runcorn sandstone and white Steetley stone, it was of the fourteenth-century Gothic style: "as though untouched by the hand of the Reformation". Constructed at a cost in excess of £40,000, the chapel was lit by oil lamps and candles. The stained glass windows were mostly prepared by Charles Eamer Kempe. As a wedding gift, the duke's tenantry assisted with the cost of those windows which are in the Lady Chapel. People of Worksop provided the money to pay for the pulpit. Superlative woodcarvings were later to be added to the building, based on the designs of the Reverend Ernest Geldart. The fine rood screen was constructed of oak and the choir stalls of walnut and cedar. This magnificent place of worship – its tower rising to a height of 180 feet – was finally ready for business on 22 October.

The Bishop of Southwell officiated at the first service, having laid the foundation stone three years earlier. Guests including the bishop's counterpart from Lincoln, whose cathedral choir (along with boys from the All Saint's Choir, Margaret Street, London) assisted in providing the vocal music. The Lincoln prelate subsequently suffering a public rebuke (a letter to 'The Times' no less) from Rev. W. K. John Kaye, his own Archdeacon, for allowing the boys to take part in such an extreme ritualistic service! This complaint was not the only adverse comment to reach the ears of the duke. Most of the letters referring to the event appear to be congratulatory; they mention the 'great beauty' and 'regal magnificence' of the Chapel celebrations. However, there was one from a gentleman who although not present on the day, had read of the service in his newspaper. Writing of his: "abhorrence of the High Church traditions, he described them as 'Mass in Masquerade' – 'Burlesque if not Blasphemic'!" The duke replied in an apparent attempt to appease the complainant but soon received another letter from this correspondent indicated that there was to be no meeting of minds on this matter. The duke's great-grandfather (the ultra-Protestant fourth duke) would have been thrilled that the remonstration had been made!

Figure 24 – Choir & Clergy arrive at Clumber Chapel.

Music for the service was provided on the partially completed organ – which eventually cost some £3,000 – and was under construction by Messrs. Gray and Davison on the specifications of Dr. Roberts, organist of Magdalen College at Oxford. The organ sounds were supplemented by a small orchestra. The duke's organist, Mr George F. Ashley, had spent some nine months in rehearsing the local choir for this event. He shared the organ accompaniment for the Dedication Service with Dr. Roberts, who was called on to supply more music than he had planned for, as the commencement of the service was delayed by the late arrival of the House party. This delay must have been even more frustrating for estate blacksmith, John Adcock, whose strong arms coped with pumping the organ bellows over his many years at Clumber prior to water-pump power being provided!

The day chosen for the Dedication Service was one of mixed weather, spells of sunshine intermingling with strong winds and heavy rain. These latter elements were used to excuse the House party's failure to appear at the appointed time – which led to comments that it might be useful to have an underground passage from the House to the Chapel – shades of Newcastle's neighbour's subterranean facilities at Welbeck? The late (and very much wealthier) fifth Duke of Portland's expensive innovations were merely a fanciful dream at Clumber!

The Vicar of Worksop's Priory Church (the Rev. Henry T. Slodden) was concerned that his parish finances were likely to be adversely affected as a result of the opening of this additional place of worship. Writing no doubt with more hope than expectation, he requested that alms collected at Clumber Chapel's opening service might be offered to the Priory. The vicar was soon to be disappointed to hear the duke's decree that the monies should instead go towards the needs of another newly-planned establishment – St Cuthbert's College, Worksop – of which, more will be recorded later.

Estate families were encouraged to attend Sunday services in the new Chapel at Clumber, and the High Church rituals favoured by the duke soon became familiar to all who worshiped there. Those local folk who wished to attend religious services, but objected to this tradition, made their way to other churches or chapels in Worksop.

Now that the Chapel was established, the duke was keen to develop the musical aspects of the services by the provision of an available and trained choir. To accomplish this purpose, advertisements were placed in appropriate publications throughout England, notifying vacancies in the Duke of Newcastle's new choir at Clumber. The ducal couple's interest in the Waifs and Strays' Society was also an opportunity to select suitable voices from the children under the care of that body. Boys between eight and twelve years of age were eligible, formal education being provided alongside the estate children in the recently constructed village school. Under the direction of the Chaplain, the boys were allocated two dormitories in his newly established Parsonage.

Rev. Walter F.B. Ward – on a stipend of £250 per year – succeeded Rev. J.E. Hatton, the estate Chaplain. The latter had resigned after only two years at Clumber (allegedly due to disagreements with the duchess, who he privately described as 'hard-nosed'). The 'Church Magazine' for this period is noteworthy for the sorrows expressed therein by both clerics at the poor attendance at the Communion services by the men of the Park! Harsh remarks are directed at these slackers: "Where were the young Gardeners, the Grooms and the Members of the Night School?" – where indeed?!

Figure 25 – The Clumber Chapel Choir of 1889.

CLUMBER'S CEDAR AVENUE AND RHODODENDRONS

Commenced in the same year as the opening of the Chapel, the picturesque walkway known for observable reasons as Cedar Avenue was said to have come from an idea of the duchess. This pleasant and enduring avenue contained fifteen pairs of fine cedars and traces its path from the Pleasure Grounds north-east of the Chapel to the southern gate of Clumber's Walled Gardens.

Mention of the Pleasure Grounds provides a reminder of the huge purchases of rhododendrons during the early years of the young duke's regime. Back then, George Farnsworth's auction sale of nursery stock at Matlock Moor had provided more than 65,000 plants: "mostly good hybrid rhododendrons" for the Clumber Estate. The purchase of so many of these shrubs has left its legacy into the present century. Copiously spread around the Park's acreage, bringing splashes of colour to set against the many shades of green, these purchases are most stunningly beautiful in their season. Unfortunately, the common variety has proved to be so insidious that they are, to a large extent, being replaced by less high-maintenance varieties.

THE DUCHESS 'CARED ABOUT DOGGIES'
(ALSO HORSES, CARRIAGES, AND MUCH MORE BESIDES)

The duke and duchess were now settling into married life together (and often apart, keenly following their separate interests) and Clumber Park was again getting used to having a firm guiding hand – usually that hand belonged to the duchess! It is more than likely that, by the early eighteen-nineties, all Heads of Departments had made the acquaintance of Kathleen, Duchess. This determined young woman had now reached her twenties. With firm ideas and an even stronger personality, she was never slow to stand-in for her husband when senior management decisions were required.

Figure 26 – Kathleen, Duchess of Newcastle.

Her outdoor interests were well publicised, especially in respect of dogs, carriages, Welsh Ponies and horses - including the occasional mildly successful racehorse. Extensive kennels were constructed to her specifications close by the Hardwick's water tower in 1891, they cost in excess of £1,000 and were described as including a 'hospital' for veterinary support. They and neighbouring overflow kennels soon housed over ninety dogs, with the main block having generously-sized tarmac-floored exercise cages. There were several other dogs in the care of the gamekeepers based at the Budby Corner cottages.

Figure 27 (above) – Hardwick Kennels – circa 1893

Figure 28 (left) – A Budby Corner cottage. Additional kennels were provided in this area of the Park, where gamekeepers had dwelt since the late eighteenth century.

The duchess is said to have joked that: "nobody who does not care for doggies has much chance at Clumber". Her nickname of 'Tatta' may be connected to this particular interest! She became an expert judge of dogs (specialising in wire-haired fox terriers), and continuing in that capacity for over fifty years, never forgetting her early experiences, when she was one of the youngest judges ever to adjudicate at the American Kennel Club Show held in Madison Square Gardens. With Princess (later Queen) Alexandra, she shared a love of Borzois (Russian wolfhounds). It was said to be due to the duchess's efforts that the first Borzois Club was established in England during 1892. She became Master of the Clumber Harriers and, by November 1896, there were thirty Borzois (several purchased from the kennels of the Czar at Catchnia), twenty-five Fox Terriers, twenty Clumber Spaniels (see Appendix One), and a pack of Harriers at Clumber. According to one newspaper report, there was also an 'American wolf' kennelled alongside the more conventional members of the canine family. This wolf – a gift from the Earl of Liverpool – adds to a short-list of unusual animals kept at Hardwick by various members of the Newcastle dynasty – the fourth duke had a leopard there during the late 1820's, and earlier, during that duke's minority, his Trustees appear to have had two buffaloes in the farm barn!

The duchess also achieved a fine reputation as a carriage driver. Whether 'doubles, tandem or four-in-hand' she was reported to be entirely confident. Shooting, angling and painting (mainly pictures of her animals) were amongst her other interests. Her prize-winning Welsh Ponies became nationally famous. As well as her definite views on the dècor and furnishings of the House, the duchess also had robust opinions as to the lines along which the ducal mansion should be run. She was eager to impose her rule on the efficient running of the kitchens and gardens. Never slow to chide any of the staff who failed to meet her high expectations, William Odd, House Steward, and Lucy Jackson the Housekeeper, were first in line for her displeasure, but were the recipients of high praise when such was deserved. Other indoor staff at that time also included two footmen, the cook, three housemaids and two housemen. The duchess had her personal maid and there were four laundry maids, a stillroom maid, coachman and six grooms. All these were to be housed in or close by the mansion, either in the stableyard accommodation or estate cottages.

'THE OPEN ROAD – THE DUSTY HIGHWAY'

Three years into his marriage, the duke again broke loose from Kathleen, Duchess – this time, not to visit America or Europe, but to travel around the South of England – *IN A HORSE DRAWN CARAVAN*! His friend, Doctor William Gordon-Stables, had been the first to purchase a 'land yacht' from the Bristol Wagon Works and named it 'The Wanderer'. The duke was determined to emulate this and, at the same time, apply his photographic hobby by recording his travels on film to the fullest extent (Oh where? Oh where? are those much praised photographs now?). The caravan was built to his specifications and complete with many luxuries – 'with nothing whatever forgotten' – including a piano and a wine cellar (the latter being a box chest, slung between the axles, with a trap-door access from the living area of the van)!

Perhaps as an indication of the duke's resolve to live as independent a life as possible, the twenty-five foot long caravan was named the 'Bohemian'. Drawn by two hefty dray horses (at a top speed of around four miles per hour) the vehicle required additional horsepower whenever steep hills were encountered. One such occasion was in the summer following the duke's new purchase, when he visited Kent and Surrey with his companion, Gambier Bolton. The travellers wished to call at the 'Globe and Rainbow' public house at Kilnton, which stood (and is still just about recognisable) at the top of a lengthy incline. To achieve this, it was necessary to hire five extra horses from a farm at Trillinghurst. The sight of this unique vehicle, weighing some two tons and pulled by the seven straining animals, was reported as causing: "quite a sensation in the village".

It is tempting to speculate that Kenneth Grahame, author of 'Wind in the Willows' fame (which he was drafting during the 1890's) must have heard of our 'little duke's' escapades! Grahame was well-acquainted with the Cranbourne and Winkfield area, especially the Fernhill estate, in Windsor Forest. Members of the duchess's family already had a home in the same parish and it was not to be many years before the duke purchased Forest Farm, a property adjoining Fernhill Park. Grahame had lived at Fernhill Cottage as a child, and his favourite uncle was a curate at the local church. Could our diminutive nobleman have been the model for the famous 'Mr Toad'? – it is most improbable that Grahame would have admitted it!

Like Toad, the duke (currently: 'a gentleman gypsy') was soon to be captivated by the promise of the motor car age. Although the exact date of the duke's conversion to the new-fangled world of the internal combustion engine is not recorded, it is known that he had taken to the motor car by the turn of the century. One of his coachmen, Albert Johnson, took on the role of chauffeur and stayed in that job for over thirty years, coping with a wide array of these pioneering motor vehicles.

Figures 29 (above) & 30 (below) – Two views of 'The Bohemian'.
As Mr Toad said '... the very finest cart of its sort that was ever built, without any exception'

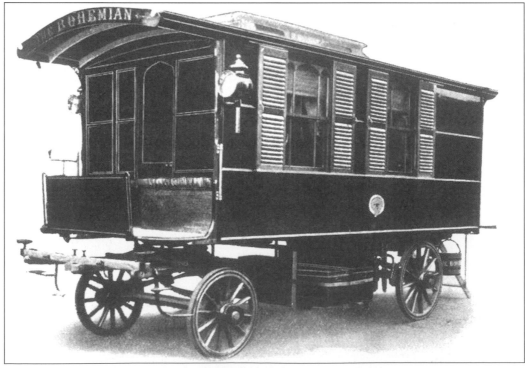

Note the 'Wine Cellar' – hung between the axles!

*Figure 31 –
Interior of the
'Bohemian' – note the
piano and the mask!*

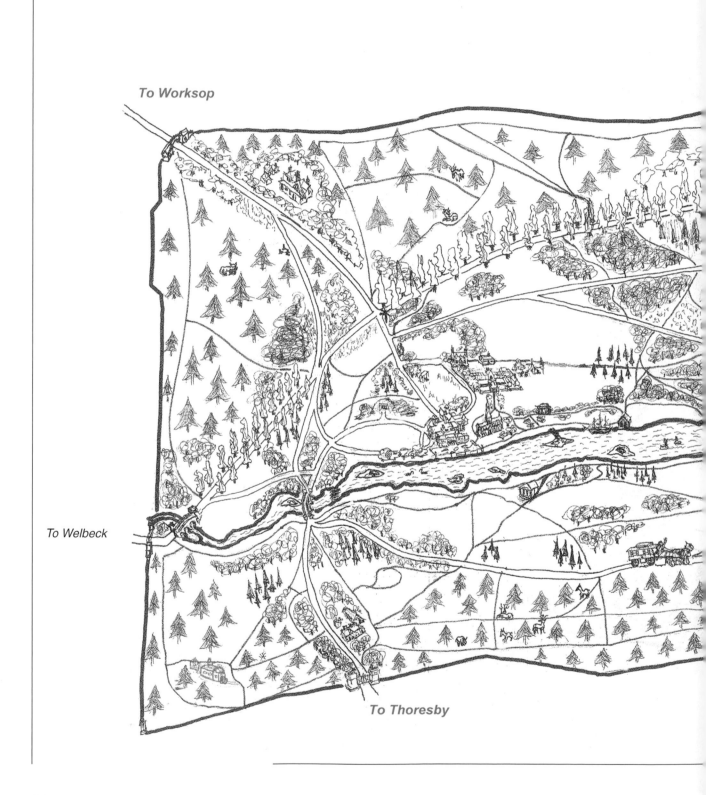

To Worksop

To Welbeck

To Thoresby

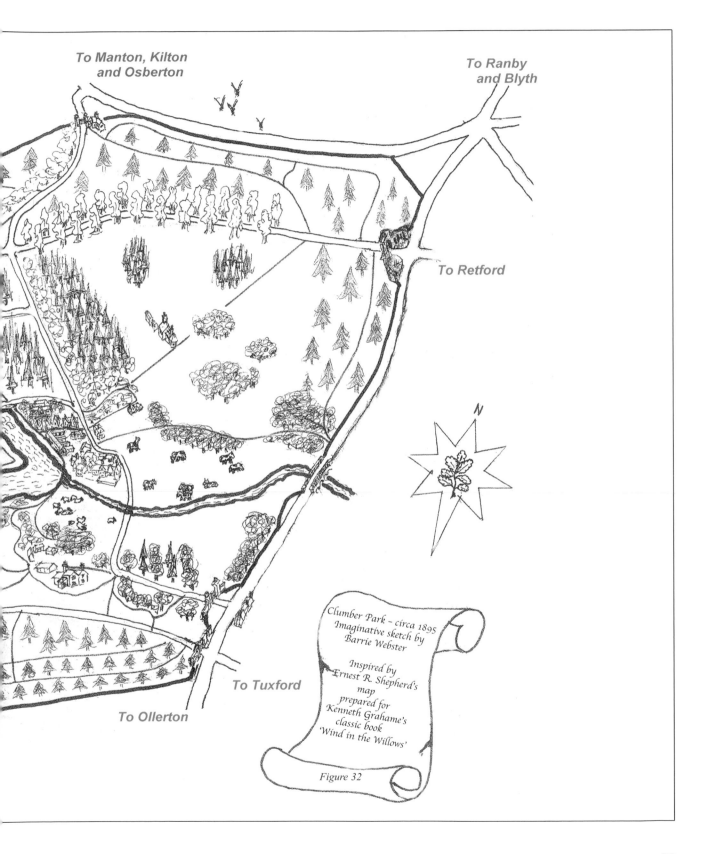

To Manton, Kilton and Osberton

To Ranby and Blyth

To Retford

To Retford

To Tuxford

To Ollerton

N

Clumber Park – circa 1895
Imaginative sketch by
Barrie Webster

Inspired by
Ernest R. Shepherd's
map
prepared for
Kenneth Grahame's
classic book
'Wind in the Willows'

Figure 32

FINANCIAL MATTERS

Estate accounts for the years of the early eighteen-nineties show a reasonably sound financial state within the duchy. Annual income exceeded £40,000 from rents and royalties – with another £1,000 received from shooting rights and the sale of game. Timber sales produced over £3,600 and the garden produce raised some £360 (mainly from the gardens at Ranby Hall). Coal mining dues at Babbington, Bagthorpe, Brinsley (where the father of author D.H. Lawrence was working at this time) and the New Hucknall Collieries brought in £4,000 pounds, with a further £8,600 from the Shireoaks Colliery Company. Royalties on the sale of sand, clay and gravel completed the list of income-raising assets. A bank balance of £10,400 is shown and the duke had taken just under £1,000 from the coffers for his own expenses during the year.

Land sales continued, usually in small pockets, such as that at Slack Walk, Worksop. However, the 1,500 acre Martin estate, north west of Bawtry was sold to Benjamin Ingham Whitaker in 1891. There had been one other major acreage release a year earlier when the duke sold 1,644 acres of Worksop Manor Park and adjoining woodlands, by auction, to John Daniel Robinson (later Sir John). This wealthy brewer, politician and philanthropist paid some £30,000 for the manor house, grounds and adjourning farm land, plus a further £25,000 for the woodlands. It is perhaps a perfect example of the changing times, that a Victorian entrepreneur should be moving into core territory previously held by two successive dukes (Norfolk and Newcastle). The 'Lordship' title was, however, not included in the sale – the Newcastle's did not release it until over a century later.

Other land sales offered much of the remaining acres of the old Worksop Manor estate, such as the Park Cottage and associated timber (sold for £4,290 to Sir Henry Watson, a Sheffield solicitor); Claylands, Gateford, Haggonfields and Hatfield Farms; Shireoaks Hall, Park and Farm; Manor Park Lodge, Shireoaks Inn, Shireoaks Quarry and the pasture land to the rear of Shireoaks Row. Also on offer were another twenty or so farms with their houses, homesteads and pasture land. The total income from these sales of just over 4,000 acres realised £143,000.

Figure 33 – Crimson Drawing Room, Clumber House – 1908
[Country Life Picture Library]

MORE PUBLIC VISITS TO CLUMBER PARK

Members of the public were now visiting Clumber and the other 'Dukeries' estates in increasing numbers. Hotels in Edwinstowe, Retford and Worksop held keys to the Park gates for their customers to be taken on guided tours through its sylvan glades. The 'Posting Proprietors Association' members could obtain admission passes and these were also available on application to the general public. The Agent, Mr Haslam, had become more concerned about the increased number of visitors to the Park, noting that the flow was 'constantly going on during nine months of the year'. In 1887 he organised a two week census on the numbers of 'conveyances' involved and reported that 95 vehicles containing 409 people had entered along Lime Tree Avenue and that 90 vehicles with 221 on board had departed in the opposite direction. There is also a strong probability that many more (uncounted) visitors entered the Park through its six other entrances known as Trumans, Carburton, South, Drayton, Normanton and Manton.

Whenever the duke and duchess were away (which was often) tours were arranged around the Park, Gardens, Chapel and House. Newspaper advertisements encouraged visitors to the Park to admire the Lake, Pleasure Grounds with their summer house temples, the formal parterres and Italianate terraces. They were also invited to visit the new Chapel and see the interior of the mansion, where the glorious rich damask flock wallpapers of the drawing rooms enhanced the fine furniture, chandeliers and ornate tiled chimneypieces. High on the most admired list were tapestries, portraits, clocks, and display cabinets containing Sevre porcelain, Delph pottery, stuffed animals, and glass and ebony collections. Amongst the many glorious rooms were the Grand Hall and the Library, where as many as 70,000 volumes were reported to be housed, many of great value.

What those fortunate visitors saw was well described in the Illustrated London News during August 1893:

> – [Clumber's] Entrance Hall is certainly, in its way, unsurpassed in England. A Hall within a
> Hall ... columns of white marble forming an inner room within this great marble atrium ...
> The State Drawing Room is well furnished with pictures ... Money value ... £25,000 ... The
> Room is close to the Entrance hall ... rich and stately ... At one end, tall Corinthian columns,
> rich in white and gold, divide off a kind of alcove. Opposite to these the high window looks
> out into the park, between long sweeping curtains whose colour harmonises with the pale
> colour of the walls. On one side is a splendid and ornate chimneypiece of the whitest marble
> ... and a steel grate, richly engraved ...

The little Breakfast Room ... with its pictures - the State Drawing Room - the Crimson Drawing Room – the small Dining Room (richly ornamented ceiling) ... anti-room to the Library (busts of Pitt and Fox)...Smoking Room (chimney from Fonthill - exquisite figures in pure white marble) ... Large Drawing Room (damask hung chandelier) ... Library (no chamber in the house is finer?).

Public admission to the House was through the door of the blue and white Large Dining Room which was situated in the north-west wing, near the Housekeeper's Room. Around the House and pleasure gardens there were notices warning visitors to 'keep off the grass'. Unsurprisingly, this increased public usage led to mischief-making by 'impudent persons' – a comment which is surely timeless! The consequences of these nuisances being that the estates of Clumber, Thoresby and Welbeck issued a joint announcement that access to the grounds would henceforth only be granted to vehicles belonging to the Posting Proprietors Association.

Figure 34 – Advertisement from a 1904 Guide Book to the 'Dukeries' area of Nottinghamshire.

Figure 35 – Clumber's Walled Gardens.

Figure 36 – South face of Clumber House.

GRAND BALL IN CLUMBER'S HALL

29 November 1892
Grand Ball at Clumber, 500 guests, 163 horses in tent.

This illustrious affair, requiring the provision of trains from Melton Mowbray to Worksop for many of the guests, was described as: "one of the most brilliant gatherings of nobility and gentry held in North Notts. in recent years". Those travelling by train were treated to dinner on the journey north and also to breakfast on their way home.

Figure 37 – Carriages arrive at Truman's Lodge on route to the festivities at Clumber House.

Apart from the duchess' family and friends from the Melton area, large parties arrived from the Duke of Portland's Welbeck estate and from the Earl and Countess Manvers' home at Thoresby. Many other local families were represented and those arriving by horse-drawn carriages found that two enormous marquees had been erected near the House stables, to provide the supplementary stabling accommodation. Dancing began at ten o'clock, to the music of the band of the Royal Artillery, Woolwich, from their lofty perch on the upper gallery of the Grand Hall. The Hall itself was resplendent in rich and gorgeous decorations. The mosaic-marbled floor was covered with a: "smooth wooden flooring ... a delightful condition for dancing". Illumination was provided by arches of tall candles in their candelabrums, and by gas lighting.

The duke and duchess received their guests in the ornate Grand Drawing Room. The walls of this imposing room were hung with rich cream satin damask. Part of the 'Prince of Wales' suite furniture included the magnificent items mentioned earlier as having belonged to the Doge's Palace, Venice and the King's Palace, Bermuda. Also used were the Yellow Drawing Room and Tea-room that adjoined the reception area. Despite this, there was only just about enough space for the many visitors. All in all, the event was a huge success. Joel Haslam, Agent, and William Henry Odd, House Steward, received much praise for their comprehensive arrangements and it was a timely dress rehearsal for a Royal event scheduled to occur a few months later.

PATERNAL CARE

Considering the rebuke that he had earlier administered to the males of his flock, the Chaplain would have been understandably elated when Christmas Day 1892 found one hundred communicants at the service in Clumber Chapel. On Boxing Day estate staff and their families, in all about two hundred and fifty of them, enjoyed tea in the Great Dining Room of the mansion. Not for the first time, the press mentioned the 'paternal care' shown by the young duke and duchess towards their employees.

The care displayed included the provision of a single storey Village Hall at Hardwick, for the use of all estate dwellers. This structure (very basic and having been completed in late-1892) was a dual-purpose building. The room's alternative identification as 'The Oratory' was due to its use as a place of worship for the weekday services. It was also utilised for worship on special holy days, in a vain attempt to encourage everyone to be present.

Close by this building was another of similar construction. This second one was variously known as the 'Billiards Room', 'Men's Club' or 'Reading Room'. As well as the obvious billiards' table (usually a good quality 'cast-off' from the mansion) the hut also housed a grand piano and the Hardwick Library. Apart from books, daily, weekly and illustrated papers were made available to (note the sexism!): "men and lads of 16 and upward residing in or at work in Clumber Park". Mr Tredaway acted as Librarian and Mr Richard Alcock (foreman joiner at the Workshops) collected the subscriptions of one penny per week, or half-a-crown [12$\frac{1}{2}$p] per year. This new Village Hall was also ideal for small social events at Hardwick, as exampled by the 'Parish Amusement' in early winter, when Joel Haslam, Agent to the Estate, arranged for a 'Conjuring and Ventriloquist Evening' to entertain the cottagers. Draughts, dominoes and cards were supplied for the use of subscribing members and, some time later, there were the added novelties of dances, whist drives and lantern-slide lectures.

His Grace encouraged the formation of Clothing Clubs, with the organist's wife, Mrs Tredaway, being nominated as organiser for the Park tenants saving schemes. Other 'innovations' included Sick Clubs and Coal Clubs. The Clumber Sick Club was formed to provide fees for one nominated doctor to attend the needs of all those in the Park, instead of the many medics (from Worksop and elsewhere) who had previously visited their own private patients. The Coal Clubs – such as the one run by the Vicar at Bothamsall – encouraged subscriptions which the duke then topped-up by an annual interest and bonus payment. All these self-help ventures offered tenants the opportunity to plan their spending on essentials.

Numerous examples are found in estate records of the duke and duchess' attention to the needs of individual members of their tenants - for instance, a cash present of five pounds seems to have been the going rate for weddings, and the attendance of one or both of the nobles at the bedside of a seriously ill tenant was the norm. However there were discretionary decisions to be made on sick pay and pensions prior to the provision of sufficient benefits by the state. Help was also given with the cost of medical operations and for such items as the: "£2.10s.0d [£2.50p] for artificial eyes for Arthur Read", the steamroller driver. £5 was spent on the provision of a pony for William Wingell, a retired employee living at the remote Tank Woodyard. An emergency payment of one guinea [£1.05p] was made to George Favill, who had been reported as being in: "great distress". A further £10 payment was subsequently recorded towards Mr Favill's funeral costs. Whether or not these payments (and many others like them) met the requirements of the various situations, or if they were well received, is not known.

When attempting to gauge human attitudes of the past, we are invariably frustrated by lack of written evidence to substantiate a general feeling that reaches out to us from the available documents. We are also beset with fables, with little chance of verification. Apart from other considerations, we know from life experiences that no two people will react the same way in any given situation. Blind faith and deep cynicism may be the opposite poles of the measure. Having weighed the many and varied components, this author's conclusion is that some few years into their control of this previously much-troubled estate, the ducal couple were attracting a genuine fondness from their tenants.

RUDOLPH SCHMIDT

Figure 38 – 'Dolph'.

There is a particular example of individual care that, although hardly typical, gives a flavour of the way the various levels of estate personnel could work in harmony.

Believed to have been born in France in 1884, Rudolph was the son of Anna Karolina Schmidt. Anna Karolina was born in 1840 at Steinmaur, Zurich, Switzerland and, at the time of Rudolph's birth, she was employed in the Paris household of the Hon. Mrs Frances Kathleen Candy, the duke's future mother-in-law. The identity of Rudolph's father is not known, although he was said (by Mrs Candy) to have been a gardener. When the Candy's returned to England in the late 1880's, they offered to bring Anna Karolina and her young son with them, to which she agreed. Anna Karoline Schmidt died in December 1890, at the Candy's home in Somerby, Leicestershire. After his mother's death, Rudolph was fostered firstly at Barsby and then in Somerby.

In the early 1890's it was arranged that the boy should be placed on the estate of the Duke of Newcastle, Nottinghamshire. At Clumber, Rudolph was entrusted to the care of the family of a highly respected Houseman, George Anderson and his wife. The Anderson's lived at Gas House

Cottages and had three children of their own: Charles, Fred and Annie. On Mrs Elizabeth Anderson's death in her early forties, George married again and he and his new bride continued to accept Rudolph as their 'adopted' son. He in his turn was happy to call George his 'Dad'. Rudolph attended the village school at Hardwick. From an early age, he was noted for his regular attendance at Clumber Chapel, where he firstly became a boy acolyte and later (in 1911) the adult thurifer.

When he reached his fourteenth birthday in 1898 Rudolph began training as a joiner in the Estate Workshops at Hardwick. Eleven years later he was selected as Clumber House Carpenter. At this time his weekly wage was £1.8s.0d [£1.40p] and he paid 10/- [50p] per week to Mrs Anderson for his board.

Figure 39 – George Anderson with his second wife. George was a Houseman at Clumber House.

Keen on sport, playing cricket and football for the Clumber Park teams, he took on the duties of the Cricket Club secretary and served as fixture secretary and Captain for the football team. He made many friends (being known to all by the nickname of 'Dolph') and enjoyed many and varied leisure time activities. These pastimes included cycling, walking, playing cards and billiards. He also attended dances at the 'Gaiety' theatre/cinema in Worksop.

The Sherwood Rangers Yeomanry Cavalry (Clumber Troop) was one of his greatest interests. Some twenty-six men of Clumber Park estate joined this force in 1909 [*See also Chapter Five*]. During training they received a gratuity of £2 per week in lieu of wages. Over four years Rudolph attended regular training sessions at the Normanton Inn and at a variety of Training Camps, including Salisbury Plain. When he had completed his agreed period with these 'Territorials', 'Dolph' volunteered for duty in the Army on 25 August 1914. By 1915, he was serving in the Sherwood Foresters Regiment and was involved in the fighting at Gallipoli. There he was injured and (after spending a month or so in hospital at Alexandria) was invalided home to England.

On Valentine's Day 1916 'Dolph' married Annie Mabel Constance Belfit in London (the duke sent £5 as a wedding present). Twenty-four-year-old Miss Belfit was from a London-based family who had originated in Worksop. She had been confirmed at Clumber Chapel on 9 March 1909. Before her marriage the bride had been employed in Clumber House for several years and had risen to the position of Head Parlourmaid.

At the time of his marriage Rudolph had adopted the anglicised name of 'Richard Smith', no doubt to avoid confusions linked to prevalent feelings about Germanic sounding names. This change was not completed legally until after his death. He was soon back on active service, being sent to France where, in 1917, he was again wounded, this time 'seriously'. Returned home again, he was (by the spring of 1918) considered to have sufficiently recovered to be returned to the front line in France. He was killed in action on Saturday, 21 September 1918 – less than two months before the end of the War - and buried at the Bellicourt British Cemetery. He is also commemorated on the Memorials at Hardwick and in Clumber Chapel. On the former he is shown as 'Richard Smith' and in the Chapel as 'Rudolph Schmidt'. In October, 1918, Clumber's Chaplain prepared a notice of Rudolph's death for the 'Worksop Guardian' newspaper, giving 'Dolph' his original name. Rudolph's son (subsequently Major Frank Richard Smith M.B.E.) was born on 20 October 1918.

CLUMBER CRICKET

Cricket had been recorded at Clumber as early as 1824, when the fourth duke noted in his diary that he had enjoyed a game with his sons and others. In 1881, an estate team was said to have played against a Worksop team on the frozen lake. Anecdotal evidence suggests that at some date during that decade, the young duke had approached the famous W.G. Grace for advice on the provision of a suitable cricket ground at Clumber. As will be obvious from later comments, a cricket team was certainly organised and matches played, although the experiment seems to have been short-lived.

In July 1893, the Chaplain recorded in the Church Magazine that cricket matches had been introduced for the boys of the Choir. The first of these being on 8th August, when a game was arranged against the boys of the Ordsall Cricket Club, in which Clumber team were the victors by eight wickets. Later, after struggling: "to find opponents of their own size", they played against boys of the Ashley House School, Worksop, as well as against a team from the estate school at Hardwick. They also had fixtures with the choir boys of Blyth, Grimsby, Harthill, Thoresby and Welbeck .

The Clumber Park C.C. has this year risen, like the Phoenix, into a new life, from the ashes of a former existence. A strong committee has been formed and a strong eleven can be sent into the field. The matches have been fully reported in the local papers, up to date 2 have been won, against Firbeck Hall and Walesby, and 2 lost, against Wheatley (home and return).

The Choir boys played a Match on June 10th, against Ashley House School. Mr. Cook kindly acting as Captain for the Clumber boys, against Mr. Johnson, who plays with the School team. The match resulted in a victory on the first innings, as under :—

CLUMBER.

	1st Innings.		2nd Innings.	
W. Stanhope b Johnson	16	c Johnson b St. Aubyn	2
H. Tredaway run out	7	c Hunter b St. Aubyn	0
H. Stanhope b St. Aubyn	0	c Johnson b St. Aubyn	0
T. Tredaway b Harris	8	c Johnson b St. Aubyn	16
G. Cook c St. Aubyn b Johnson	2	b Johnson	42
T. Bratton c Harris b St. Aubyn	7	b Johnson	0
G. Atkins not out	11	l.b.w. b Johnson	5
W. Spencer b St. Aubyn	3	c and b Bramall	3
A. Martin c Bramall b Johnson	1	c Kirkley b Johnson	0
F. Houldsworth c and b Johnson	0	c and b Johnson	1
E. Turner c Bramall b Johnson	0	not out	1
Bye 1	1	Byes 3, Wide 1	4
	56		74

Figure 40 – From the Clumber Park Church Magazine of July 1893.

Earlier in the year, the (adult) Clumber Park Cricket Club, apparently dormant since the eighties: "has this year arisen, like the Phoenix, into new life, from the ashes of a former existence". A 'strong committee' was formed, with Mr Tredaway as Secretary. The duke agreed to allow staff to prepare a permanent cricket ground on land to the west of the Walled Gardens and south of the Paddocks. A picturesque cricket pavilion was erected there and the duke's friend, William Hickson (a wine merchant, living in Clumber Cottage) later provided bowling screens to shield the shadowy backcloth of trees that surrounded the ground. The team was soon supplied with caps of navy-blue colour, centred by a white medallion shaped badge containing the initials 'C.P.'.

Press reporters recorded the first of these senior matches played against teams from Firbeck, Walesby, Wheatley and the Worksop Police. The Club boasted that it did not stray into the competitive world of cricket leagues! Instead, it chose to remain aloof, selecting the teams that should be allowed the privilege of being invited to play a 'friendly' match against the home side – also locations that the Club would deign to visit! Over the following years, matches were arranged with teams from Budby, East Markham, Rufford, Whitwell and the National Telephone Company.

It was to be more than one hundred years before the Club joined the prestigious 'Bassetlaw' league. As their identification badge – and to honour their predecessors on the hallowed cricket square – these latter-day 'Clumberites' chose to proudly wear the coat of arms of the Newcastle dukedom.

ROYAL VISITORS

Early in the 1893, the first Royal visit of the duke's 'at home' reign was noted by his Head Forester:

23 January 1893
The Duke and Duchess of Teck, Princess Mary and Prince Alexander came to Clumber.

The diary entry indicates that the popular Princess Mary (also known as 'May') had arrived at Clumber with her parents, the Duke and Duchess of Teck. The Princess had recently been in mourning following the death of her fiancé, Prince 'Eddy', Duke of Clarence, who had died in January 1892. Princess Mary was to become engaged to 'Eddy's' younger brother, George (recently created Duke of York), within four months of her visit to Clumber. On George's succession to the throne in 1910, the Princess became his Queen Consort and was subsequently known as Queen Mary. She died, aged eighty-five, in 1953, just three months before her grand-daughter's coronation as Queen Elizabeth II.

The visitors stayed at Clumber for five nights and were entertained right royally, with hunting parties and a choral evening. The latter was provided by the English Opera Singers in the magnificent surroundings of the Grand Hall. Before leaving, the Royal party was reported as: "having assembled on the lawn and planted cedar trees ... to commemorate the happy week". Wilson proudly mentions that he held a Mount Atlas Cedar for Princess Mary to plant near the church.

OUR GUIDE'S ACTIVITIES AND OTHER HAPPENINGS

Wilson continued to note the events most relevant to his family and his work. His seventy-year-old mother-in-law's death and her funeral at Worksop brought sadness at Christmas 1892. In the New Year, Haughton Chapel and the Drayton Avenue were the subjects of conversations between the forester and his master. As a consequence, the Chapel was: "to be kept tidy and the Avenue to be planted with new trees"

***

Then it was 'party in the park' time again, to celebrate the wedding of his recent royal acquaintance:

6 July 1893
Royal Wedding Day – Prince George and Princess Mary's.

In respect of this event, a General Holiday had been proclaimed across the land and the folk of Clumber were not to be denied their share of the festivities. Over 700 children enjoyed a 'School Treat' there, with various sports, a Punch and Judy show and a tea being provided. The duchess handed out a present and a silver-gilt medal to each of the children following these more lively activities.

Wilson was active with the long established Clumber Troop of Sherwood Rangers Yeomanry at this time. Their regular meetings took place at the Normanton Inn. Many of the estate tenants had become members, including the Clerk of Works, William Stanhope (carrying the rank of Sergeant) and the Estate Blacksmith, George Salmon (who lived at Budby Corner and had recently been appointed as Sergeant Quartermaster). Rifle shooting matches were arranged between the 'Clumber' and other Troops in the Nottinghamshire and Yorkshire areas.

In August, Wilson enjoyed a five day organised trip with the Royal Scottish Arboricultural Society. Their travels took them to the Windsor area, also to Cliveden, Burnham Beeches, Southampton, Lyndhurst and the New Forest. Moving on to London, they stayed at the Grosvenor Hotel. On the final day, they visited Kew Gardens and the Earls Court Forestry Exhibition.

***

22 November 1893
Saw the first wedding at Clumber

The bride at this first celebration of a marriage service in the four-year-old Chapel was Lady Aileen Hastings. She was the second daughter of the late Earl of Huntingdon and a cousin of the Duchess of Newcastle. The bridegroom was Colin George Campbell, a distant relative of the duke's.

***

Our senior Woodsman then made his presence felt in the duke's lands closer to the Town ('City' from 1897) of Nottingham – twenty-five miles south of Clumber Park. During 1894, Wilson was occupied in marking out timber for sale from the Brinsley area, then visiting the Basford 'Garden'. He also attended to the supplying of new gates for Nottingham Park's prestigious development, having supervised their construction in the workshops at Hardwick-in-Clumber. September was marked by the birth of another son for the Tomlinsons, Cecil, who joined his eight siblings at Cabin Hill. Wilson attended timber sales and rent audits during the year and, during August, entertained a group from the English Arboriculture Society who were visiting all the substantial estates in the 'Dukeries' area.

7th December 1894
With the big shooting party and getting ice.

Figure 41 – Ice-breakers at Clumber Lake.

This 'getting ice' comment refers to the requirement to collect this useful resource, whenever the conditions were suitable, which seems to have been at least twice a year. The slabs of ice were then carted to the icehouse north of the Pinetum.

***

During the 1895 and 1896, Clumber's workmen worked on new stabling at Ranby Hall and were also busy with tree plantings in Worksop, especially alongside the new road by the ancient Priory. As Worksop's Lord of the Manor, the duke had financed the re-routing of this thoroughfare, to prevent the endangered Priory Gatehouse from collapse. Over several centuries, vehicles passing through its archway had severely shaken the foundations of this ancient structure. Clumber's Clerk of Works, William Stanhope, with some of his men, undertook this project. The duke also provided lime trees for the area of the Priory grounds adjacent to the Gatehouse.

Figure 42 – Alterations at the Worksop Priory Gatehouse – 1896.
The bowler-hatted gent is William Stanhope.
Clerk of Works at Clumber.

CLUMBER HOUSE.

230

INSTRUCTIONS IN CASE OF FIRE

When a Fire breaks out, the alarm should be raised at once, the big bell rung, and the Captain of Fire Brigade sent for.

If in the House, run to the nearest fire-cock, take down the hose from the board and unroll it. Screw branch pipe on male end of hose, then unscrew the cap on fire-cock and with the hose key attach the hose to the fire-cock. If the hose is not long enough to reach the fire run and fetch another length and screw it to the first; then open the fire-cock, turning it to the left with the hose key, and direct branch pipe on to the seat of the fire.

All doors and windows close to the outbreak should be shut wherever possible, to avoid unnecessary draughts.

Remember that a bucket of water at the commencement of a fire may be sufficient to put it out and so prevent a serious fire.

Curtains on fire should be pulled down, rolled up and trampled upon.

To put out the clothing of a person on fire roll him up in a blanket, carpet or rug.

All buckets to be kept full of water and in their places.

At drill the length of rubber-lined hose, provided for the purpose, should be attached to the fire-cocks, and the water turned on, the branch pipe being brought to a window. The fire-cock should not be opened with the unlined hose attached, except in real cases of fire, to avoid damage from water.

If the fire can be got at from the outside, run to the Fire Station, put on helmet, and belt with axe, take to the hydrant nearest fire one stand-pipe, branch pipe, one or two lengths of hose, also hydrant key and hose key.

Fix stand-pipe, unroll hose, fix branch pipe and turn on water.

See that there are no kinks or sharp turns in the hose.

As it is of great importance that the water should be got on to the fire as quickly as possible, it may be best to act independently at first, to save time, but directly the Captain comes he will take the command and must be obeyed in everything.

As soon as he can spare a man, the Captain should send him to the turbine house to open the sluice on inlet to turbine as far as possible.

After the hoses have been used they must be hung up to dry before being put away again. This is best done by taking them in the middle and hanging them to a cross timber which is drawn up by a tackle so that the ends of the hose are just off the ground. The leather hose should be rubbed with dubbin before being put away and if they are not often used, they should be oiled at least four times a year.

Newcastle Estate Office, 1st March, 1893.

Figure 43 – Fire Instructions at Clumber House in 1893.

***

Wilson's summer travels this year took him to Edinburgh, from whence he travelled to Bremen with a party from the Royal Scottish Arboricultural Society. They then went on to visit Berlin, Potsdam and Hamburg, before returning home after a very full fortnight's sightseeing holiday.

LORD FRANCIS HOPE – HEIR TO THE DUKEDOM

Lord Francis (the duke's brother) made the headlines in 1894, with two quite separate subject matters. The first related to his wretched money problems – describing him as having failed to live within his means during the previous seven years. This appears to have been a major understatement! On an admitted income of £16,000 per annum, he had accumulated gross liabilities of £657,942. These debts included £10,000 from his university days, plus £70,000 on betting escapades! He was declared bankrupt (the first of three similar happenings in his life). His mother, Henrietta, the dowager duchess, now had control of certain of the 'Hope' monies and with her assistance he eventually obtained discharge by offering 10/6½d (roughly 53p) in the £1 to the creditors. The description 'a chip off the old block' comes to mind!.

His second headline was in connection with his marriage to an American actress and singer, Mary Augusta Yohé. Mary, said to be of Dutch and Red Indian parentage, was from Bethlehem, Pennsylvania. One report suggests that she was a descendant of William Penn, of Pilgrim Fathers' fame. Lord Francis and Mary were married at Hampstead Register Office on 27th November: "after setting up home together sometime earlier"! The wedding was not publicised, which suggests that the couple were well aware that the duke and his sisters disapproved of this liaison.

Little more is recorded of their lives together except that, during the early years of their marriage, Mary is reported to have made the gaffe of wearing the infamous Hope Diamond, along with her costume jewellery, whilst on stage. This somewhat dubious story was certain to make a lurid headline and front-page story. She told the stage magazine reporter that she had been: "in an ecstasy of terror"!

Their first years together were said to have been happy ones and they enjoyed a world cruise in 1900. However, during the following year, whilst Lord Francis was visiting Florida with his brother, Mary had a liaison with another man. Divorce followed in March 1902 – based on the grounds of her adultery. Her marriage to Lord Francis had been childless. Mary was to marry twice more, but subsequently (conveniently blaming everything on the influence of the Hope Diamond) expressed regret at having left her British aristocrat.

Figure 44 – Mary Yohé, Lady Francis Hope.

Within six months of their divorce, British newspapers were announcing the engagement of Lord Francis to his cousin, Kathleen Beatrice Ricketts. This liaison was short-lived, wedding plans were aborted, and the heir to the ducal title was soon seeking solace elsewhere.

Whilst looking ahead in Lord Francis's life, we can note that he was to sustain a serious leg injury in December 1901 when out shooting with Lord Aylesford at Packlington. One of the servants accidentally fired a gun the result of which was that Lord Francis's ankle was shattered. The duke's heir then followed his elder brother's example and underwent an amputation, losing his left foot. No doubt some would argue that the unlucky recipient of an interest in the 'Hope Diamond' should not have been surprised by any misfortune that befell them! For more on the story of the fabulous gem with the ill-starred reputation see Chapter Four.

ST CUTHBERT'S COLLEGE, WORKSOP

The newly-built St. Cuthbert's College (later to become known as Worksop College) then featured in Wilson's diary:

4 September 1895
At the luncheon at St Cuthbert's College, Worksop – the opening day.

The duke had recently become a major benefactor of a Woodard Foundation school, this one close to Clumber Park, and built upon Newcastle land. Back in 1887, quite unsolicited and unexpectedly, he had provided some ninety acres of land for this establishment. He also agreed to finance the preparation of a driveway, and supplied the cedar trees that lined this fine approach. Many years later it was noted that the legal deed that conveying the land to the College authorities had inadvertently included the mineral rights – an expensive error!

The new public school had now been erected: "for the education of the lower and middle classes ... enabling young boys to go to university and enter holy orders". The duke laid the foundation stone, praying:

'... that within these walls hereon be raised, bearing the name of St. Cuthbert, the true faith and fear of God, together with brotherly love and sound learning, may ever flourish and abound'.

Some three hundred people sat down to lunch (2/6d [12^1/$_2$p] per head: "wine not included"), in the marquee erected in the grounds of what became known as 'Worksop College'. Exactly five years later, following severe difficulties in raising the finances, the Bishop of Southwell presided at the dedication of the completed building. The duke and duchess were amongst the 500 present at this service. Nine days later, five masters and forty-four boys were in place to begin the life of the college.

Around fifty years later, a suggestion was made by the headmaster, that the school be renamed 'Clumber College'. This was subsequently declined on the (unexplained) grounds of 'family feelings'. There is still a 'Newcastle Scholarship' and a 'Pelham House' within its establishment.

A NEW CHAPLAIN-IN-WAITING

One major consequence of the establishment of St. Cuthbert's was the arrival there of a College Chaplain; thirty-two-year-old Rev. Frank Hawkins. Not only was he of the High Church tradition that so appealed to the Clumber duke, he was also an excellent cricketer! Both of these attributes were (some six years later) to lead to Father Hawkins permanent transfer of his ministry from the College to the Parsonage at Clumber. He was to retain this privileged Newcastle living for over thirty years.

MORE ABOUT THE DUKE

Now into his early thirties, already titled Earl of Lincoln and Duke of Newcastle-under-Lyme, the duke had added to his noble designations, acquiring appointments and offices that included Master Forester of Dartmoor and Keeper of St. Briavel's Castle, Gloucestershire. He was a Deputy Lord Lieutenant of the County, Lord of the Manors of Newark and Worksop, Lord High Steward of Retford, Fellow of the Colonial Institute, Knight of Grace of the Order of St. John of Jerusalem in England and a Justice of the Peace for Nottinghamshire. All these no doubt put him on a pedestal that his diminutive height belied.

The duke had also settled into his position as patron and role model. His reputation as a kind, gentle and religious man had quickly developed and was matched by his and the duchess's generosity to good causes. A minor (but altogether representative) example of the twenty-one-year-old duchess's duties is offered by the record of her attendance at the East Markham Bazaar, held on 14th July 1893 in aid of the Church Bells Fund. Apart from attending and speaking at the opening of the event, she was said to have made 'extensive purchases'. The newspapers also reported that the duke had made a contribution of £1,000 towards the restoration of the ancient village church. It should be remembered that he had responsibility for several other churches within his duchy (as detailed below) and he gave considerable support to All Saint's, Margaret Street, London as well as his own Clumber Chapel. He and the duchess also gave generous support to the Church of England Waifs and Strays Society.

On church matters, the duke was still very active. He had become a lay rector of the Priory Church at Worksop and was a leading advocate of changes to the Lady Chapel there, which alterations he eventually financed to the tune of one thousand pounds. Incidentally, the advowson (the right to present clergy to a living) of the Priory had been conveyed by the duke to the Cowley Fathers in 1891.

He was also President of the local branch of the English Church Union. Although Worksop Priory took his particular attention, he was involved in the affairs of his other parishes such as: Bevercotes, Bothamsall, Brinsley, Cromwell, East Markham, Egmanton, Elkesley, Greasley, Kirton, Maplebeck, Markham Clinton, Shireoaks and West Drayton. His Grace had made a particularly thrilling find amongst these 'livings' – this was at the parish church at Egmanton. In 1897 he financed the Anglo-Saxon Chapel's restoration to the tune of at least £2,000. The church was structurally repaired and the Shrine of Our Lady of Egmanton re-introduced, having previously existed there until its destruction in 1547.

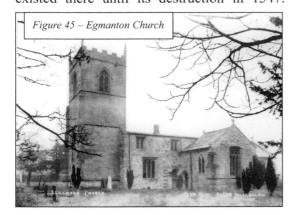
Figure 45 – Egmanton Church

There is no doubt that the duke, with his 'Pre-Reformation' leanings, would have been very excited to assist in restoring such a site of ancient pilgrimage. He was not to observe the full fruits of his beneficence, as it was only in the year after his death that the pilgrims of more modern times began to travel there, the first to arrive being on Easter Monday 1929.

His hobbies were the subject of much comment. As mentioned earlier, he was an enthusiastic photographer and one of the earliest 'modern day' caravanners. The duke was also a keen fisherman who, whilst on a trip to Avalon, California landed a fifty pound yellowtail tuna: "'the second heaviest ever taken with rod and line". He had the prized catch encased as a preserved specimen and shipped back to Clumber House for display. Many of his family, friends, neighbours and tenants saw the fish, when they were subsequently invited to various celebratory events. They would also have seen the numerous other cases containing hundreds of stuffed animals, birds and fish collected by the family for over one hundred years and more. Clumber's reputation in that respect, and his as a generous host, must have soon spread. Throughout his Nottinghamshire estates, the duke's influence was evident, not only through his agreement to rent reductions in times of need, but in increased activity to improve the condition of dwellings owned by him.

A NEW HYMNAL, A MARRIAGE AND A DIAMOND JUBILEE

For George Tredaway, Clumber's schoolmaster-choirmaster-organist, Easter 1896 was an exciting time. It was then that the first editions of his 'Clumber Hymnal' were published, specifically for Clumber Chapel and the Oratory at Hardwick. The previous year his 'Vade-Mecum for Church Choirs' had been published, but a major interest for him over several years had been in editing this new hymnal that brought together some 460 hymns, carols and litanies considered suitable for High Anglican devotions.

***

Mr Tredaway must have also been delighted that he had found a new wife-to-be, in Lucy Ann Jackson, the Clumber House Housekeeper. It was Mr Tredaway's second marriage, his first wife having died two years earlier. Following the wedding service (held in the Chapel in April 1897), a 'breakfast', attended by some seventy guests, was provided in the Grand Hall of Clumber House. The duke, duchess and Major Candy (the duchess's father) made their appearances for the toasts to the bride and groom. The newly-weds then left for London and on to the south coast for their honeymoon, leaving the house servants to enjoy a dance in celebration of the happy event. Mrs Agnes Kidd succeeded Lucy as Housekeeper.

***

Presumably, Mr and Mrs Tredaway were home by June, and in time to enjoy the occasion of Queen Victoria's Diamond Jubilee festivies. A unique Clumber medal was struck for this special event and these were issued to selected families of the duchy. Wilson noted that one thousand children were provided with a 'school treat' at Clumber. This was followed by a Garden Party for the adults at Mr Haslam's home, Park House, Worksop.

Figure 46 – Clumber 'medal' – 1897

Clumber House on fire in March 1879

John & Sybil Weth, also the *Illustrated London News*

Charles Barry's design sketch for the new Grand Hall at Clumber House, 1879

R.I.B.A. Library Drawings Collection

Clumber Chapel, opened in October 1889
Cecil Brown Collection

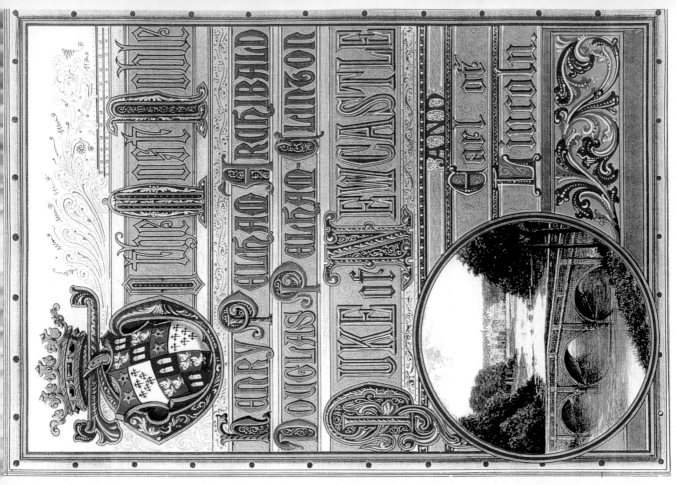

Depictions from the 'Loyal Addresses' presented to the 7th Duke of Newcastle-under-Lyme on his Coming-of-Age in September 1885

Manorial Society

The Silver Wedding casket presented to the 7th duke and duchess in April 1914
Manuscripts and Special Collections Department, University of Nottingham

Clumber Spaniels
Bill Ironside

The Reading Room and Library at Clumber House, empty and awaiting demolition – 1937

Charles J Stableforth, also A.C. Cooper (Colours) Ltd.

THE FORESTER'S ACTIVITIES – CONTINUED

A selection of items of the Forester's diary entries for 1896 and 1897 will assist in rounding off this high-activity decade, and also provide a further indication of the widespread character of the estate at this period. Working duties at Barnby, Cromwell, Crookford Farm, Eaton Hall, Elkesley Vicarage, Hawton, Holme, Lound Hall, Manton, Mattersey Hall, Newark, Ranby Hall, and Retford involved planning and erecting new fencing and gates. He was also kept busy pollarding old elm trees at Tuxford Vicarage. Timber sales and Rent Audits continued, requiring visits to the Normanton Inn and the Lion Hotel at Worksop. On the Park's forestry front, beech trees (alternate purple and green) had been planted in Beech Avenue, Ash Tree Field and poplars at the Kennels area of Hardwick. Roads through the Park were sorely in need of attention, many (like the Carburton Road) were still merely: "grass tracts full of deep ruts", mercilessly churned up by the forester's efforts whilst carting timber to and from the workshops and sawmills.

Despite the continuing agricultural depression the position of the Newcastle estate finances had somewhat stabilised since Wilson's early days there. His own work was highly appreciated and his status and self-esteem enhanced by the representative duties he undertook, which included his regular attendance at meetings and outings of arboricultural societies, in England, Ireland and Scotland.

So, as the second decade of the Head Forester's time at Clumber Park was almost completed, his family's tenth and final child, Aylmer Erling, was born in June 1897. Aylmer was to attend Retford Grammar School, then be apprenticed as a joiner at Hardwick and finally to be commemorated on the Clumber's War Memorial as being sacrificed for his country, at Ypres, twenty years after his birth. Over the two previous years Wilson had travelled widely, having been to many noble estates. One of these was Buchanan Castle, the home of the Duke and Duchess of Montrose, where he met them both. Then to the Marquis of Bute's home at Mount Stewart and on to many more splendid landed estates. The following year whilst in Ireland (where he had worked some twenty years before) he received an invitation to lunch with Lord Ardilaun and Lord Edward Fitzwilliam. He visited the estates of the Duke of Leinster, Lord Kenmare, Earl of Meath, Lord Milton and many others: "not bad for a lad from Manton, Worksop!"

**

Figure 47 – The Tomlinson family, photographed at Cabin Hill in 1897.

***

The twentieth century was fast approaching and the duke's estates were looking far healthier than had been the case when he inherited the title. Much had been accomplished in restoring respectability to the Newcastle name and he, his family, tenants and employees probably anticipated some stability and security for their futures.

Figure 48 – Yellow Drawing Room, Clumber House – 1908.
[Country Life Picture Library]

Figure 49 – South face of Clumber House, displaying the upper and lower terraces.

CHAPTER FOUR

1898 to 1908

Clumber's finest hours? – Noble 'Doings' – 'Economies, economies, economies' – A dead statesman and lively royalty – Into the twentieth century – Motor cars arrive in Clumber Park – The forester was still travelling – Clumber Shows – Fire at neighbouring Welbeck – Queen Victoria died – Coronation 1902 – Life goes on for the estate workers – Lord Francis v the Hope diamond – Duke robbed by his lawyer – Routine, yet changing times – A New Agent & a New Year – Royalty motor in Clumber – Estate staffing – Electricity introduced – The duchess was not amused – The daily round – A loss and some gains for the Pelham-Clintons.

CLUMBER'S FINEST HOURS?

A S THE TWENTIETH CENTURY APPROACHES, we enter the thirteenth year of the 'little' duke's move into the command of his Nottinghamshire estates. Finances, although still finely balanced, were as favourable as the Newcastle estate had achieved since the days of Georgiana, fourth Duchess, from 1807 to 1822. That wealthy woman's monies had bailed the estate out of eighteenth century excesses, but the spendthrift attitudes of her husband had led to a deteriorating financial situation which was later aggravated by the sixth duke's gambling and his subsequent bankruptcy. During the seventh duke's minority, Trustees had worked hard to produce a situation from which the now sitting peer could regain some approval for his family name.

Clumber Park was looking good again and the duke has consolidated his position as one of the county's leading landowners. Debatably, this was to be Clumber's finest decade since its creation at the beginning of the eighteenth century. The early 1890's had seen the establishment of many new initiatives at Clumber. The mansion's reputation as a beautiful stately home was spread far and wide, as was the magnificence of the Chapel, with its colourful ritualistic services and impressive music. The Choir School was now a permanent feature and Hardwick's new Village School well set up and receiving good reports from visiting Inspectors. Substantial amounts had been spent on many of the duke's properties throughout the county and his standing with most of his tenantry appears to have been high.

With the books now balancing as well as they had ever done, moves aimed at consolidating the duchy's land holdings had increased soon after the 1894 Parliamentary Bill to raise the target of Death Duty taxation. Under the terms of that Bill, all forms of property, whether landed or otherwise, were brought into the reckoning. Significant portions of the Newcastle estates were sold off during the duke's first decade. It was a time of heavy demand by the railway companies for yet more land. The Great Central and Great Northern Railway Companies were successful in acquiring portions of the estates which adjoined the station at Worksop. Increasingly, housing requirements had led to the sale of many farming acres at Worksop, especially the northern fields of Sparken Farm. These had long been the base for Agents to the Dukes of Norfolk and Newcastle. Some lands close to Nottingham had been released, such as those at Brinsley and Heanor, also at Haydn Road and Dob Park, Basford.

In the dying years of the old century a new colliery was sunk to the east of Worksop. The workings were owned by the Wigan Coal and Iron Company and known as Manton Colliery. The duke had leased the coal rights of some thirty thousand acres of his land to the company in 1896. As the pit reached full working order in 1907, the local press reported that its official name would be: "Newcastle Main, Manton Colliery". Although not in general use, this title was certainly applied to the headed paper of the colliery up to the start of the Great War. Whatever designation was used, the duke benefited from the mineral royalties on coal, gravel, sand and water extracted. Quite early on in the new century several of the duke's properties were reaping the inconveniences caused by mining subsidence.

It is interesting to note that, despite the local availability of this fuel, the duke insisted that more 'domestically-friendly' coal should be transported for use in Clumber House from the Langwith Colliery, some ten miles further away than Manton. This delivery was undertaken with the aid of the estate's traction engine! On arrival at the mansion this fuel was conveyed to the various floors by barrows and the use of water-powered lifts.

NOBLE 'DOINGS'

On a personal level, the duke had become involved in local church matters. He was Vicar's Warden at the Worksop Priory and Branch President of the English Church Union. Still visiting North America and Europe regularly, the duke was generous in his financial gifts to various churches abroad as well as in England. One example of this benevolence is the provision of an organ for the American Episcopal Church at Sault Ste. Marie, Michigan in 1915. He had been a member of the London School Board for three years from 1894. On the national scene, he had no apparent centre stage inclinations (such as those of his grandfather who was a senior Cabinet Minister during the 1850's). Hansard reporters were rarely troubled by his outpourings in the business of the House of Lords. His main contributions to national debates were in connection with opposition to the reform of land tax, remarriage of divorced persons in Church, disestablishment of the Church and the abolition of the use of the birch at Eton College. He gave evidence to a select committee on the 'Derbyshire and Nottinghamshire Electric Power Bill', emphasising his support for the measure. He saw it as likely to bring: "great industrial development" to the area and that it would be: "for the benefit of his tenants". To those who suggested that the Bill would bring devastation to the rural idyll of Sherwood Forest (and said that his enthusiasm for the measure was based on his own financial welfare) he responded that he had: "too much reverence for history and tradition to allow the haunts of Robin Hood to be marred by colliery smoke and commercial bustle".

Newcastle and his duchess (known as 'Linny' and 'Tatta' to their intimates) were well known and popular, despite a reputation amongst their peers for shyness and infrequent attendance at formal functions. At various times he was a member of the Carlton, Garrick, St. James' and Whites clubs. He had two homes in London, one in Hayes Mews and the other at 11, Hill Street, the latter being a splendid five-storied house bought from Baron Alfred Rothschild. In that property the duke and duchess occasionally held lavish parties, with members of royalty attending. Numbered amongst the guests were the Duke and Duchess of Connaught (Queen Victoria's favourite son, Arthur, and his shy consort, Louise Margaret). The duke's widowed mother, Henrietta, Dowager Duchess, was much praised for her charity work with the Catholic Social Union. This was performed amongst the poorest classes in the Whitechapel district of the East End and she lived in St. Anthony's House there, but also occasionally resided at the duke's more opulent abode in Hill Street. In the latter property he had set up photographic rooms that matched his facilities at Clumber House.

Figure 50 – 11, Hill Street, London.

It was around this time that the duke began a search that was to lead to his purchasing a substantial property in the area of his beloved Eton. He eventually decided on Forest Farm, in the vicinity of the Great Park at Windsor.

'ECONOMIES, ECONOMIES, ECONOMIES'

Notwithstanding the overall satisfactory financial accounts, there were areas of concern and it was clear that landowners were becoming the target of even greater taxation plans. At the sharp end of the duchy - meaning the Newcastle Estate Office at Worksop and the various offices of Clumber Park Heads of Departments - there was a pervading mood of 'economy'. This was to continue for many years. The financial records of the early 1900's grouped the retained areas of Newcastle ownership into three blocks. Firstly 'Clumber', which meant the 'Park' and surrounding lands, such as those at Bothamsall, Elkesley, Normanton, Ranby, Shireoaks, Tuxford and Worksop. Secondly 'Newark', referring to Balderton, Besthorpe, Coddington, Farndon, Girton, South Clifton, South Scarle and Winthorpe (amongst others) as well as Newark town itself. Finally there came 'Nottingham', including Basford, Brinsley, Flawborough, Heanor and Hucknall. Despite the land sales mentioned earlier, income from rents was listed as £45,000 for the year ending March 1900 (as against £33,000 ten years earlier). Some reductions had occurred in receipts from mineral royalties, £10,800 (previously £12,000) and timber sales £2,000 (down from £3,600).

At the luxury end of financial spending, expenditure on the kennels was now an important factor, running at over £1,100 per year. The stables were an expensive but apparently unavoidable necessity for a ducal estate. Nevertheless, forty-five-year-old Head Groom and Coachman, George Cook, was being urged to stringent economies, despite the conflicting demands of producing the horses in peak condition at all times. Income from the sales of produce from the Gardens was also down, with yet more spending on replacing panes in the Glasshouses. Costs involved in maintaining Clumber House had increased significantly. The almost twenty-year-old rebuilt property now required much re-decoration and maintenance.

Reductions in the considerable acres of timberland at Worksop Manor Park must have led to a lessening in responsibilities for the foresters, although Wilson Tomlinson's diaries do not indicate this to be so. He was far more interested in recording his plantings at: Ash Tree Avenue, King Charles Breck, Crookford, also in Tank Wood and at Manton, where under the direction of the duke's relative, Mr Lister-Kaye, he was forming some: "small triangular plantations". Nottingham and Bagthorpe timber required his attention, as did the culling of trees at East Markham Vicarage. There were also more decorative activities, the Forester delivering a substantial six-foot diameter bunch of mistletoe to Retford Town Hall for the County Ball in January. Later in the year he took quality evergreens to Newark for the Town Hall display.

The following year, in an attempt to cut costs, the estate introduced a new approach to the work of the foresters. Outside tenders were sought and contract woodsmen brought in to undertake the planting of around thirty acres at Haughton Warren at a cost of £8 per acre. Unfortunately, Wilson does not record his reaction to this tendering process or whether he had any control over the project. It is inherently improbable that he welcomed the change!

A DEAD STATESMAN AND LIVELY ROYALTY

Yet another diary entry now catches the eye, this one involving William Ewart Gladstone, an important personage long associated with the Newcastle Estates. Wilson recorded that the famous statesman had died on Ascension Day and then, a few days later:

> *28 May 1898*
> *Her Grace planted a Purple Beech near the Paddocks, from a pot at my request,*
> *on the day of the burial of Mr Gladstone.*

Figure 51 – William Ewart Gladstone.

William Gladstone had first visited Clumber Park sixty-six years earlier, as the favoured candidate to represent the fourth duke's interests in the Newark election. Whilst at Oxford University, the young hopeful had become the trusted friend of that duke's eldest son, Lord Lincoln. On Lincoln donning the ducal coronet in 1851, the friendship was maintained. Gladstone and his wife assisted with the care of the children during the fifth duke's marriage breakdown. When that duke died in 1864, Gladstone was entrusted with the roles of senior Executor and Trustee. As such, he was largely responsible for the restoration of financial order following the bankruptcy, departure and death of the sixth duke. From 1869, Gladstone's home at Harwarden Castle had become a regular refuge for the present duke and his siblings.

Wilson Tomlinson had met Mr Gladstone on several occasions and he was now showing his admiration of the man in guiding the duchess to plant this commemorative purple beech tree that has survived into the twenty-first century. Why the Paddocks were chosen for this gesture is not known. Since his appointment in June 1894, Head Gamekeeper Walter Harrington had been living in the Paddocks Cottage with his young family. Walter received a wage of £78 per annum (later to rise to £130) plus free rent, coal and gas and a further £1.10s in lieu of a pig! He had six permanent assistants plus another four during the rabbit-killing season – but that is probably more information than the reader wanted!

***

Next, a Royal event:

> *9 November 1898*
> *Preparing for a Ball at Clumber ... at night seeing to traffic.*

The Duke and Duchess of Connaught were foremost amongst the 500-plus visitors to a Grand Ball at Clumber House on a very foggy winter's night. The royal couple had enjoyed several days in the 'Dukeries' area, staying at Welbeck and shooting on surrounding estates including Clumber. The reasons for holding the Ball were twofold, firstly to acknowledge the royal visitors' presence and secondly the 'coming-out' of Miss Lois Lister-Kaye (later to become Lady de Vesci), daughter of the duke's sister Beatrice.

The affair seems to have been everything one would expect of a royal event. All major apartments were in use, especially the State Drawing Room, Grand and Little Dining Rooms. Dancing took place in the white-marbled Grand Hall, with music played by the Royal Artillery Band. Huge fires roared from each fine chimney-piece. Thousands of candles lit the mansion – except in the Library, where gas lighting was flickeringly reflected in the highly polished mahogany woodwork of shelving and gallery. Clumber's chef, Mr Landermare, excelled himself with the supper menus. In this his final year in the Park, head gardener, Charles Slade, was complimented on the flower arrangements that graced the many rooms. Local hotels in Edwinstowe, Ollerton, Retford and Worksop, were full to overflowing with guests to the Ball, many of whom had travelled from far and wide, including Scotland and Ireland.

Figure 52 – Western Corridor of Clumber House – 1908
[Country Life Picture Gallery]

Figure 53 – Eastern Corridor of Clumber House – 1908
[Country Life Picture Gallery]

INTO THE TWENTIETH CENTURY

18 February 1899
Mr S. Barker, gardener came to Clumber.

Head Gardener Charles Slade having now departed with a Golden Handshake of one hundred pounds, his replacement arrived in February 1899. The new man was thirty-year-old Samuel Barker, born at Woolley, in Derbyshire. He had come from Baroness Burton's Rangemore Estate, near Burton-on Trent with a high reputation for horticultural skills, particularly in producing carnations and quality indoor fruits. Over the following thirty-five years Mr Barker was to lead an eventful life at Clumber. Beginning with an annual salary of £150, he found himself in charge of some twenty-nine gardeners and labourers, with a wage bill of £1,400 per year. The Walled Gardens and Glasshouses had been improved over the previous twenty years but were now undergoing further expensive attention. New Carnation Glass Houses were erected, at a cost of £716.

***

After that brief excursion into the head gardener's empire, we return to the head forester's activities. For his well-earned holiday in 1899 he travelled with other woodsmen to Manchester and Liverpool. From there he boarded the vessel the 'St. Tudno' for an outing to Llandudno, Beaumaris, Bangor and the Menai Bridge. On return to Clumber he worked on substantial tree plantings at Haughton Warren plus a multitude of other duties.

Wilson does not record how he and the family celebrated the arrival of the twentieth century. However, we do know that his noble master was away again, this time in North America. Whilst there, the duke purchased Cotton Woods tree saplings for Clumber. The Forester noted the practical results of this transaction, which were that he was required to plant these new species close by Clumber Bridge.

MOTOR CARS ARRIVE IN CLUMBER PARK

On his return from America in early May 1900, the duke and his duchess took a holiday at Ditton Park, Surrey, which they rented from Lord Montague (whose name was to become so famously connected with the motor car). In their absence from Clumber Park they had missed the novelty of an early-days 'Rally'. Some fifty or so automobiles passed along Lime Tree Avenue: "at 20 to 30 miles per hour" as a section of their route from Sheffield to Lincoln. The 'Worksop Guardian' announced the event on Friday 4 May 1900:

The motor cars in the great trial now proceeding will leave Sheffield ... at about 7.30, and travel to Worksop at the rate of about 12 miles an hour, arriving here about 9. They will be checked and timed by members of a local committee at Gateford Villa, and will then go to the next checking place, Sparken Hill at a pace of 8 miles an hour, thirty minutes being allowed for breakfast. At Sparken Hill, the competitors will separate, some proceeding through Clumber Park and Hardwick to Normanton Inn, and thence along Drayton Avenue to Markham Moor, whilst those possessing the faster vehicles will go to Welbeck Park, where, by permission of the Duke of Portland, a speed trial will take place.

On 11 May, the 'Retford and Gainsborough Times' contained the following report:

The arrival of the motor cars was not an imposing pageant. There were many people in the streets. It was a raw afternoon, and they stood until their teeth "chittered" waiting for the "procession". But there was no procession. One car came early, sang its little song, gave off its spurt of steam somewhere around the wheels, and passed on. Another did ditto, after a ten minutes' wait. Then two might come together. One gentleman was privileged to have a lady on the seat with him. He seemed all right, and went past prettily. The lady had done the whole route. The best-looking car, to my mind, belonged to a Sheffield gentleman, who had a friend with him.

Far be it from me to endorse the definition of an enemy who said "a motor car was a thing that barked like a dog and stank like a cat". Yet, of a truth, they are not lovely. Elegance is conspicuous by its absence. A journalist told a friend of mine that the riding was delightful – it gave all the pleasure of going fast on a bike, without the pain of pedalling. But my friend said he saw him in Pinstone-street looking as if there was not a drop of warm blood in his veins. The motor car has no doubt a future; and it is economical to have a horse that needs no forage, no meal and water, no groom, and no ostlers to tip. But, on the whole, should fortune favour, my preference is for the old order. A carriage and pair would be good enough for me.

In 1903 the duke had a new 'motor house' erected at Clumber, but by then he was well into the own motoring life – horse-drawn caravans were a distant memory! He seems to have started with steam-engine cars, and he certainly bought an early paraffin-powered 'Serpollet' – a vehicle which had already achieved trial speeds of over fifty miles. He spent even more on a Clément-Panhard 'Gladiator' and an early 'Anglian'.

It was not long before he was involved in a motor accident. In this so-called: 'unavoidable crash', the duke's car (reportedly travelling at twelve miles per hour) managed to kill a grand total of eight sheep being driven along a road at Babworth, near Retford. By now, and just like Kenneth Graham's owner of Toad Hall, the little duke seems to have been fully converted to the newest: "only way to travel ... O poop poop!"

Figure 54 – Albert Johnson transferred from Groom to Chauffeur.

Figure 55 – Coachmen and footmen at Clumber found time for a game of cards – circa 1900.
Head Coachman/Groom, George Cook is seated on the right.

THE FORESTER WAS STILL TRAVELLING

During 1900 the Head Forester's summer trip was to Ireland with the Scottish Arboricultural Society. No doubt along with the rest of the party, Wilson dined with Lord Dufferin and the Duke of Abercorn. He also met Lord and Lady Annesley. He then visited Portrush and the Giant's Causeway, and having found everything either: 'fine', 'very fine' or 'splendid', he completed his week's break by sailing back from Belfast to Barrow, and on by train to Sheffield and Worksop, in time for the next big happening at Clumber.

CLUMBER SHOWS

25 August 1900
My mother died at Shafton at 10.10 p.m. ... I was in bed ill till 28th. .

Following his reaction to this sad loss, Wilson was well enough to attend the very first 'Clumber Show' in September 1900.

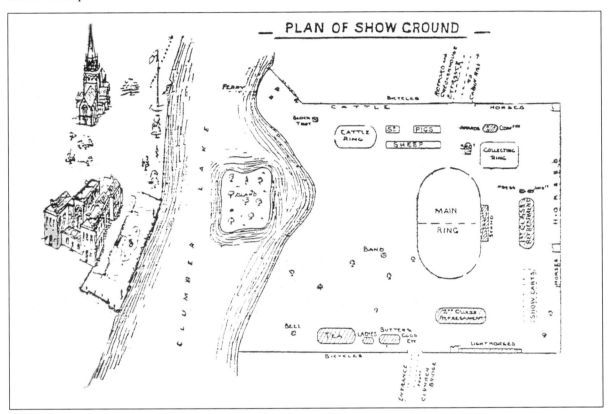

Figure 56 – Sketch plan of the Showground, as published by the 'Worksop Guardian' newspaper.

Initially titled the 'Newcastle Estate Tenants Agricultural Show' the Shows were announced as being sponsored by the duke: "to promote a general improvement in your livestock and create a rivalry which may be beneficial". Horses, cattle, sheep, pigs, poultry, butter and eggs were amongst the categories being judged. His Grace financed the prizes for each class of entry, and the duchess presented the winners with the cup trophies or cash prizes, usually of two or three guineas. Lectures were presented in the 'Bee Tent'. Agricultural Turnouts and Driving Harness Classes were not overlooked and Her Grace's famous collection of dogs was also on view - especially Borzois, Fox Terriers and a few Clumber Spaniels.

Held on the South Lawns, the shows were well-supported affairs with around two to three thousand people attending. The main Grand Stand faced the lake, and the First and Second Class Refreshment Marquees squared off two sides of the Showground. Similar events were held almost every year until the final one on 4th August 1914, the day the First World War commenced. This last Show broke with tradition and moved to a site at the Cow Pasture, nearer the Kitchen Gardens – the site of modern day events. 1912 was the only year the Show had to be cancelled, due to an outbreak of foot and mouth disease.

Figure 57 – The 'First Class' Luncheon Tent at the Clumber Show.

Figure 58 – A scene from the Clumber Show – the duke and duchess escort members of their house party

LORD EDWARD AND THE DEATH OF QUEEN VICTORIA

22 January 1901
Queen Victoria died at Osborne.

*Figure 59 –
Lord Edward
Pelham-
Clinton.*

The Newcastle dukedom had a particular interest in this event.
Lord Edward Pelham-Clinton (son of the fifth duke and uncle to
the present one) was a main player in the proceedings following the
death of the Queen.   He was Master of the Household to Her
Majesty. Our Forester had often met him at Clumber Park during the
years of the young duke's minority, when Lord Edward had acted as
a Trustee and advised on the re-shaping of the Estate's fortunes.
After the formalities of the funeral at Windsor, Lord Edward was the
only non-royal invited to be present at Frogmore Mausoleum for the
private interment. Lord Edward wrote in his diary: "The King most
kindly allows me to throw the earth on the coffin, during the well-

known passage in the burial service: the last, the very last act that could be performed for the Queen". This was creditable testimony to his own high standing within the Court circles and demonstrated the respect that his father had earned in his service of Queen Victoria and Prince Albert. The fifth duke had once been described by the new monarch (when a young Prince of Wales) as: "the finest man that ever lived". Lord Edward was initially appointed as Master of the Household to King Edward VII but (probably due to failing health) was replaced after six months and appointed as a Groom of the Household.

After the demise of the eighty-one-year-old monarch and the involvement of the Newcastles in the events in London and Windsor, life at Clumber seems to have settled down to the routine format. Money was still tight, 'economy' was the watchword and the duke and duchess were frequently absent. The hunting and shooting continued, particularly when the duchess was at home, and during 1901 there was at least one music concert held as a money raising event in aid of British troops involved in the Boer War conflict.

Her Grace gained some publicity during that year with the publication of her article in the January edition of the 'Pall Mall Magazine'. This sang the praises of Clumber's Mansion; Treasures (including the three Chelsea vases placed in the State Drawing Room and valued at £20,000); Pleasure Grounds; 14th century styled Chapel; also the Terraces and Gardens. The Kennels feature large in the piece, with the reasonable boast that the duchess's borzois (having achieved some four hundred 'Firsts' in shows over the previous five years) had almost cornered the market in prizes. Photographs taken by the duke enhanced the narrative.

Figure 60 – The cover of 'Pall Mall Magazine' for January 1901.

The duke was again away in North America for the Christmas period, on this occasion he visited California and Winnipeg. In the summer following his return, the Forester noted (without further comment) certain new-age travellers and their modern transport modes:

> *31 July 1902*
> *Met the Lincoln Automobile Club at Normanton Inn.*

CORONATION – 1902

One week after the Clumber Show, the duke and duchess were in London to attend the Coronation of King Edward VII. The glittering but abbreviated service (due to the King's recent appendicitis operation) was the first occasion that the Newcastle dynasty had the Court of Claims' permission to present the 'Worksop Glove' to the monarch. The glove was for the monarch's right hand (into which hand is placed the Sceptre with the Cross). As the glove was subsequently gifted to the recipient, a new glove is required for each coronation. This ancient practice had been included in the ceremony since the thirty-third year of the reign of Henry VIII. The Earl of Shrewsbury obtained the privilege of presenting the glove in the seventeenth century in an exchange with the Crown for lands and privileges at Farnham Royal, Buckinghamshire. That earl was also owner of the 'Lord of the Manor of Worksop' title. Since his days, possession of the title had come into the Newcastle's hands some time after the fourth duke's purchase of the Worksop Manor estate from the Duke of Norfolk. Newspapers now recorded that the seventh duke was appointed as 'Bearer of the Sceptre' for the coronation but that the Glove presentation was one of the items removed from the proceedings in view of the King's weakened state of health.

LIFE GOES ON FOR THE ESTATE WORKERS

Whilst the duke and duchess were in London at the heart of the Coronation celebrations, woodmen at Clumber were fixing a new entrance gate to Haughton Hall. These activities bring us back from the dizzy heights of royals and dukes and provide further examples of the normal daily routine of a busy and extensive landed estate. We can be sure that if a Head Forester's life was working to a fixed pattern, that of his men must have been doubly so. That Wilson was able to combine a working trip to Bagthorpe, Basford and Nottingham Park with a visit to the Nottingham Theatre Royal may not have been an opportunity that all his men could enjoy. It is however a reminder of the many levels of estate hierarchy and how near or far each was from imitating their noble masters' pursuits.

Nevertheless, they could all participate in the Coronation festivities in Clumber Park, financed by the duke. Marquees were erected near the School and at the Cricket Ground. At the conclusion of a cricket match, children's sports – including 'Boots Hidden in Clover' (a find-the-needle-in-a-haystack-type competition) – and a 'Punch and Judy' show preceded the tea. A 'Phonographic Entertainment', children's games and a conjurer followed this. Then came the adult sports, including a tug of war, three-legged race and an obstruction race (with a tarpaulin, cross-bars and horse-collar amongst the obstacles).

Later, Mrs Haslam, wife of the Estate Agent, presented the prizes. These ranged from 3 pence to 5 shillings (2p to 25p) and there were Coronation gifts on behalf of the ducal couple. Each woman on the estate received a handsome book titled 'King Edward's Realm'. Every child was given a 'Foley China' engraved mug, bearing the portraits of the King and Queen and the royal coat of arms. The youngsters also received a medal to commemorate the event. The day ended with a further 'Ventriloquial performance', followed by dancing to the sounds of the Welbeck Band and the singing of 'God Save the King'.

The Coronation meant that more money was released from the duke's coffers. In addition to his own attendance in London and the party for people of Clumber Park, all his various parishes made their separate requests for monies to provide parties for tenants. The duke's Estate Agent (having checked with his Welbeck counterpart to compare levels of largesse) agreed to disperse amounts averaging three guineas to the smaller parishes. Babworth and Ranby were combined for this purpose and received five guineas. Worksop (including Shireoaks) attracted a massive £50 contribution.

Later in the year, there was another party they could all share when a 'welcome home' was arranged for men of the area who had recently returned from military service in the Boer War. On 13th November, the duke unveiled a Memorial Tablet at a Worksop Priory service and Wilson noted that a privileged group (including the Head Forester himself) was also invited to dine at the Worksop Town Hall, where his master again presided. The Memorial contains the name of Lieutenant A.G. Williams, 10th Company (Sherwood Rangers) Imperial Yeomanry, who had died at the Battle of Boshuf in April 1900. This officer was a member of the previous Newcastle Estate Agent's family.

LORD FRANCIS v THE HOPE DIAMOND – AND THE WINNER IS?

It was the year before the Coronation that the duke's brother (and heir) Lord Francis was declared bankrupt for the second time. His debts were said to be due in large measure to his Turf gambling and his speculative sponsorship of theatrical productions. To provide some relief from his troubles, Lord Francis had (after several applications and facing opposition from his siblings) obtained the court's permission to sell various heirlooms. He had sold eighty-three pictures from the Hope Collection in 1898, raising £121,000. Now he had made further representations, appealing for permission to sell a very special heirloom. This was the fabulous, albeit allegedly dangerous, Hope Diamond, in which he had a life interest under the terms of his grandmother's will. Simon Frankel, a New York City jeweller, bought the gem in 1901. The price paid has proved difficult to establish, as quoted sale figures ranged from £29,000 to £120,000!

If we are to bow to the legend, the damage that this $45\frac{1}{2}$ carat sapphire-blue jewel [*See Colour Plate 5*] had allegedly inflicted on Lord Francis and his family was probably too severe to be mended by its selling. The mishaps laid at its door might be stretched to include:

– The divorce from his first wife and the early death of his second.

– The shooting accident leading to amputation of his foot.

–- His several bankruptcies.

– His brother's (the seventh Duke) leg amputation.

– The subsequent demise of the countryseat of Clumber.

These and all other illnesses and misfortunes which befell the Newcastle family and their Estates can be conveniently blamed on this fabulous gem. The record of subsequent owners after Lord Francis – and their misfortunes – included the following:

– Prince Kanitovski, a wealthy Russian - Assassinated.

– A Greek jeweller – Killed (with wife and family) in an accident.

– Sultan Abdul Hamid – Deposed in the Young Turk revolution.

– Habid, Persian diamond merchant – Drowned in the French liner La Seyne,
  near Singapore.

– Edward B. McLean, American multi-millionaire – lost his wife and his son,
  killed in a road accident.

The infamous Hope Diamond is now in the Harry Winston Gallery of the Smithsonian Museum, Washington D.C. – hopefully they will keep it secure! A far less threatening replica can currently be found in the Mineral Gallery of the Natural History Museum in London.

DUKE ROBBED BY HIS LAWYER

Wilson wrote:

> *29 January 1904*
> *Mr G Marshall, solicitor of Retford, lost £12,000 of the*
> *Duke's money ...*

Figure 61 – George Marshall.

67 year-old George Henry Marshall of Mount Vernon, Retford, had been the duke's solicitor for some twelve years. During 1902 he was involved in the sale of 11 Hill Street, London. The monies raised from this transaction amounted to some £40,000, which Marshall placed in his firm's safe, awaiting further instructions. In December 1903 he was again in London on behalf of the duke. He had with him £18,000 of the duke's cash, as he was now under instructions to pay this as deposit on the purchase by mortgage of Forest Farm, near Windsor. He then reported to the police that £12,000 of the cash had been stolen from his wallet whilst it was in his room at the Hotel Metropole. National newspapers had a field day, 'Bank Note Robbery' being the usual headline, with some hint that a gang of well-known London criminals might be involved. However it was not long before other speculation and accusations gathered momentum. It became clear that Marshall's law firm was insolvent (owing around £24,000) and he himself was deeply in debt. Eventually, this led to Mr Marshall's arrest and court appearance, where he was charged with misappropriation of the cash.

In July 1904 the case went to a three-day trial at the Nottingham Assizes. The duke appeared as a witness, and asked that his: "old servant be treated as leniently as possible". The case was proved, with the jury also recommending mercy because of age. Despite this, the judge commented that this five-time Mayor of Retford, senior Alderman and Justice of the Peace, had seriously betrayed the trust placed in him and an example needed to be set. The maximum sentence for the offence was seven years penal servitude. The judge imposed five years.

The Lincoln's Inn, London, firm of Messrs. Francis and Crookenden were then appointed as the duke's solicitors. They were to look after him and his successors well for the whole period covered by the remainder of this book, and beyond.

ROUTINE, YET CHANGING TIMES

The Head Forester's life moved on, beginning 1904 by attending the funeral of his friend, George Philips, lately landlord of the Lion Hotel, Worksop. Wilson then resumed his work: clearing and selling the duke's timber from Apleyhead Wood, planting new maple saplings at Black Hill Clump, on the Clumber Road, and visiting the Newark and Nottingham Park estates. This was alternated with shooting rabbits on the South Lawns at Clumber (around fifteen thousand were being killed each year), and the fixing of a paddock fence at Ranby Hall for Lady Rossmore (grandmother of the duchess). By this date, Wilson was also responsible for the considerable task of improving roads within the Park. There were more than sixteen miles of tracks designated as 'roads' which had for over a century been formed with cobbles collected from local farmlands, puddled into an irregular and bumpy surface. Now, with the provision of waste from the ever-expanding Manton Colliery, the Woodsman and his men – especially those of the Gabbitas and Read families who drove the estate's steam-roller – were charged with bringing these ancient and modern thoroughfares into the new century.

On the lighter side, Wilson attended the April races at Retford along with the Hardwick's latest Farm Bailiff, William Beattie, who had been appointed to that position six years earlier. In June, Wilson and his family went to the Yeomanry Sports at Welbeck. He then undertook a business trip to Cleethorpes – staying at the Dolphin Hotel. Whilst on this 'jolly', he visited both Grimsby and Brocklesby, noting that estate's: "Pelham's Pillar ... was erected in 1849 to commemorate the planting of 12 and a half million of trees – the year I was born".

Back at Clumber in time for the Annual Show, he was pleased to record that he had: "dined in the duke's tent". A further entry, during this summer, gives the first indication that Wilson's family had been introduced to the motor car being used at their level of society, when friends arrived on a 'motoring' visit from Huddersfield. These early moves away from the horse-drawn carriage age were also exampled by his July mention of travelling on 'trams' – this being whilst in Sheffield, where the city's tram system was then less than five years old. His experiences of the transport revolution presumably mirrored those of his contemporaries.

In August, changing times were again emphasised to Wilson and many other interested locals. They witnessed the visit of Joseph Chamberlain to Welbeck Abbey to speak in support of radical proposals for tariff reform. The ex-Cabinet Minister had held the posts of Secretary of State for the Colonies and President of the Board of Trade. The following month, the forester went to see King Edward and his party arrive at Lord Savile's Rufford Abbey – a royal visit arranged to coincide with the racing at Doncaster. At the end of the week, Wilson and his ladies again travelled to Rufford and: "saw the King and party dining". Presumably the royals were under open marquees in the Abbey's extensive grounds.

Routine times for the duchess meant that she was on duty at Newark Town Hall during October. In the absence of the duke, and travelling by motor car, she journeyed there to speak at the first R.S.P.C.A meeting to be held in that town. She also accepted the invitation to become the organisation's local president for the following year.

***

The opening of a Post Office at Hardwick on Monday 16th of May 1904 was one of the major events of the year for Park residents. The postmistress for this new venture was Mrs Mary Alcock, the fifty-year-old wife of the Estate Foreman Joiner. Their cottage formed part of the Workshops complex at Hardwick village and the small bay-windowed front room was now to be given up to the needs of her new duties as a government official. The facility was linked to the town Post Office in Worksop and Mrs Alcock was supplied with a hand-stamp to record the 'Hardwick'

Figure 62 – Mrs Mary Alcock, Clumber Park's first Postmistress.

impression on postcards and letters. Her shop also offered basic provisions such as tinned groceries, as well as sweets and other luxuries. She retained these duties until the beginning of the Second World War.

To supplement the service provided by Mrs Alcock, Worksop tradesmen visited Clumber Park with a mobile service of provisions. Amongst them was a certain William Straw, later to become famous following the purchase of his semi-detached suburban house by the National Trust. Mr Straw cycled the four miles from Worksop every Monday evening (his bike complete with carbide lamp) to collect orders for items from his grocer's shop at the town's Market Place, which he then delivered by pony and trap later in the week.

Figure 63 – Hardwick Post Office

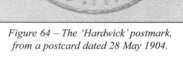

*Figure 64 – The 'Hardwick' postmark,
from a postcard dated 28 May 1904.*

A NEW AGENT AND A NEW YEAR

The strain of handling problems in connection with the theft of the duke's monies mentioned earlier seems to have been the final straw for hardworking Agent, Joel Haslam. A loyal servant of the Newcastles for around forty years, it was in August, soon after the annual show, that he fell ill with what sounds very much like a nervous breakdown. He never returned to work and died within three years of his retirement. Mr Haslam's replacement, Arthur Elliott, arrived in October 1904, and was to stay for some thirty years, to see the estate through yet more major traumas and fast-changing times. Mr Elliott's six-monthly Estate Reports to the duke have proved invaluable in piecing together the story presented here.

*Figure 65 – Arthur Elliott
(Agent from 1904 to 1931)*

***

The Head Forester's work programme for the autumn of 1904 is a reminder of some of the areas still under the duke's ownership. Woodsmen undertook work at Worksop (a hedging competition), Newark and Flawborough (fixing barbed wire), East Markham (marking timber) and fixing a fence at Walesby School. They spent time in the autumn applying tree-lime to trees along the Lime Tree Avenue, Wilson recording that: "it caught hundreds of thousands of grubs and moths".

The New Year began with a timber sale at Worksop, raising a welcome £2262.10s which enabled Wilson to purchase 150,000 unspecified plants from the Handsworth Nurseries. Other activities included beech hedge planting at the Park Street Estate Office, the planting of a cedar tree near Clumber's 'Summer House' at the 'Rocks' (close by the Bridge and more latterly known as the 'Grotto') and various shrubs in the Clock Tower Yard.

Two weddings added some diversity to the year for Clumber's residents. The first was that of Wilson's daughter, Gertrude, who was married to Mr J.P. Crowther at the Worksop Priory. Rev Frank Hawkins, the duke's latest chaplain, officiated and many members of the estate attended the service and the wedding breakfast.

The second event was the marriage of the duke's niece, Lois Lister-Kaye, daughter of Beatrice Adeline, the duke's elder sister. Her bridegroom was Lord Oxmantown, who had served in the South African Wars and was heir to the Irish town of Birr. The ceremony took place in Clumber Chapel and Heads of Departments were invited to attend. Wilson particularly enjoyed mixing with old friends from the Womersley and Denby Grange areas of Yorkshire, the location of the bride's family home. There was a sad occurrence linked to this event. Estate worker John Read was said to have died as a result of catching cold whilst tending the bonfires and burning torches that had been placed alongside the park roads. It had been normal practice to light the way for evening visitors to Clumber House, particularly along the route from Worksop via Truman's Lodge. The night of the wedding was exceptionally wet and John had been on duty throughout the downpour. His cold turned to pneumonia and he died a few weeks after the event.

ROYALTY MOTOR IN CLUMBER – BUT NO ONE WAS HOME.

On Thursday 14 December 1905 the King and Queen (who were staying at Welbeck) made a motor trip through the Dukeries, accompanied by the Duke and Duchess of Portland. Their route took them into Clumber where the Queen and the other ladies visited the Church (the King staying in the car). Neither the Duke nor Duchess of Newcastle was at home when the royal party called. The King's first visit had been in 1861 and his second twenty years later. Clumber mansion's south-facing 'Prince of Wales' suite of rooms had been so named in honour of his stay on the earliest of these two visits.

Figure 66 – The Grand Drawing Room (part of the 'Prince of Wales' suite) at Clumber House.
[Country Life Picture Gallery]

ESTATE STAFFING

At the time of the new Agent's appointment in 1904, numbers of outdoor staff comprised: the Clerk of Works' Department – sixty: the Forester's Department – forty-nine men and boys. The Head Gardener had twenty-nine staff, and the Farm Bailiff thirty-six. A further six gamekeepers and unspecified grooms brought the total to little short of two hundred. Additionally, thirty servants were more directly attached to duties in Clumber House. The annual wage bill was approaching nine thousand pounds.

The duke's instructions to the new Agent were clear and had a time-less ring – 'reduce the costs of running the duchy'. This directive was difficult to fulfil, especially when it went alongside apparently contradictory instructions that included: "renew heating arrangements at the Glasshouses and in the House Billiard Room – build two new cottages near the Cricket Field – and, [by the way!], plan for the installation of electricity at Clumber, which will mean taking down and selling the old gas plant, removing the cottages and blacksmith's shop to the north of the House, and erecting a new generating station in the stone mason's yard!" No one had told Mr Elliott that his new job was going to be easy!

ELECTRICITY INTRODUCED

Following much pre-planning – and commencing in 1906 – the first comprehensive electricity supply was installed at Clumber House. Initially, the project was thwarted by the absence of building plans for the twenty-five-year-old rebuilt Mansion. Fresh plans were belatedly drawn up – these also included the many-roomed stableyard and outbuildings including the Chapel and the Parsonage.

The electrical installation caused considerable disturbance to normal routines and that Christmas was the first for many years that the servants and other estate workers had not been invited to have dinner (or even a tea party) in Clumber House. Their consolation prize was an allowance of one and half pounds of beef for all those who were deprived of the annual treat.

Mr W. H. Massey of Twyford, Berkshire, undertook supervision of the electrical improvements. A generation plant was installed just one hundred yards from the north entrance to the House which meant that underground cabling was kept to a minimum. Some 1,400 electric lights were provided for the House, together with many hundreds more for the Stableyard, Offices and

Parsonage. The duchess' approval was sought for the wax-coloured electric candles to be fitted in the Library. Problems in hiding the cabling below the Library Gallery handrail seemed endless, but were finally resolved to her satisfaction.

The electrical supply was provided by the use of a suction gas plant (manufactured by Crossley's of Openshaw, Manchester). This comprised a gas producer and two gas engines installed in a newly erected building forming an extension of the stable premises. Anthracite coal was used to fuel the new generating plant. The battery room adjoined the engine room, from where lead concentric mains were carried underground some 270 feet to the back of the house and approximately 600 feet around the west end of the house, to the middle of the south front facing the lake. Inside the house, the main was affixed to a switchboard on the ground floor.

The new power supply – and the fire appliances, which were part and parcel of the installation plan – led to a review of fire insurance costs. Newly drawn-up risk-assessments give a clear description of the arrangements. Fire appliances consisted of two six-inch rising mains with hose and hydrants on each floor. Both were supplied with water from the reservoir in the Paddock, which was kept filled by the use of a turbine pump worked from the lake overflow. However, there was a 'very grave defect' in the arrangements. The reservoir was insufficiently higher than the House to provide a strong water pressure and required considerably more engine power. There were six hydrants around the mansion and stables, to be operated by the estate's nine volunteer firemen – who were required to attend drill practice once a fortnight. The insurance company representative was not at all impressed by the available fire-fighting resources and recommended, as a minimum, the provision of sufficient 'Minimax' extinguishers on each floor. He also gave the strongest hint that a 'steam fire engine' (such as he had noted at Welbeck) was essential to provide the best solution for attacking fire at the highest levels in the House. However, although the duke authorised the purchase of the small extinguishers, he would not agree to the financing of a steam fire engine. The extinguishers were placed in the Clinton Corridor, Grand Corridor, Mezzanine Corridor, North Corridor, Yellow Satin Corridor, the Servant's Landing, and the top of the Lincoln Staircase and the Laundry. Unprotected areas were listed as the Stables, Motor House, Power Station, Chapel and the Parsonage.

By the autumn, Clumber was full of visitors for the week of the Doncaster racing. No doubt they were duly impressed by the improvements, little realising that their presence was causing the excavations for cabling work to the Chapel to be being delayed for some weeks.

THE DUCHESS WAS NOT AMUSED

The duke was away in the early months of 1907, this time escaping from the worst aspects of the electricity installation upheaval at Clumber House. He sailed to America on the 'Lusitania', the brand new (but ill-fated) liner that had been launched the previous year and was to be sunk by German torpedoes some eight years later.

Whilst he was abroad the duchess stayed at their recently purchased property at Forest Farm, or at their Berkeley House flat. She also called on her relatives at Sysonby Lodge, Melton Mowbray. Increasingly involved in the dog show world she had (during 1906) parted with almost all of her Borzois. With the exception of her six favourites (named Velsk, Tzaretsa, White Tzar, Nags, Stonefield and Olga), the remaining twenty-four animals had been sent to the Manchester Show along with their Russian pedigree documentation. Selling these dogs was partly done on financial grounds, but mainly because she had become increasingly involved with her hobby as a leading breeder and eminent judge of wire-haired Fox Terriers. She was also still spending on her Welsh ponies.

On her return visits to Clumber, she kept a watchful eye on the estate. Very little escaped her attention! One day, when travelling home from Welbeck, she noted something that resulted in her contacting the Agent. She had only occasionally entered the Park through the Carburton Lodge gateway during her eighteen years at Clumber and, on this visit, was surprised at what she found there. The 'Wilson' family (not 'our' Wilson Tomlinson's) had been housed rent-free at the Lodge since before her Grace arrived in the Park. To supplement their modest earnings, they provided a small shop service for the sale of refreshments (such as mineral waters) to the public who visited the Park. In an attempt to advertise the facility 'a tin placard' had been nailed up at the Lodge and it was the sight of this brash commercialism which roused the duchess to action.

The Agent, who helpfully noted that the Wilson's had been providing the service for very many years, was urged to notify all tenants of the Lodges around the Estate that no similar unofficial and unseemly enterprises should be undertaken and above all that no such signs displayed. Not only that, but the area outside the Carburton Lodge was to be tidied up, the road widened: "untidy grass done away with and semi-circular flowerbeds introduced"

On the duke's return, he pronounced himself delighted with the House electricity installation which was almost completed. However, he was less than pleased to hear that the removal of gas supplies meant that the purchase of four new coke-fuelled cooking stoves was now required.

THE DAILY ROUND

Whilst all this change was going on around them, Clumber estate workers continued their daily round of common tasks. Wilson's 'doings' again give us such a good flavour of the way his and their lives were an interesting mixture of work and leisure.

Work obviously meant more plantings and sales of timber and it is interesting to note the extent of these activities. Fourteen acres were planted in Manton Wood during 1906 and a further twenty-five acres the following year, Handsworth Nurseries again being the suppliers. This brought total plantings on the Clumber estate to more than four hundred and fifty acres over twenty-four years. Visits to Basford, Bagthorpe, Claypole, Egmanton, Gamston, Ranby, Retford, Newark, North Muskham, Nottingham Park, Tuxford, Walesby and Worksop Forest were necessary to check on a variety of issues. These included matters connected with boundaries, fencing, valuing, damage caused by railway and other fires, also: "willows taken down in error".

There was also a picturesque aspect to these arboreal matters. On the duke's instructions three Sugar Maples were to be planted in Clumber Park opposite the Cricket Ground (at the corner of Ice House Wood) and six Pin Oaks in the area close by the Turbine House near Clumber Bridge. Both of these varieties had been ordered from America in the previous November. Quercus Palustris oaks and Berberis Stenophylla hedging shrubs were planted alongside Clumber's newest road, which is the closest to the lake on the route from the mansion site to the bridge. Apleyhead Lodge was provided with a selection of ivies, and evergreens were cut to enable the annual gift of festive decorations to be chosen for St. Paul's Cathedral.

The two cottages by the Cricket Ground were built at this time. The site had been marked out in 1905 and G.G.Middletons of Worksop completed the construction just over a year later. J.M.Thompson of Kirton Hall prepared the impressive Newcastle coat of arms on the front of these cottages. The first occupier was the newly-appointed estate electrician, Mr J.W. Rungay.

Figure 67 – Clumber's 'Cricket Ground Cottages', built on the southern edge of the 'Paddocks'.

Certain estate residents found light relief from their working lives by joining shooting parties with the Grove and Rufford Hounds. Locations identified for their sport are Apleyhead, Ash Tree Hill Wood, Boat House Wood, Burnt Oak, Culloden, Haughton Decoy and Warren, Normanton to Blackcliff, Sharpe's Hill, South Lawns and Worksop Forest.

Many members of the 'Dukeries' estates enjoyed horseracing at Aintree, Ascot, Retford and Rufford. Outings to Cleethorpes, York and Scarborough, Bolsover Castle, the Royal Show at Lincoln, and a dance at Welbeck, made up some of the other entertainment. Gertrude Treadaway, daughter of Clumber's organist, choirmaster and headmaster, was wed in August 1906 and this no doubt provided the icing on the cake.

A LOSS AND SOME GAINS FOR THE PELHAM-CLINTONS

Lord Edward Pelham-Clinton died on 9 July 1907. Previously introduced here as the Master of Household to the late Queen, he was the last surviving child of the fifth duke, and had lived through so much change at Clumber. His parents had separated when he was in his early teens and later (unlike his four siblings) he had achieved high office and much respect. He was buried at the Brookwood Cemetery, west of Woking. A memorial service was held for him in Clumber Chapel and soon afterwards the duke financed a stained-glass window for the Chapel, in his memory.

***

Lord Francis, brother of the duke, had divorced in 1902. His eight-year marriage to Mary Yohe had been childless. It was soon after this that his engagement to his cousin was announced – and then abruptly unannounced! He had now remarried and his second wife was Olive Muriel Owen, formerly Shaw [née Thompson]. They had three children, the eldest being Henry Edward Hugh who was born on 8 April 1907. Daughters, Doria Lois and Mary Hope, were born in 1908 and 1910 respectively. The young boy (invariably known as 'Pelham') was destined to become ninth Duke of Newcastle-under-Lyme in the 1940's, but it would have taken remarkable foresight at this stage to guess that he would be instrumental in the demise of this Nottinghamshire-based ducal estate.

CHAPTER FIVE

1908 – 1918

A Liberal Budget & other irritants – Minerals, Cars & Investments – The Gardeners & the Inland Revenue Inspector – Clumber's 'Normanton Gates' – The Alcock Family – National publicity for Clumber's glories – The Forester's Activities – Demands of Royalty – Clumber Troop of Sherwood Rangers – Leased & Tied Cottages – Leisure Pursuits – A Funeral & a Wedding – Coronation 1911 – Estate events and family matters – National Insurance – The fire of 1912 – Terrace Ornaments – The London and Fort George Land Company Ltd. – Hardwick Village School – Clumber's Choir School – The Dowager Duchess died – Army Training in Clumber Park – Garden Parties – Silver Wedding celebrations – Royals visit Nottinghamshire again – The realities of War – Belgiums, Canadians and Others – Yet more Financial Adjustments – Wartime effects on Schooling at Clumber – There was always the Timber – The duke's and duchess's London interests – Our first Guide retires.

A LIBERAL BUDGET AND OTHER IRRITANTS

WE NOW COMMENCE A DECADE that will conclude with the retirement of our current Head Forester – and the end of a World War! This period begins with continuing agricultural depression. Farming incomes had fallen by some 25% since the days of the sixth duke, attracting low farm prices and rebated rents for tenant farmers. Along with other major landowners, the Duke of Newcastle would soon feel additional pain from the effects of the Liberal's 1907 budgetary measures that introduced taxes on undeveloped land – and a National Insurance Act. Many landowners would also be stung by the government's plans to remove the power of the House of Lords' veto (doesn't that sound familiar!). There were soon to be other problems, such as cutbacks in manpower and the additional demands of an imminent war, even if timber was likely to be at a high premium once war began.

An overall deficit on annual accounts was calculated at around £3,000, with the Clumber/Worksop figures recording a substantial excess of expenditure amounting to around £19,000. Expenses of £6,000 had been involved in the switch from gas to electricity in the mansion. This gloom was marginally brightened by better news from Newark and Nottingham, with excesses of income respectively of £4,500 and £12,000.

To cut the losses at the Clumber's 'Home Farms', such as Hardwick Grange Farm; Haughton Farm and also Clam Cat Farm, it was decided to reduce the unprofitable arable on these properties by about a third. This increased the grasslands to around five hundred acres, leaving something less than six hundred acres for rotational crops: barley, oats, potatoes, rye, swedes, turnips and wheat. A farm sale of surplus 'livestock' (cattle, pigs, horses and implements) was also arranged, as was the sale of twenty-three shire horses. These measures raised a welcome £3,000.

Lime trees in Clumber's famous Avenue were again under attack by the winter moths. Year after year, experts were called in for advice on this matter. Contradictory recommendations were received. One example being that soil should be removed from around each tree and fresh soil applied mixed with gas lime. Stout paper, coated with cart grease and soft soap, was then tried. Also considered was the extreme use of arsenic spray or explosive bisulphide. The latter suggestion was discarded on the grounds that it was: "too risky for the average labourer"! Even more money was spent on the problem and (as no magic remedy was found) the black grease bands became a permanent feature. There were many other items of estate expenditure. These included a new drainage system for the fourteen terrace cottages at Hardwick, ongoing repairs to properties and fences, the purchase of a new steamroller and a replacement ferryboat. Also, a new dairy had recently been constructed and located next to the main Grange Farm complex. Mother and daughter, Jane and Jane Olivant (who lived at Manton Lodge – and later at Schoolmaster's Cottage) controlled milk-marketing operations at Clumber's new facility. Estate families called at the dairy for their supplies but the 'big House' received pony and trap deliveries of both milk and butter.

MINERALS, CARS AND INVESTMENTS

Income from coal royalties (charged at around sixpence [$2^1/_2$p] per ton) had decreased by roughly half, mainly due to those received from the failing resources at Babbington Colliery, near Nottingham. Another sinking fund was that of royalties on sand, gravel and water. A notable example of this was the seven-eighth of one 'old' penny received on each thousand gallons of water pumped out of Manton Colliery to the newly-built reservoir and treatment plant off Lower Sparken Hill. As a director of the Wigan Coal Company the duke was also entitled to a portion of the three pence per gallon that the company received. Water from the 'Number One Shaft' – magnesian limestone bed source – was particularly hard and pure. Total daily water extraction at Manton was reported at the incredible rate of four million gallons per day! It was piped to Belph and Whitwell, then on to the villages of Barlborough and Clowne, some ten miles to the west of Clumber. Somewhat ironically, the River Poulter has its source at Clowne and had provided water for Clumber Lake supply since the development of the Park in the 1760's.

On a personal level, His Grace's investments (a frequently changing portfolio, but amounting to around £10,000 at this time) appear to have attracted interest payments of around four per cent. Also, the knowledge that apart from other heirlooms he had '16 Chests of Plate' stored at Coutts the Bankers in London must have been a comfort to him! After considering the overall financial situation, the duke was not deterred from purchasing a 'Leon Bollé' motor car for a mere £750 (less £200 for his traded-in 'Clements-Panhard Gladiator' and a further £47 for a paraffin-powered 'Serpollet' vehicle). This was soon followed by the acquisition of a second-hand Mercedes (£450, less £150 for his 'old Anglian').

GARDENERS & THE TAX INSPECTOR

Figure 68 – Head Gardener, Sammy Barker (seated, centre of the front row) with his team of 'gardeners'.

117

Clumber Gardens continued to be another drain on resources, with problems arising over the Palmhouse construction. Unseasoned wood was blamed for the latest spending, although the accused firm loudly denied the charge. Also, new Glasshouses had been recently provided at a cost of almost £1,000 and a new boiler and pipe extension fitted in the Carnation House.

On the personnel front, Gardener's Licences gave much concern during this period. This was all due to the government's requirement that employers should apply for 'Male Servant Licences'. It was also a matter of the grounds for exemption from obtaining such certification – when was a 'Gardener' not a 'Gardener'? That was the nub of the argument made by Sammy Barker, Head Gardener. Mr Barker said that only four licences were required, one for himself and three for his nominated 'Under Gardeners', Messrs. T. Rigby, W. Skinner and T. Smith. He was adamant the other twenty-five staff under his control were not 'Gardeners' but merely 'apprentices', 'improvers' or 'labourers' and, therefore, in the exempt category.

The Inspector from the Inland Revenue's Sheffield office called during May 1908. He listened to arguments as to whether potting and sowing seeds, striking cuttings, planting out plants in the Pleasure Ground and attending to those in the Glasshouses, fitted the job description of a gardener. After the Revenue man had visited the sites of these activities he returned to Sheffield to consider his verdict. Unfortunately, no record has been found indicating the result of this negotiation between civil servant and Clumber's finest. It seems likely that a compromise was reached and something more than four (but less than twenty-nine) licences were obtained!

CLUMBER'S 'NORMANTON GATES'

Mrs Dallas-Yorke of Welbeck had 'set her heart on' the ancient gate pillars at Shireoaks Hall Farm. In April 1908 she instructed her Agent to make enquiries of the Clumber hierarchy with a view to purchasing them for Welbeck. Mrs Dallas-Yorke's timing was unfortunate! Her Agent's letter was received at Clumber when the duke was away but the duchess was not! Despite the fact that these stone pillars had been neglected ever since the four hundred acre farm had come into the possession of the Newcastle family nearly seventy years earlier (as part of the Worksop Manor purchase), the answer was a resounding 'no'.

After Calvert Wheeler, Estate Architect, had been sent to Shireoaks to make a sketch of these objects of desire, it was decided that the almost forgotten gate pillars were: "now too good to remain in their present position". They were abruptly uprooted from the potato field in which they stood and transported ten miles to the eastern boundary of Clumber Park, opposite the Normanton Inn. This move inevitably meant that Mrs Dalles-Yorke would not see them so frequently and may soon recover from her disappointment. The previous wooden gates were replaced by new metal ones and fitted to the coveted pillars. This historic and impressive gateway was given a new lease of life as the 'Normanton Gates'.

Figure 69 (above) – The gates in situ at Shireoaks Hall Farm.

Figure 70 (right) – Young John Alcock 'guards' the Normanton Gates to Clumber Park in the mid-1930s.

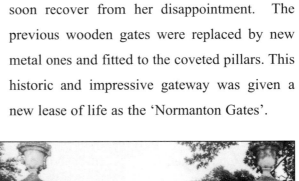

THE ALCOCK FAMILY

The Alcock family had been associated with the Newcastle estate since at least the early 1880's when Richard George Alcock was the foreman joiner at the Hardwick Workshops. As mentioned earlier, Mary, his wife, had been appointed as the estate's first post-mistress when the position was established in their Workshop's cottage in 1904. Mr Alcock (better known as 'George') was highly respected on the estate. He had served as the 'banner bearer' at Clumber Chapel since its opening. On his death in 1918 the coffin was watched over throughout the night in the Chapel. The Requiem Mass that followed was attended by Kathleen, Duchess and her two young nieces, Doria and Mary, together with many family, friends and colleagues. His eldest son, Charles (known as 'Tip') followed his father as foreman joiner and in 1946, when

Figure 71 – Richard George Alcock.

the estate was sold to The National Trust, went with the ninth duke to his new estate in Wiltshire.

The youngest son of the family, Richard, was the Alcock's fourth child and, in 1906, found favour with the estate hierarchy due to his promising achievements at the village school. During 1906, the Sub-Inspector of Schools (a Mr J. Hall BA) had noted Richard as a: "clever boy" and his good results continued with a special distinction award during the following year. Arthur Elliott, the Agent, passed the Inspector's opinion up the line to the duke, with a recommendation that the young boy: "worthy of help ... be offered ... a couple of years at Worksop College as a Day Boarder". The duke agreed and Richard began his studies in a public school environment in late January 1908.

Figure 72 – Richard Alcock (on the right) with a fellow pupil. Both boys are sporting their Worksop College Boxing Club blazers – circa 1912.

Having been selected for such special treatment, Richard was a resilient enough character to withstand the teasing of his former fellow-students at Hardwick village. At the college, his mark was quickly made as an outstanding sportsman and student, becoming Captain of both Cricket and Boxing at the College and moved on to high achievements as Head Boy. He represented the College at such prestigious events as the Silver Wedding celebrations of the Duke and Duchess of Portland at Welbeck.

During the war he served as an officer with the 9th Battalion of the Sherwood Foresters and subsequently, following training in Dublin, became a schoolteacher. In 1930 he married Christine Mary Cole at Worksop Priory and they had two children, John and Gillian. Christine was the only daughter of William Cole, a long-serving employee of the estate – groom, drayman and gatekeeper at Truman's Lodge being amongst his duties. Christine had also attended the Hardwick school. Her mother, Catherine, attended to the domestic needs of the single men who lodged in the Clumber Garden's 'Bothy'. On marriage, Richard and Christine lived at the Post Office cottage with his mother. They later moved to Manton Lodge and finally New Cottages.

After attending teacher's training in Dublin, Richard had a variety of appointments until, in 1936, he moved to Gatehouse School in Kingston-on-Thames, which became his favourite teaching post. After periods at Macclesfield and Uttoxeter, he returned to Kingston-on-Thames until his retirement in 1965 at the age of seventy.

In contrast to his energetic sporting pastimes, Richard was a regular church attender and whilst on leave during his army service acted as: "Thurifer in khaki" at services in the Chapel. In the 1950's, he wrote the first Guide Book for the Clumber Chapel. He also excelled at the art of photography and his talent with the camera has been of benefit to us all. On returning to Clumber during the 1920's and 30's, he spent many hours at this hobby, recording and cataloguing his 'snaps'. His unique record of ordinary life within the boundaries of Clumber Park has been saved on many hundreds of negatives, on both film negatives and glass slides. Richard died in 1978, and his children have passed his archive to the National Trust for safe-keeping. Many of his depictions are already in the public domain.

NATIONAL PUBLICITY FOR CLUMBER'S GLORIES

After due appointments had been negotiated, the famous 'Country Life' magazine sent a reporter and photographer to Clumber Park in 1908. The whole of the Mansion's exterior woodwork had been painted just in time and was looking at its best. The journalists were well practised in the art of recording the splendours of Britain's great houses and estates. Their efforts indicating the glories of the 'big house' complement the work of the excellent amateur mentioned above. Large-scale pictures of many aspects of the mansion recorded forever (albeit in black and white) the magnificence of this ducal residence. These photographs are scattered throughout this volume and include views of the terraces, chapel, lake and pleasure ground.

Figure 73 – Samuel Barker, Clumber's Head Gardener (1899-1935)

On the subject of 'glories', Clumber's Head Gardener, Samuel Barker, was earning accolades from a 'Gardener's Magazine' contributor in June 1910. Mr Barker's expertise was lauded in all aspects of the management of his empire. The terrace gardens were said to be: "affording some of the finest examples of the Italian style, as applied to garden design, to be found in the United Kingdom". The report especially highlighted his displays there of heliotropiums, dracaenas, bamboos, hydrangeas and fuschias. The walled kitchen gardens: "flanked by broad borders of hardy herbaceous plants ..." came in for special praise, noting particularly the carnations, phloxes, hollyhocks, sweetpeas, roses and the fifteen hundred chrysanthemums grown in pots. Under glass were Malmaison carnations and single and double varieties of violets. In the fruit houses were figs, grapes (including Muscat of Alexandria, Madresfield Court and Gros Colmar) peaches and nectarines. The loganberries were said to be excellent and some three thousand strawberry plants were grown annually. Vegetable plots were extensive areas, with a whole acre (of the total seven) given over to the asparagus beds.

THE FORESTER'S ACTIVITIES

Now around sixty years of age, our Forester, Wilson Tomlinson, continued his energetic leisure pursuits. January was hunting and shooting time for him and his fellow seniors in Manton Forest, also at Ash Tree Hill, Apley Head, Burnt Oaks, Culloden and Haughton. They rode to hounds at Gamston and with Lord Lonsdale's party at Clumber. With family and friends Wilson attended Retford races, went on a trip to Southwell Minster (calling at Merryweather's Nurseries) and had a picnic at Hardwick Hall. He also enjoyed a visit to Earl FitzWilliam's Wentworth House. Shortly after this no doubt he received grateful thanks for having found the earl's silver hunting horn at Heron Hill, on Clumber's northern border. In mid-September, Wilson took his wife and daughter to Rufford Abbey, there attending a meeting of the Primrose League. Five days later he motored from Newark to Farndon to organise the planting of lime trees on a piece of land owned by the duke, who was Lord of Farndon Manor. The following April, Mr F. Mitchell (son of the Head Forester at Woburn) was employed as assistant to Clumber's Head Forester, a sign that the duke was looking ahead to the day when his long-serving woodsman would retire.

Other work-related duties included fixing a new oak fence at Carburton Lodge and more fencing at the new cemetery at Bothamsall. Some six-hundred trees had been blown down in a storm during January 1908. No doubt this made available even more timber to weigh down the market and keep prices low. Plantings were made at Manton, Normanton Old Larches and three timber sales held at the Lion Hotel, Worksop, raising an average of £2,000 per sale. At this time, Wilson proudly noted that, with the Agent, Arthur Elliott, he had travelled 'in a car' to check the timber at Bevercotes and Tuxford.

During the years covered by this chapter, Wilson's family events included the marriage of Emma (June 1908) and Maud starting work at Oakham Post Office (January 1909). Youngest son, Aylmer, began his schooling at Retford Grammar School, leaving in September 1913 to begin training as a joiner at the Hardwick Workshops. Cecil had begun work at Clumber Gardens and Percy found employment at Sandbeck Hall.

Figure 74 – Herbert Tomlinson. Born at Clumber in 1892, he is shown here working aboard the 'Lincoln' frigate.

Wilson was also still journeying to other estates, where he was pleased to be invited to judge various aspects of country activities, such as a 1911 'hedging' competition at Lilleshall Hall, Shropshire, property of the Duke of Sutherland. Along with his wife and daughters, Wilson travelled there in the Duke of Newcastle's car.

Spotting foreign visitors to England seems to have been a secondary occupation for our Forester during the summer of 1911. Firstly he noted some one-hundred and fifty Australians at Ranby House [*searches through press reports of the day (including the cricketing pages!) have failed to reveal who these visitors were, or why they were in England*]. A few days later he recorded three-hundred and fifty Germans as motoring along Lime Tree Avenue on their way from Welbeck to the Apley Head Gateway and beyond. The size of the German's 'peaceful invasion' also has a puzzling aspect, as it is somewhat difficult to reconcile with the local press reports. The latter merely reported the presence of: "between sixty and seventy German and English motorists" with a possibly maximum of sixty-four cars. They were taking part in a tour promoted by Prince Henry of Prussia, brother of the Kaiser. Participants were also testing the reliability of the cars, whose drivers were members of the Royal Automobile Club and the German Imperial Automobile Club. Whether non-participants made up the number is not known, but this early-days 'RAC rally' was certainly a foretaste of what the Park was to experience in later years.

Early in 1912, Wilson visited the duke's estate at Cromwell in respect of new plantings on the banks of the River Trent. His journey involved a boat trip from Newark to Carlton Ferry. Babworth Hall was next on his list, regarding the boundary line with Eaton, where Newcastle Agents of the late eighteenth century had lived. The duchess also discussed with him desirable improvements at Clumber's waterfall and pleasure grounds. In November, when King George V and his Queen visited Welbeck, Newcastle's estate staff helped to erect the decorative archway at the gateway to Worksop Manor (and close by the Estate Office, an area known locally as 'top-of-town'). Prepared on the duke's instructions, the archway was designed by estate architect, Calvert Wheeler. This archway became the talk of the town and was much admired by the royal party. During the following year Wilson toured Scotland by motor car with the Royal Scottish Arboricultural Society, taking lunch one day at Balmoral Castle: "by the King's command".

DEMANDS OF ROYALTY

During September 1908, the King and Queen stayed at Rufford Abbey. There they were entertained by Harry Lauder, the most famous comic singer of the day. For their further amusement, a motoring tour of the 'Dukeries' had been arranged. They visited the Welbeck estate and then Clumber Park where the Duke and Duchess met them and tea was served in the 'Grand Saloon'. The Queen took a particular interest in the magnificent Library, after which the royal party left, travelling over Clumber Bridge and on through Thoresby Park on their return to Rufford.

In the spring of the following year a surprise royal request was received from Marlborough House that the 'Clumber Cup' might be sent to the Prince of Wales for his inspection. It seems that this Cup was an important family heirloom, dating back to the 1707 Act of Union. In that year, John Holles (Duke of Newcastle-upon-Tyne in its second creation; Privy Seal and a Commissioner of the English Union with Scotland) was presented by Queen Anne with a two-handled cup manufactured from the melted-down metal of the Privy Seal of England that was being replaced by a Seal of the new union. Needless to say, the Prince of Wales's request was heeded and the Cup sent to London, to be returned with royal thanks on the same day, 10th May 1909.

CLUMBER TROOP OF SHERWOOD RANGERS

Figure 75a – Sherwood Rangers, at a Salisbury Plain Training Camp [circa 1910.]

As part of on-going army reforms and the formation of the Territorial Force from Yeomanry and Volunteer categories of earlier days, the Sherwood Rangers had a boost in 1909. First mentioned in estate manuscripts dated some one hundred years earlier, members of newly titled Clumber Troop of the Nottinghamshire Imperial Cavalry then had (in those earlier days) had the 'unhappy reactionary' fourth duke as their Major Commandant. At that time the training and social activities of the Troop were based at the White Hart public house at Ollerton. Over the intervening decades the fortunes of the Troop (sometimes 'Squadron') waxed and waned but from the 1860's had a fairly regular standing. In addition to the 'unfortunate' fifth Duke of Newcastle and Colonel Welfit of Langwith, a long-standing (or 'mounted') commander was Lord Galway of Serlby. Up to fifty men formed the backbone of this rather privileged group.

Regular troop meetings were held at the Cattle Market Hotel on Worksop's Bridge Street and their annual training camps rotated around Mansfield, Newark, Retford and Worksop. Whilst at the latter venue, the camps were centred on the land at Worksop Manor Hills known as Plain Piece.

Now, in 1909, the attraction of time-off work to attend training (not to forget the cash training allowances) seems to have been a strong incentive. Regular drill and firearms training was held at the Normanton Inn and at a variety of venues in Worksop. An unexpected – albeit predictable – outcome of the attempts to strengthen their numbers had led to protests by the duchess that, whilst commending the efforts to find new recruits, she was reluctant to agree that her grooms and kennelmen should spend time away from their normal duties! The annual camp of two weeks now entailed travelling to Salisbury Plain and other distant locations. Other camps and sports days were held near Newark and provided a very popular diversion for the volunteers and their families.

The new recruits of the Clumber Troop of Cavalry Volunteers had an opportunity to demonstrate their prowess on Empire Day (celebrated on Monday 24 May) when they paraded in Worksop at an early hour prior to moving on to their camp at Coddington, some twenty-five miles away. Lieutenant Wade-Palmer was their leader, with Sergeant Major Bowler as his second in command.

Figure 75b
Men of the Sherwood Rangers, Notts. Imperial Yeomanry, Clumber Troop.
At the Coddington Camp in May 1909

LEASED & TIED COTTAGES

In July 1909, wine merchant William Hickson died. A friend of the duke and tenant of Clumber Cottage, he was the most recent of the Park's 'Shooting Tenants' and had been on the estate since 1880. On an annual rent of twenty-five pounds, the property boasted two female servants plus a male groom. The cottage also had a tennis court. Rights to shoot over some seven thousand acres of the duke's land had been included in his lease. Mr Hickson also sub-let certain Keepers Cottages and a few grass fields. Mrs Hickson had died six year earlier and her niece, Miss Evelyn de Jersey Morris, was now to take over the tenancy of this delightful cottage, albeit without the shooting rights. Miss Morris continued to reside there until the late nineteen-twenties, describing her abode as: "the dear little house that I love". On her death in 1936 Miss Morris was buried alongside her aunt and uncle in a prominent plot outside the east doors of the Markham-Clinton Mausoleum.

A 'musical chairs'-type shuffle during 1913 provides a small but typical example of life in accommodation tied to employment on the estate. Even heads of departments such as the Clerk of Works were not exempt from these exercises. 'Her Grace suggests' begins the Agent's letter to Sammy Barker, head gardener. The duchess's good idea was that gamekeeper Bloomfield be moved from his cottage at the 'Aviaries' to 'Tarr's Lodge' (more commonly known as 'South Lodge', and Mr and Mrs Tarr having recently died). Despite its isolated position, the 'Aviaries' cottage – on a site prepared around 1809 and then known as 'the (4th) Duchess's Garden' – could then be offered to gardener Samuel Brown and his invalid wife. After which, Joe Gabbitas, currently one of Wilson Tomlinson's woodsmen, would be moved into the Brown's cottage. Size of family and a new circumstance (such as widowhood) could bring about this sort of regular 'flitting' about the Park – and he who shouted loudest did not always get the best deal! These moves were put to the participants as 'suggestions' but there is an underlying sense that refusals would not be welcomed!

LEISURE PURSUITS

4 September 1911
A very enjoyable day. Weather very fine.

So wrote Rudolph Schmidt (introduced in Chapter three above). 'Dolph' was referring to the Clumber Cricket Club and supporters having travelled to Sheffield on this sunny Saturday. In the morning they had toured the John Brown and Thomas Firth steelworks (where development of the new 'stainless steel' was underway) and then lunched at the Grand Hotel. Following this they were off to Norton Hall to play their match against the 'Norton and Atlas' team. In the evening 'Dolph' went to the Sheffield Hippodrome with Joe Gabbitas – the latter having now been promoted to the estate's much-envied job as steam-roller driver.

Figure 76 – Clumber Park Cricket Club 1912
Front Row (from the left):2nd – Joe Gabbitas, 3rd – Rev Frank Hawkins (Chaplain)
Back Row (from the left):1st – Rudolph Schmidt? (Joiner), 6th – George Tredaway (Headmaster/Organist).
Back Row (from the right): 3rd – John Adcock (Blacksmith), 5th – Arthur Elliott (Agent)

Cricket events played a large part in filling leisure-time during the summers, providing many opportunities for sport and travel. During the nineteen-eighties, the cricket ground had been re-positioned from an area east of the House and pleasure grounds to a site overlooked by Leeping Bar Wood. On the re-forming of the cricket club in the following decade, 'Little Jimmy' Chapman of Budby Corner was appointed as the groundsman. An attractive pavilion had been built (the duke insisting that heather be used to thatch its roof) and the first sightscreens were provided – and paid for – by William Hickson of Clumber Cottage.

Figure 77 – Rudolph Schmidt (centre of the front row) captains the Clumber Park football team of 1912

The Clumber Football Team had been allocated a playing field at Hardwick, behind the Village School and with changing facilities in the Reading Room. Clumber's Fishery Club had been active for over five years, with Worksop's Vicar, Rev. Canon d'Arcy (having replaced the late Rev. Slodden) as a leading participant. The cleric was keen to offer advice on the re-stocking of the lake, suggesting that more pike, roach, perch and eels be purchased and that opposite the Lincoln Terrace deeper holes be dug, downstream of Otter Island. Fishing was permitted from boats on the lake although only the privileged few were invited aboard the 'Lincoln' frigate for this purpose.   The 'Lincoln' was over-hauled at this time, being in a very bad state of repair (the duchess expressing the view that the boat was: "a disgrace ... rather past repair"). New rigging and repainting quickly followed Her Grace's intervention, some two hundred pounds being spent on this work carried out by Tomlinsons of West Stockworth.

Figure 78 – Repairs underway near the lake arm at Hardwick.

Figure 79 – This is not the servants' Billiard Room! It is the duke's palatial facility off the east corridor within Clumber House. His first such leisure room had by this time become known as the 'Duke's Study'.

Indoor activities included billiards. The House servants and grooms were able to set up a Men's Billiards Club, in a room allocated in the Stableyard accommodation (the current site of the Clumber Park Clocktower Shop). With an annual membership subscription of two shillings and six pence [12$\frac{1}{2}$p], all men over seventeen years of age were eligible for membership. Messrs Warwick and Richardson of Newark provided the beer, and best bitter sold at one shilling and two pence [6p] per pint. Over the three years ending 1911, the average annual beer consumption was one thousand, four hundred and sixty four pints!

Figure 80 – The Duke's Sitting Room (circa 1908) – originally the Billiard Room, it is nowadays known as the 'Duke's Study.

If the estate dwellers required more commercial entertainment, they had several options in nearby Worksop. One favoured novelty was the 'Gaiety Picturedrome'. This new-style cinematographic delight had a programme that changed three times each week. An example of the tempting fare was entitled 'The Salving of the Soul'! The admission charges were six pence [$2^{1}/_2$p] for the circle, four pence the stalls and two pence the 'pit', with half prices for accompanied children. These costs should be set against an average weekly wage of around £1.5s.0d [£1.25p] for a Clumber Park workman.

The duchess being acquainted with Baden-Powell on the Duty and Discipline Committee [see *The duke and duchess's London interests' later in this Chapter*], it is no surprise to find that a Boy Scout troop had also been introduced at Hardwick with eager recruits from the duke's choir as well as the estate families. Formation of Girl Guides, Brownie and Wolf Cub packs soon followed.

Figure 82 – Brownies and Girl Guides of Clumber Park – circa 1918.

A FUNERAL AND A WEDDING

The death of King Edward VII (who had a long association with Clumber) occurred in May 1910 and the duke and duchess attended the funeral. However, their London visit was combined with a somewhat happier event. This was a wedding of two good friends of the ducal couple, and the bride had asked to duke to 'give her away' at the ceremony. She was the 'incomparable' Adeline Genée, the most famous dancer of the day. Her bridegroom, solicitor Frank Isitt, Master of the Old Union Lodge and a church organist, was well acquainted with the duke and his brother, Lord Francis, in both business and leisure activities. A favourite of Princess Alexandra, Adeline had also known Lord Francis and Mary Yohé in the 1890s and early 1900s. Eventually, as Dame Adeline, she became President of the Royal Ballet (to be succeeded by Dame Margot Fonteyn).   Clumber's Chaplain, the Rev. Frank Hawkins, assisted at the wedding service which took place at the ornate church of All Saints, Margaret Street, London, the scene of the duke and duchess's marriage some twenty-one years earlier.

Figure 83 – Adeline Genée – knitting socks for First World War soldiers during a break between acts in the ballet. Sketched by Alice Boughton in 1914.
[National Portrait Galley, London]

CORONATION 1911

At the Coronation of George V in June 1911 the duke again presented the traditional velvet 'Worksop' glove for his sovereign – [*for more detail on this matter of the glove, see Chapter Four above relating to the Coronation of King Edward VII nine years earlier*].

For this year's event, the two hundred and eighty residents at Clumber Park were treated to a General Holiday on Coronation Day. After a Thanksgiving Service in the Chapel, a cricket match was played against the Norfolk and Atlas Works team from Sheffield. Then came a 'Children's Tea' followed by organised sports for children and adults. The youngsters competed for prizes ranging from three pence [2p] to a shilling [5p] and their events included a sack race and: "boots [*hidden*] in clover". Women could win up to two shillings for top placings in the egg and spoon or the potato race. Men were offered up to three shillings for success in the half-mile cycle race, and shared the magnificent sum of six shillings in the tug-of-war team (eight men a side). Senior staff – Heads of Department in most cases (Chaplain, Rev. Hawkins; Messrs Barker; Beattie; Elliott; Stanhope; Tomlinson and Tredaway) acted as judges and administrators throughout the day – and of course, their decisions were final! After the distribution of the competition prizes and a Coronation Gift to all the ladies of a: "cheap and cheerful" commemorative cup and saucer, the adults were treated to 'Dancing in the Tent', with music by Mr G. Duncombe's band until 10 p.m. They then moved to the lake-arm to enjoy fifteen guineas' [£15.75p] worth of fireworks.

ESTATE EVENTS AND NOBLE FAMILY MATTERS

The break-up of the Newcastle estates continued in 1911, led by the sale of several of the duke's Nottinghamshire properties, notably those in Flawborough (for £16,618), Cromwell, Holme and Muskham. He had also had released some of his Worksop land for the new church of St. Anne's – a project financed by Sir John Robinson of Worksop Manor. The Gloucestershire estate, inherited from the Hope family, was sold during this same year. The duke also proposed the building of a church at Manton, where the recently developed colliery had attracted the construction of two hundred dwellings for the miners and their families.

Soon, several unhappy events brought gloom to members of the leading family of the estate. Lord Francis had again appeared in the Chancery Division Court, requesting permission to sell yet more of the Hope family heirlooms. He was said to again be in financial difficulties and pleaded that the sale of twenty pictures valued at £24,750 would be of great benefit to himself and his family. He already had a firm offer for purchase of these items and, despite the fact that the duke and his sister, Lady Beatrice Lister-Kaye, had made representations cautioning against the disposal of family heirlooms, the judge allowed his claim.

In May 1912 there was another death, on this occasion that of Lady Olive Muriel Hope at the early age of thirty-five. Lady Olive was the second wife of Lord Francis and in line to be the next

Figure 84 – Lady Olive – mother of the 9th duke.

Duchess of Newcastle. She died (reportedly from leukaemia) whilst on a recuperative holiday at Montreux, Switzerland. Her funeral was at the Hope family mausoleum at the Deepdene, in Surrey.

***

This sadness was shortly followed by the death of duchess's grandmother, Lady Rossmore. The eighty-five-year-old had (since 1895) lived at Ranby Hall with her youngest son, Hon. Peter Craven Westenra. Since that time she had been a regular attender at Retford's Roman Catholic Church. Her Grace's father, Major Henry Augustus ('Sugar') Candy, had died in July 1911.

Figure 85 – Lord Frances with his son and eldest daughter, around the time when their mother died.   *Figures, 85a – The 7th duke and his nephew (later, 9th duke) in 1914,*   *Figure 86 – The duke's nieces, Doria & Mary.*

The children spent much time at Clumber and Forest Farm following the death of their mother.

NATIONAL INSURANCE

The state was encroaching even further onto ground previously considered a sacred part of the good landowner's prerogative. Culminating in the National Insurance Act 1911, Health Insurance and Old Age Pensions' regulations meant that compulsory insurance costs had now become a fact of life in respect of the thirty-one house servants at Clumber House together with the outdoor estate workers. The Estate Agent noted that he was holding around two hundred and fifty National Insurance cards. Stamps had to be purchased, licked and placed on individual record cards. All Estate Sick Pay was to cease from January 1913 and a 'Clumber Park Sick Club' formed. Staff were to be recommended to take out additional insurance through such organisations as the 'Oddfellows' and 'Heart's of Oak' Societies at a cost of around ten shillings [50p] per quarter for the majority of estate workers.

THE FIRE OF 1912

Figure 87 – The 'back door' of Clumber House, with smoke clouding the damaged roof.
Boys of the Clumber Choir School were amongst the earliest spectators.
[Photograph from the Daily Sketch dated 27 April 1912]

Figure 88 – 'Little Henry' Thompson waves to the photographer as he and John Adcock (estate black-smith) escort the fire chief to inspect the aftermath of the blaze.

Figure 89 – One of the fire damaged upper-storied rooms.

On 25th April 1912 yet another fire caused damage to the House. Fortunately, this one was on a lesser scale to the 1879 disaster although, initially, staff feared the worst. Discovered at about six in the evening by the head coachman, George Cook, the fire affected the roof: "over the back door" of the north-west Wing together with the first floor 'Lincoln Rooms' and much of the furniture contained therein.

The matter of further provision of fire appliances had been discussed for years, with still no substantial decisions made. Some four years before this current fire, Arthur Elliott, the Agent, had informed the duke that no reduction in the fire insurance costs would be achieved simply by the provision of more handheld extinguishers. However, a discount of up to fifty-five pounds per annum might be possible if a fire engine was purchased for the estate (together with: "an organised Brigade to work the same"). The net result of Agent's efforts was an instruction from the duke to order an extra ten 'Minimax Hand Fire Extinguishers'! It should, therefore, have been no surprise that Clumber's fire hydrants proved ineffective for the latest conflagration and fire appliances had to be called in from Retford, Sheffield, Welbeck and Worksop. The Sheffield contingent travelled the twenty-plus miles in forty minutes. The first of these machines arrived just thirty minutes after the outbreak and the fire was reported to be under control within three hours. Welbeck's fire team stayed overnight to keep watch and were rewarded 'with gratuities' by the grateful duke. Electrical systems throughout the House were badly affected by the water used to douse the fire. The duke's Agent recorded some £3,820 worth of damage.

No one was injured and the art treasures were unharmed. The top floor nursery was destroyed and the ground floor area containing the Grand Dining Room suffered considerable damage to the elaborately decorated Adam's ceiling. A further review of the fire apparatus led to extinguishers being purchased for the Mezzanine Corridor, Grand Corridor, Clinton Corridor, Yellow Satin Corridor, North Corridor, Servants' landing, the top of the Lincoln staircase and the Laundry. It was noted that this left several locations unprotected, such as the Stables, Motor House, Power Station, as well as the Chapel and Parsonage. Yet still no fire engine was purchased, despite the preparation of a catalogue of paintings for insurance purposes. This list showed that the 569 pictures in the Clumber Collection were valued at £71,000 and included Gainsborough's 'Beggar Boys', Hogarth's 'Southwark Fair' and Rembrandt's 'An Orator'.

TERRACE ORNAMENTS

Unconnected with the fire, repair and cleaning work was urgently required on many of the Terrace vases, urns, statues, etc. In 1912 there were over ninety such items that needed attention – many were more than eighty years old. Some had been brought to Clumber from Worksop Manor in the 1840's and may well have been transported from Arundel Castle to Worksop much earlier than that. Seven of the stone vases: "on that side of the Lincoln Terrace farthest from the lake" (presumably meaning the left-hand side on the lakeside walkway from the House site towards the boathouse basin), had new bases prepared to replace the cracked ones. The mosaic tiled semi-circular seats, near the steps on the Lincoln Terrace were thoroughly cleaned. Depictions of storks and dogs were replaced altogether, the former from the lakeside edge of the Terraces and the latter from the foot of the steps near to the House. The duke limited the spending on replacements to the extent that they were cast in cement, rather than Portland stone.

Figure 90 – Storks, vases, etc. on the steps from the lakeside terrace at Clumber Park - c. 1920

THE LONDON AND FORT GEORGE LAND COMPANY LTD.

It was in 1913 that the duke invested in the newly-registered 'London and Fort George Land Company'. The company consisted of twenty-nine shareholders and its main activities at that time were concerned with land investment in Canada. The duke bought one thousand shares and became a director, thereby joining the duchess' uncle, the Earl of Rosse, in the new enterprise. Frank Seymour Nelsson Isitt was also a director. As recorded earlier, the duke had attended Mr Isitt's 1910 wedding to the dancer, Adeline (later 'Dame Adeline') Genée, and had given away the bride. None of the friends or business partners involved in the company could have dreamt that almost the whole of the duke's properties would be sold to this company within fifteen years.

THE VILLAGE SCHOOL

The children of the Clumber Park estate had their own school, variously known in official records as 'Clumber School', 'Hardwick School' or 'Village School'. Up to eight years of age, children

139

travelled to the infant school at Carburton village. From then they attended lessons at the Hardwick School until they were fourteen years old. The school (previously mentioned here on its opening in August 1889) was built to house up to one hundred children, but appears to have had an average complement of around sixty. There were six 'Standards' (or 'Years') and the annual examination results recorded those pupils in each 'Standard' who achieved 'distinctions'. Since 1892 (when two assistant teachers supported him), George Tredaway had filled the role of headmaster. He had also undertaken duties as the Clumber Chapel choirmaster and organist. Tredaway managed the school with a variety of assistants and was praised by the Schools' Inspector for his efforts, although there was a clear intimation that he was in need of additional teaching resources if standards were to be maintained or improved.

Widowed in 1913, Mr Tredaway soon found himself under investigation for alleged rough treatment of the pupils, one father wrote of: "the measure of his vindictiveness". After further enquiries Tredaway was very upset by the decision that he must leave his positions, and also depart from Clumber Park. The appearance of this dark cloud was a great pity, as Tredaway had been such a force in establishing high quality music for the Chapel, especially his fine work in producing the 'Clumber Hymnal'. He had also given the village school as good a reputation as most estate schools could hope for. Despite canvassing parents of his past and present pupils, to support his petition to be retained, he realised his protests were doomed to failure. Several estate parents withdrew children from the school to display their opposition to the headmaster's dismissal, sending them instead to Worksop schools. Faced with having to accept the inevitable, Tredaway left Clumber and moved to Glastonbury. He died three years later.

CLUMBER'S CHOIR SCHOOL

Since shortly after Clumber Chapel's dedication, it had boasted a splendid choir. Proposed in 1889 and formed four years later, it was in fine voice by the time the Rev. Frank Hawkins began his lengthy assignment as Chaplain. Father Hawkins had been at the nearby Worksop College since 1895 and was appointed full time at Clumber in 1901, having occasionally assisted there since his arrival in north Nottinghamshire.

In the early years the boys lived at the Parsonage or in various estate cottages. Some were from estate families and there were a number recruited from the 'Waifs and Strays' homes, which the

THE NATIONAL TRUST
CLOCK TOWER SHOP
CLUMBER PARK
M1953702   TID26623700
AID : A0000000031010
VISA DEBIT

DELTA
4462 7823 0293 1106
EXP 10/07
ICC

SALE

AMOUNT   £9.50
VERIFIED BY PIN
THANK YOU
11:08 11/09/05 40DLR6:00
AUTH CODE: 989573
RECEIPT 9279

duke and duchess supported. At an early stage, it was decided to advertise more widely for choristers and, much later, to build a 'hostel' for the recruits to be housed and educated. To help plan arrangements for this new accommodation, Mr Tredaway had been dispatched to Newlands Choir School (the location of this establishment is uncertain, but perhaps at Middlesborough) to investigate the arrangements made for such private choirs – in respect of both housing accommodation and education. He returned from Newlands to enthusiastically report his findings to the duke.

The Clumber choirboys moved into their purpose-built accommodation at Hardwick early in 1913. Known initially as the 'Hostel', the building was (some twenty years later) re-named 'The Chantry'. It was large enough to house the regular intake of twelve boys, along

Figure 91 –
'The Hostel' in 1913.

with the sequence of matrons and their deputies, Miss Hartenstein and Mrs Jaggs, who were followed by Mrs Hubbard and her sister, Miss Whitehead. Constructed by Thomas Barlow and Co. of Nottingham at a total cost of £2590.13s.9d (including £354. 7s. 8d for furniture), the Hostel, complete with its own tiny chapel, was ready for occupation from 20 January 1913. With an initial intake of five boys, aged between nine and eleven years of age on joining, the occupants lived by the light of oil lamps. During school holidays, Worksop Priory provided a small replacement choir for Clumber Chapel.

When their voices broke, the boys had the option of accepting a two-year scholarship that the duke offered at Worksop College (previously known as St. Cuthbert's College), or other 'Woodard' Schools. He awarded a bursary of £45 per year for each boy who chose to attend these establishments.

Figure 92 – Mr Tredaway with Choir School boys at Hardwick Village School – circa 1910

THE DOWAGER DUCHESS DIED

Figure 93 –
Henrietta Adela,
Dowager Duchess.,

The duke's mother, dowager duchess Henrietta Adela, died on 8th May 1913. She had lived out her final years on the Estate, and had seen remarkable changes at Clumber from the days of the 1860's, when her husband, as sixth duke, had filled the estate stables with unsuccessful racehorses and recklessly ordered the building of a Chapel alongside the House.   He had then been declared bankrupt and barred from any control of the Newcastle estates.   Their separation and marriage annulment in the early 1870's (and his death at the end of that decade) had led to her marriage to Thomas Hohler, followed twelve years later by her second widowhood. A convert to Roman Catholicism, she had spent many years engaged in charity work in the Whitechapel area of London where she was the subject of much gratitude and praise for: "her visits to the sick, watching by the dying and bringing comfort and hope wherever she went". A Requiem Mass was held for her in Westminster Cathedral. The youngest of her three daughters, Lady Florence Pelham-Clinton, was to follow her mother's example in charity work for Londoners.

ARMY TRAINING IN CLUMBER PARK

Figures 94 – The Duke and Duchess of Newcastle inspect the Sherwood Foresters in Clumber Park.

During 1913, Wilson had more near-neighbours than he was used to, when the 6th Battalion of the Nottinghamshire and Derbyshire (Sherwood Forester Territorials) held their training camp near Cabin Hill. The site had been selected to allow the Clumber Show (held on 5th August) to take place on the South Lawns as usual.

Figures 95 & 96 – The Duke and Duchess of Newcastle are pictured here with members of the 6th Battalion, Sherwood Foresters.

The recruitment campaign for the extra Territorials having been so successful that it was necessary to organise a large training session. Other camps (for the 5th, 7th and 8th Battalions) were being held at the same time on grounds at Worksop Manor, Welbeck and Thoresby respectively.

GARDEN PARTIES

In August 1913 a Garden Party was organised by the duchess for the Crippled Children of Newark. Some eighty-five youngsters attended for a memorable day out. Having had an interesting tour of Central Nottinghamshire on their way to Clumber Park, they were invited to partake of: "a sumptuous tea" on the lawns, whilst the Shireoaks Brass Band provided musical accompaniment. Then the children were taken on the Lake in rowing boats and afterwards played in the picturesque Pleasure Grounds. On returning to the House they found bottles of sweets, food and fruit parcels to eat on their return journey or to take home. This event and similar parties for organisations such as the Church of England Waifs and Strays Society were notable features of the seventh duke and duchess's 'ducal watch' at Clumber.

SILVER WEDDING CELEBRATIONS

Celebrations to mark the Silver Wedding of the duke and duchess went ahead in April 1914. Shortly before the festivities began and (following a complaint by the duke) George Lines, the forty-six-year-old House Steward, checked the wine cellars and noted that the contents of some five hundred bottles of 1895 Burgundy were substandard. They were hastily returned to the London supplier and replacements demanded. Happily the Volnay and Barsac vintages were in good condition!

The celebrations were held over three days, when the Tenants of Clumber, Newark and Worksop properties; Officials and Workpeople; also the Mining Lessees at Shireoaks, Babbington and Worksop, made their presentations and received generous hospitality. Along with members of the Posting Proprietors Association and the parishioners of Worksop Priory, they and others gifted silver caskets, albums, loyal addresses and assorted presents. Retford Town dignitaries were keen to express their affection, loyalty and respect for the Newcastles despite the dukedom having no direct financial interests there.

A silver casket took pride of place, presented by the tenants of Clumber, Worksop, Basford, Cromwell, Holme and North Muskham [*See Colour Plate 6*]. It was mounted on a substantial plinth and inscribed:

> To his Grace the Duke of Newcastle and her Grace the Duchess of Newcastle.
> We, the undersigned tenants of the Newcastle estates, hereby desire respectfully to offer to
> you our hearty congratulations upon the commemoration of your silver wedding day. You

will receive at this interesting time many congratulations and good wishes from your numerous friends, but we assure you that none will be more sincere and heartfelt than those of your own tenantry. We trust and pray that you may yet be blessed with many years of happy married life, and we take this opportunity of thanking you both for the many acts of kindness, good-will, and sympathy which in past years we have received at your hands.

As well as more elaborate dining arrangements for the house parties, the obligatory marquee was erected in the pleasure gardens to the east of the mansion. 'Meat teas' were served there to the six hundred visitors who came to help mark the event over two of the three days. From the warmth of the speeches made on these occasions, it is apparent that there was a genuine respect and even affection in the relationship between the parties concerned.

During the week, the duke and duchess visited Newark in order that His Grace could be presented with the freedom of the town. With their houseguests, including the duke's friend, Sir George Arthur (whose claim to fame was that he had once been interviewed by police investigating the 'Jack the Ripper' crimes!), they stopped off at Newark Bridge to view the Castle and field opposite. This area has variously been known as 'Loonie', 'Luny' or 'Riverside' Park, the first two designations hinting at the public's reaction to the fact that (within one month of its opening) it became flooded by the overflowing River Trent! The duke had gifted the two and a half-acre field to the Town during George V's Coronation year. Now he expressed his delight regarding the stipulation that the public should have use of this amenity in perpetuity. This meant that nothing should ever be built there that would spoil the view of the Castle from across the river.

Newark's Alderman Knight proposed that the Freedom of the Town should be awarded to: "Our Duke" and he emphasised the close links of the area with the Newcastle duchy over several centuries. He was particularly complimentary in regard to the present duke's benevolence to the town, its schools (especially that for Science and the Arts), hospital, gardens and the Newark Provident Clothing Society. The alderman described the duke as a good man who: "ardently sought to promote all those things which tended for the good of the community". The proposition met with the full approval of all present and in responding to the meeting, the duke expressed his regret that he had inherited: "very old and poor property" in Newark, which he was keen to continue to make: "sanitary and more homelike". Soon after this visit to the town, he sent a cheque for £200 to Newark Parish Church funds.

Back at Clumber and on behalf of all officials and fellow workpeople, eighty-five-year-old George Thompson was selected to present the couple with an album containing an Illuminated Address and signed by all of the two hundred and fifty employees. For sixty-one years George had worked at Clumber as a woodsman, farm labourer, horseman and (latterly) gatekeeper at the Normanton Gate. This meant that he began his working life when the Secretary of State for War was the fifth bearer of the Newcastle-under-Lyme coronet and the Crimean War had not yet begun! Most members of the Clumber-based staff were at the 1914 event, together with representatives from Forest Farm, also from Nottingham Park and the duke's Berkeley House flat in London. The duke and duchess were very moved by the old man's presentation as well as by the gift itself.

George Thompson died in the following year and from the tenor of the Chaplain's remarks in the Clumber Park Magazine there is no doubting the sincerity of mood for the loss of this old Park dweller: "that good old man, as we used to speak of him ... was a religious man ... in spite of his years he always hobbled down, when possible, to take his part in the Lord's service ... He set us all a noble example ...". The funeral service was held in Clumber Chapel and then at his graveside in the cemetery at Carburton.

Figure 97 –
George & Annie
Thompson at Tank
Cottage, Clumber.

Figure 98 – Lord FitzWilliam (on the left) joins the Silver Wedding hunting group.

Figure 99 – Members of the House Party on the same occasion.

ROYALS VISIT AGAIN – WAR DECLARED

King George and Queen Mary visited Nottinghamshire again in June 1914. They journeyed north to stay at Welbeck and at the end of their stay arranged to pass through Clumber's Lime Tree Avenue on the way to Retford railway station. The children of Hardwick School were assembled at the crossroads north of the Paddocks and estate keepers were put on patrol duty. This gesture seems to have been appreciated by the royal couple, which was a happier circumstance than that which had met the duke and duchess on the previous day in Nottingham. As part of that day's royal events a dais, providing seating for distinguished guests, had been set up in the Old Market Square. The Newcastle's had stayed overnight at Wollaton Hall with Lord Middleton. They then travelled to the city in their own car, with long-serving Albert Johnson as chauffeur. On approaching the Market Square, the car had been stopped by a young police officer, and, as the duke had forgotten his tickets, the officer obeyed his clear instructions to turn away anyone who arrived without such documentation. The couple reluctantly motored back to Wollaton Hall and awaited the return of their hosts and the royal personages, probably with less than keen anticipation!

It transpired that the Clumber Agent belatedly realised the duke had left home without the required tickets and he took the precaution of contacting Nottingham's Town Clerk. The Town Clerk acknowledged the Agent's message and everything seemed to have been catered for. Nevertheless the disaster had occurred. Many letters were written over this embarrassing episode, the Town Clerk protesting that he had told everyone – apparently with the one exception of a certain young police officer! The constable perhaps allowed himself a wry smile when informed of his 'error', if so it was one of the final moments of amusement prior to the outset of a 'war to end all wars'.

Clumber's Annual Show took place during the same month as war broke out, but it was to be the last until the final decade of the twentieth century. With only six hundred visitors and gate money of £56 it is perhaps surprising that it was declared to have been a success! However its new siting, on the area known as Cow Pasture (to the east of the Walled Gardens) was a move introduced to make it more convenient for the luncheon arrangements, as the Lake had been a major obstacle to the previous site on South Lawns!

THE REALITIES OF WAR

War with Germany being declared in August 1914, life on the Clumber estate was to see unprecedented changes. Not only were families to be devastated by the absence of so many of their men folk on military service but injuries and deaths were to bring long-term grief to many.

Shortages of commodities may not have been as noticeable as in urban areas, but as men volunteered for war service, reductions in the estate workforce were certain to have an effect on levels of income for families as well as the duchy. Each department, whether Repairs, Woods, Gardens, or Game, was to be affected. War Bonus payments for employees below heads of department levels provided a slight offset for doing the extra work of those joining the armed forces and not being replaced. The Bonus remained at two shillings [10p] per week until 1917 when it was increased in two stages, to six shillings. An Estate 'Clothing Club' was organised at the start of the Great War. One shilling per month was the usual contribution and the duke added a bonus of three or four shillings provided that the contributor maintained regular payments for a full year.

The duke, along with so many other landowners, was expected to encourage his employees and tenants to heed their country's plea that 'Your Country needs *YOU*'. To that end, on Tuesday 15th September 1914 and along with his neighbour, the Duke of Portland, he travelled to a meeting at the Newcastle Arms, Tuxford. The full content of his speech can be found at Appendix Two but the gist of it emphasised: "... the justice of our cause in the terrible war in which the greater part of Europe is now engaged ... rally to Lord Kitchener's standard and give him the great army for which he asks ... the war, I fear will be a long, a very long one ... let us not relax our efforts until the enemy is crumpled up like a withered leaf, and Europe breathes freely once more".

Figure 100 – Richard Alcock (standing at the rear) with fellow officers of the Sherwood Foresters.

With the close-knit nature of a landed estate community it is difficult to imagine how any but the most determined could have failed to offer themselves for duty in the armed services. The demands had been growing for years, with the recruitment and training of Territorials being a feature of Park life. No doubt this pressure had been similar throughout the whole of Newcastle's Nottinghamshire duchy. Many were to follow the call to arms.

Despite the injuries to, and slaughter of, eleven out of the first year's intake of thirty, the various departments of the Clumber estate continued to provide more soldiers and sailors for the rest of the war. Those listed as having joined the fray (as of December 1915) were: Fred, Charles and William Albones; Richard Alcock; John W. Allan; Fred Anderson; Vernon Armitage; Fred Carrott; George Carter; Ernest Chappell; William Cope; John Crutchley; Charles P. Elliott; John Gascoigne; James Harrington; Frank Knight; Alfred Mendham; Ernest Merrils; 'Billy' Pratchett; Charles and John Read; William Robertson; Charles Simmonds; Rudolph Schmidt; William Tarr; Arthur Tidbury; Cecil, Fred and Herbert Tomlinson; Charles Wilson and John Wing. Disturbingly, only Tarr and Tidbury were still 'active' at this mid-stage of hostilities. Most of the injured were sent back to active service after treatment, as was exampled earlier (in Chapter Three above) when recording the injuries and death of the Sherwood Forester, Rudolph Schmidt. Eventually, fifty-seven men of Clumber Park had joined the forces during those four dreadful years.

BELGIUMS, CANADIANS AND OTHERS ARRIVE

From October 1914 accommodation was found at Clumber for twelve Belgium refugees. The duke also allowed five pounds per week for their household expenses. The group was a tiny portion of some one-hundred thousand Belgiums who had arrived in Britain following the German invasion of their homeland. Unfortunately, due to some unrecorded mis-behaviour involving an estate tenant, this small contingent was dismissed from its Sherwood Forest safe haven after only nine months and returned to London.

There was a more permanent overseas presence in Clumber from the early months of the war. As hostilities continued, men of the Canadian Forestry Corps began work at their newly-constructed sawmill. Their tented camp was south east of Carburton Lodge, alongside the sawmill that was situated just inside the Clumber Park gates. Estate records also indicate the stabling of Canadian horses that attracted a government allowance of twenty-five shillings [£1.25p] per animal.

As with so many service activities in the Park (during both First and Second World Wars) estate records are tantalisingly short on detail; for example when recording that Clumber Lake was used by the Royal Engineers for pontoon bridge practice during the later years of the 1914 to 1918 conflict. Why were these soldiers based in Clumber? – was it purely a training exercise or were new ideas being tested? Other records indicate that a brigade of Infantry were encamped at Carburton village and, along with the troops based in Thoresby and Welbeck, they were permitted to use Clumber lands for training purposes. A designated area was set up from the Normanton Inn to the Lake and along the south side of the water as far as Carburton Bridge.

Towards the end of the war, a Training Centre for women land workers opened at Clumber. Nottinghamshire County Council had requested and financed this facility for ten students. The duke agreed to pay the wages of a housekeeper and one maid, also to provide a room for meals and sleeping accommodation. The trainees lodged over the Lincoln Stables and in other properties alongside the mansion. They were also: "given the run" of the Home Farm at Hardwick. The end of the war brought a closure to the Training Centre, although there was to be a similar facility for women offered some twenty years later.

Figure 101 – Unnamed officers at Clumber during the 1ˢᵗ World War.

WARTIME EFFECTS ON SCHOOLING AT CLUMBER

At the Village School, thirty-six-year-old Fred Leeson had succeeded George Tredaway as headmaster in 1914 (but without the musical duties of his predecessor) and was soon earning high praise for the standards of his leadership. Mr Leeson came to Clumber from

Figure 102 – The Schoolmaster's House (on the right) stood next to the Choir Hostel.

151

his post as Headmaster of Corby School and accepted a salary of £150 per annum (rising by annual increments of £10 to £180), free accommodation and a B.S.A. Model H2 motor bike with sidecar, costing £142. His home was to be in the brand new house next to the Choir Hostel. This building, together with its two adjoining cottages, was ready for occupation in the winter of 1914 and cost almost £2,000 to construct.

Military conscription having now replaced the voluntary system, Mr Leeson learnt that he had been granted a short period of exemption but would be required to report for army duty in July 1916. This caused a major re-think regarding the future of the Village School arrangements, especially as to whether the Choir should be disbanded. The outcome of the deliberations was that Mrs Leeson (with one female assistant) undertook to teach the estate children, whilst the Chaplain, Rev. Hawkins, was put in charge of the choirboys schooling, assisted by a Mr H.S. Bourne. The choirboys' lessons were then held at the Hostel rather than in the Village School. This was the first time that the choir had been separated from the Park residents, a move long advocated by the parents of some choristers.

Leslie Rupert Pike had been appointed to take on George Tredaway's role as organist and choirmaster. With a salary of £150 per annum, Pike – who also taught the choristers – lodged rent-free with the Clerk of Works family at Hardwick Grange until he joined the armed forces in April 1916. On Mr Pike's departure, Mr Bourne was appointed as deputy organist but was soon replaced by Miss E Rainbow.

MORE FINANCIAL ADJUSTMENTS

In the six months prior to the start of the war, Hardwick Farm finances were a mix of good and bad news. The Agent wrote to the duke that the prices of stock had done: "very well indeed". Mangolds had shown an upward trend in value but corn and turnips were fetching a poor return. Determined efforts were to be made to reduce the annual cash loss of Clumber's Home Farm. All Shire horse breeding was ceased and the sale of most of the duchess' prize herd of Welsh Ponies gave a clear message of the financial requirements of the time.

Figure 103 – The duchess's Welsh Ponies, as depicted on the cover of the 1915 Sale Catalogue.

The Grand Dispersal Sale of the duchess' Welsh Ponies, Kerry Cattle and Shire-horses took place in August 1915. Of the pony herd, only three-year-old 'Grove Elfin' and four-year-old 'Hardwick Conqueror' were kept for breeding. Since the Stud had been started in 1897 with six of the finest, the duchess had developed a splendid stable full of quality ponies. From 1894 an equally fine herd of the pure bred Kerry cattle had been raised but the duchess had now decided to turn to the breeding of Red Poll cattle. Many show prizes had been won and the decision to sell was said to be a very popular one with the buyers, who turned out in goodly numbers for the auction.

Most of the costs involved in maintaining the dog kennels were transferred to the duchess at this stage, presumably a gesture indicating that the dogs were a mere hobby of hers, rather than an estate necessity. Despite the cutbacks elsewhere, several new features were now added to Clumber House, Chapel and Gardens. Additions to the West Front and a new stone chimney in the Yellow Room cost over £4,000. Also, almost £3,000 was spent on new bedrooms for servants. In the Kitchen wing new pastry ovens and grills were provided, in addition to three new sinks (one stone and two copper) and the flues were altered above the scullery hot plate. The cost of repairing faulty heating apparatus in the Chapel, with the provision of a new warm air stove, was an unwelcome expense. In the Gardens, where several span-roof plant houses had recently been erected by Messrs Foster and Richardson of Beeston, much painting was now required. The vinery and palm range of the glasshouses, the range of carnation and eucharis houses, lean-to stove, melon frame, four violet

153

frames and three old lean-to frames, cost £263. Within two years, the Palm House was found to have rotting wood and being in need: "of rebuilding and lowering".

The estates finances (as at Lady Day 1916) were recorded as:

Clumber and Worksop Estates:		
Rents	–	£22,000
Royalties on Minerals	–	£17,400
Interest on Investments	–	£ 7,000
Woods	–	£ 2,500
Tax repayments	–	£ 800
Total	–	£49,700
Nottingham Estate	–	£ 8,945
Newark Estate	–	£ 3,650
GRAND TOTAL	–	£62,295
PAYMENTS	–	£61,145
SURPLUS	–	£ 1,150

Almost £16,000 worth of American securities were also sold at this time, as were many of the duke's investments (amongst which were 'Mappin's Masbro' Old Brewery' shares). September 1917 saw another sale of Newcastle lands within the Newark estate. Some 2,206 acres were on offer at Cromwell, Winthorpe, Holme and Muskham. A small pocket of the duke's land at Wellow found a new owner during the following year.

THERE WAS ALWAYS THE TIMBER

In the forestry department, instructions arrived at the beginning of the war to the effect that His Grace did not wish any large trees to be felled unless they were dead or dying. Silver birch could be sold. Larch obtained from Budby Corner and the Apleyhead Wood was to be supplied for the needs of Manton Colliery. Messrs Godley and Goulding of Worksop were granted rights to fell and remove the timber required for pit props and other essential wartime requirements of local industry. Any new plantings were to be carried out only on grounds described as 'sheltered' and 'lie high' places, and at a rate of three to four acres each year.

Caterpillar damage was again reported as affecting the trees along Lime Tree Avenue. Once more, grease bands were fixed but proved ineffective (probably because they were allowed to dry out). The tree trunks were then washed with a solution of 'Soft Soap and Paraffin'. This was no more successful, so grease bands were re-applied. At this time, the majority of the trees were approximately seventy-six years old and the duke ordered a major thinning to be undertaken during 1914. Every alternate tree (totalling 650) was removed in each of the four rows, leaving space for remainder to breathe.

Mention of the Avenue is a reminder that it was now one of Clumber's fifteen and a half miles of metalled roads. Although many cobbled roads had been formed, some of the thoroughfares were described as merely: "grass tracks full of deep ruts". Steam-roller drivers, John Read, (followed by his son Arthur) and Joe Gabbitas, had pummelled down some two hundred tons of colliery waste provided by Manton Pit as the hardcore base for their improvement. Travel through the Park was now a smoother ride than at any time since its enclosure in the early eighteenth century.

During the spring prior to the outbreak of war, twelve acres of new trees were planted along the Thoresby border. This was followed by eight acres at Apley Head Wood and the replanting of a triangular piece on the corner of Hardwick Wood near the Lime Tree Avenue. The 'filling in' of woodlands continued at Manton Wood, Farley's Wood, Oak Square and Bevercotes Wood. Wilson and his men then learnt that there were to be no new plantings during the following two years. With staffing shortages in all departments, no doubt the foresters were found other duties without too much difficulty.

In 1917 a new three-acre tree Nursery was introduced near Cabin Hill. During the final two years of the war, timber was taken from many parts of the duke's estates, but the majority came from the areas of Budby Corner, Thoresby Border, Burnt Oak Plantation and Hardwick Wood, all within Clumber Park. From outside the Park boundaries it came from Lodge Brake Plantation at Babworth, Manton Forest North at Worksop and Apleyhead Wood in Elkesley.

A calculation of income from the sale of estate timber for the war indicates that, over those final two years of the war, the Government (through its Timber Supply Department) paid more than £69,000 for this essential commodity. Larch, scotch fir, oak, ash, beech, birch, chestnut, sycamore and elm had been felled, with a mutual agreement that the total was not to exceed 700,000 cubic feet. This was said to be in line with contributions made by other estates for the war effort. It is interesting to note that the area of lands now called Clumber Old Wood (close by the Truman's Lodge) had been known as 'Warr Wood' some three hundred years earlier. Northern acres of Sherwood Forest were again playing their part in the nation's history.

THE ROYAL FLYING CORPS MOVE INTO RANBY HALL

The duchess' uncle, Major Peter Westenra and his wife had left Ranby Hall in June 1916. This 450-acre property had been in the Newcastle family for over 120 years. It was now put under military occupation for the use of officers of the Royal Flying Corps who were training on the 'Green Mile' (also known as 'East Retford') aerodrome from 1917 until the end of the war. This arrangement brought the unprincely sum of four pounds per week into the duke's coffers.

THE DUKE AND DUCHESS'S LONDON INTERESTS

Although quite an illusive character for any researcher to track down, the duke's capacity for shunning the limelight was occasionally thwarted by various newspaper reporters or other scribes within the nation's capital. The reports of the 'Church and Parish Paper' of All Saint's Church, Margaret Street, London were generally of a low-key nature. However, the worthy journal repeatedly recorded the generous nature of one of their main benefactors, 'the Duke of Newcastle of Clumber, Notts.'. It is clear that, apart from being Vicar's Warden there, the duke – along with his youngest sister, Lady Florence Pelham-Clinton – were active in many and varied aspects of London church life.

It is perhaps his interest in ensuring the financial wellbeing of the All Saints' Church Choir that is most note-worthy. Remembering that his commitment to the Clumber Chapel Choir School was absolute, it is somewhat remarkable to find that he also offered around six thousand pounds for the benefit of the London boys when they left the Choir of All Saints. The money was offered as a loan, and this became known there as the 'Newcastle Trust'. The interest on this money was used to provide assistance to boys who continued into higher musical education. Incidentally, when the All Saints' authorities wound up that Trust in the 1980's, the ninth duke agreed that they should keep the original capital. It has subsequently been combined with other monies and now forms part of a 'Choir and Music Trust Fund'.

Amongst the boys who benefited from the duke's largesse at All Saint's was a nine-year-old by the name of Laurence Kerr Olivier – much later to be knighted for his services to the theatre and then further ennobled as a life peer. Olivier had joined the choir school at All Saint's in the autumn of 1916 and it was at Christmas that he met the choir's main benefactor. He found himself to be one of a party of boys and masters who were taken by the duke to a London pantomime 'Babes in the Wood' at the Strand Theatre. After the excitement of the performance the school party was conducted backstage to meet the cast and enjoy the atmosphere. Who knows how much this experience influenced young Laurence's choice of profession? This example of the duke's paternal attitude echoes the visit made by his Clumber Choir to the pantomime at Sheffield during the previous winter.

At this time, the duke also endowed a Prize Fund at Eton College. The prizes there were to be awarded for the encouragement of learning Russian and other foreign languages. They are still a part of the reward system at the College.

With somewhat wider press coverage, London's Savoy Fair was held on 6th December 1917 and the duke was able to offer his services for the day as a portrait photographer. The newspapers reported that he was kept busy and was ably assisted by: "his charming assistant, Miss Adeline Genée". This was his 'unadopted daughter', the young ballerina he had supported on her wedding day some few years earlier and whose glittering career he had helped to promote. Adeline was of Danish decent, and was said: "to be to dance what Jenny Lind was to song". This is particularly fascinating for students of the Newcastle dynasty, as Miss Lind (the 'Swedish Nightingale') had entranced the widowed fourth duke during the late 1840's. He had written: "I cannot disguise from myself the sentiment of deep interest which I entertain towards her". Now, some seventy years later, his great grandson, the present duke, had been captivated by the charms of the latest theatrical goddess.

Meanwhile, the duchess was still being perfectly proper and active with her good works to raise monies for the troops serving overseas. During the war she also took on the role of co-President of the Duty and Discipline Movement – an 'Empire and loyalty' organisation with the famous Baden Powell on its committee. The aims of the movement were: "To combat softness, slackness, indifference and indiscipline, and to stimulate discipline and a sense of duty and alertness throughout the national life, especially during the formative period of home and school training" and "to give reasonable support to all legitimate authority".

In sharp contrast, Lord Francis, heir to the dukedom, was yet again seeking financial help from the Court that cleared the way for him to sell even more of the Hope heirlooms. Sotheby's were engaged to conduct the auction and their two-day sale in July 1917 raised in excess of £135,000 for paintings, classic marbles and other items. Of these monies, the duke had – by bidding at the sale – contributed more than £9,000 in an attempt to save at least some of the 'family silver'!

OUR FIRST GUIDE RETIRES

Two months before the end of the war, Wilson Tomlinson, the Head Forester, retired having served just over forty years on the estate. To mark the event, Mr John Storr of Upper Morton Grange (a senior tenant of the estate) chaired a special presentation. The meeting was held in the Normanton Inn during February 1919 and Wilson was awarded an 'Illuminated Address'. The frame was of Clumber Oak and had been made in the Hardwick Workshops. It contained a prominent portrait of a grateful duke, together with a message from the forester's colleagues:

> To Wilson Tomlinson, of Cabin Hill, Clumber Park, Head Forester and Wood Steward, to his Grace the Duke of Newcastle. We, the undersigned tenants and employees of the estate of his Grace the Duke of Newcastle, congratulate you on the completion of 40 years service as Forester and Wood Steward. Upon your retiring from that position we wish to express our appreciation of the courtesy and consideration, faithfulness and geniality manifested by you in our mutual relationships and, as a token of our esteem, we ask your acceptance of the accompanying wallet of national War Bonds. We also earnestly and sincerely wish you and Mrs Tomlinson much happiness and comfort, and a good old age full of peace, honour and blessing.

Figure 104 – Wilson Tomlinson.

Wilson responded with emotional farewells to his work-colleagues and estate neighbours of so many years. He mentioned the singular honour done to him by the organisers of this event, noting that this was the first such award ever given to anyone on the Clumber or neighbouring estates. Commenting that his career had involved the supervision of planting over one thousand acres of young plantations, he added that: "some of these had now been chopped down to help win the war".

Fifteen years older than his master, the Head Forester had closely observed the 'little' duke throughout his first four decades in office. From His Grace being that fourteen-year-old schoolboy who had inherited a very distressed and humbled duchy, Wilson Tomlinson had watched him become a much-respected 'patron', and had played his own part in establishing the estate's good standing. This ex-Head of Department was now sixty-nine years old and Henry Pelham Archibald Douglas Pelham-Clinton (the duke) was fifty-four.

The ex-forester had six more years to live – the duke had ten.

*Figure 105 –
The sculpture
'Thetis dipping the
Infant Achilles in
the River Styx', by
Thomas Banks R.A.
and displayed in a
corner of the Grand
Hall at Clumber.*

*It is currently on
view at the Victoria
and Albert Museum,
London.*

*[Country Life
Picture Galley]*

CHAPTER SIX

1918 to 1928

Several new Guides – The aftermath of War – Comings, Goings and Pensions – Financial Matters – Home Farm – Duke and Duchess – More changes in School arrangements – Sales and Other Money matters – London and Fort George Land Company [L.F.G.] – The Duke's Last Will and Testament – The death of the 7th Duke.

SEVERAL NEW GUIDES

THE FORESTER'S RETIREMENT led to his move from Clumber Park to 10 Station Road, Tuxford, where (on a pension of £150 per year) he and his wife were to live until his death on the Palm Sunday of 1924. His departure causes us to turn elsewhere for first-hand evidence regarding the situation of the Newcastle duchy.

Firstly, there is the work of the admirable Arthur Elliott – the Estate's Agent – who was still producing his regular informative 'Reports' for the duke. These records not only contain detail of the major items, but also such fascinating minutia as the weekly rainfall measurements taken on the gauge in the Clumber Gardens. Mr Elliott's formal records will help guide us through this important decade in the life of the Estate. They will be especially useful in following the story in a fairly orderly march towards the liquidation of what was a substantial but largely unprofitable enterprise.

Secondly we can also turn to the more informal documents within the Newcastle archives. These include internal reviews, letters, and even scribbled notes plus proposals between the various levels of estate hierarchy. They often reveal far more than the published texts ever did.

Our third group of witnesses will be members of selected families living at Hardwick during the relevant period. Amongst these are the descendants of the Adcock, Alcock, Allbones, Brown, Hile, Olivant, Read, Schmidt, Sissons and Smith dynasties, who have been extremely generous in offering their archives, including photographic collections and miscellaneous artefacts. These records relate to both home-life and work in Clumber's Clerk of Works, Woods and Garden departments. Also available are newspaper reports of the age where, despite their numerous contradictions and journalistic embellishments, events are well outlined.

THE AFTERMATH OF WAR

Post-war records indicate a few incidents of war damage caused to the Newcastle estates. One of these was that which affected St Mark's Street, Hull, where the duke owned six cottages. During a Zeppelin raid in 1915, more than one hundred people were killed or injured when a bomb was dropped from this airship and exploded close by these properties. Only trivial damage was recorded to the fabric of duke's buildings. Also in that same year, a naval bi-plane crashed on his land at the Worksop golf links whilst attempting to fly from Leeds to London. Minor injuries were sustained by one of the airmen involved. The wreckage of this new-fangled flying machine was left on the course for some time and must have been a major talking point for the town's folk.

Apart from small claims elsewhere, mainly connected with accidental damage and dilapidation as a result of the Army's billeting at Newcastle properties, the most severe damage had been to the health of volunteers and conscripts (and their families) who had endured this four-year conflict.

In the aftermath, the duke made donations towards the cost of the War Memorials at Shireoaks and Worksop. The latter grant was part of a promise made some years before to assist with the renewal costs of the Lady Chapel at the Priory Church. A portion of the monies had been paid on this original intention before the duke observed that no one else was being urged to contribute! He ordered the Agent to withhold further payments until this matter was rectified. However, as it had now been decided to use the Lady Chapel as the Parish War Memorial, the duke was persuaded to continue his gifts. These eventually amounted to £1,000 for the new purpose.

Together with the costs of building a 'Calvary' memorial at Hardwick, these grants are a poignant reminder of men who had died in the recent Great War. Fifty-seven men had been recruited from the Newcastle estate and nineteen of them had perished. The sacrifice made by these men extended to all those families grieving for their loved ones, and no doubt many others coming to terms with physical or mental afflictions that were consequences of the hostilities. Estate records also allow us to follow the happier moves necessary to re-locate newly returned workers, many of whom were outwardly unscathed following their release from the armed services.

Figure 106 – Clumber's 'Calvary' at Hardwick village – 1921
Blessed on the 25 September 1918, the structure was designed by Mr W.E. Tower
and constructed by architectural sculptor, William D. Gough (both of London).

COMINGS, GOINGS AND PENSIONS

It was a period of many comings and goings. Obviously, the comings included all those returning from war service. The changes they found and the unsettled nature of the various departments must have been disturbing, each man having looked forward for so long to the return home. There were also new recruits arriving to replace those who were leaving. These 'goings' were a mixture of redundancies, retirements and voluntary transfers to other work. Some moved to the urban life-style, where the lure of higher wages in the factories and commerce beckoned. In particular, several of the daughters of estate families (including two of Wilson Tomlinson's girls) moved to office or shop work in local and more distant towns.

The re-building of the estate's fortunes over the twenty-year period from the late eighteen-seventies meant that many of the staff, then newly employed, were now approaching retirement. Wilson Tomlinson is the obvious first example of this trend. His replacement as head forester, Robert Fernie, left in 1924 to be succeeded by a Mr H. Palfrey, whose salary was £150 per annum, plus a free house, £10 out of pocket expenses, six tons of coal, firewood and paraffin.

Others were also ready to take their pensions. George Lines, House Steward at Clumber House since the late 1890's, had retired and from Lady Day (25th March) 1919 was replaced by George Brookfield (brother of the duke's Valet) on an annual salary of £178, which included the cost of his board, food and washing.

***

Figure 107 –
William Stanhope, Clerk of Works

Seventy-four-year-old William Stanhope, Clerk of Works, died in 1920, having been on the estate for thirty-seven years. Mr Stanhope had served as a sergeant in the Sherwood Rangers Yeomanry, and was in the escort party for the duke's wedding celebrations in 1889. Twice married, he had eight children (seven by his first wife). His second wife was a Miss Levick, previously the cook at Clumber House, although originally from the Welbeck estate. Head Gardener, Samuel Barker had been best man at their wedding. The only child of this second marriage was Barratt Stanhope, born in 1905 and lived at Clumber until the 1950's. Barratt was trained in the joinery workshops and later followed his step-brother, Sydney, as the carpenter designated to work in Clumber House. As recently as the late-1990s, Barratt was proud to point out his handiwork in the window frames of the 'Duke's Study' and also in the highest points of the Chapel's spire: "from where you could see as far as the church at Laughton-en-le-Morthen".

Figure 108 –
The Hile family, outside their home at
Cabin Hill, Clumber Park (circa 1933).

Randolph Hile succeeded William Stanhope as Clerk of Works. On arrival at Checker House Station, near Ranby, and fresh from his previous work as Assistant Clerk of Works at Woburn, he was met by Clumber's farm bailiff and driven to the Park by pony and trap. Thirty-three-year-old Mr Hile and his wife Emily (a thirty-year-old, born on the Earl of Bradford's Weston Park estate in Shropshire) firstly lived at the Clerk of Works' house in Hardwick Grange. They were later removed to the Cabin Hill house and subsequently, in the 'musical chairs' game played with tied-cottagers, came back to the main residence at Hardwick Grange. By this time they had three children, Philip, Constance and Richard. Some years after, the family moved to one of the Cricket Ground Cottages on Clumber's 'Paddocks' area.

Starting on a salary of £225 per year (which rose by annual increments of £10 to £275) plus a rent-free house and a motorcycle with sidecar, Randolph Hile had a staff of thirty-six men and boys. His department's budget was around £7,500 and included the wages for himself and his workers. Most of the men worked in the Repair Shops and were responsible for the maintenance of farm buildings and cottages. Others were employed at the Sawmill and creosoting plant near Cabin Hill or as drainers, whose main duties were in weeding rivers and also repairing their banks and arterial dykes. Painting contracts had now been put out to tender, with the estate providing the materials in another attempt to save money.

Figure 109 – Bill Salmon (blacksmith)

Figure 110 – Sydney Stanhope (joiner)

FINANCIAL MATTERS

Between 1917 and 1921 the duke sold almost 10,500 acres of agricultural land, leaving himself with some 14,350 acres. £160,000 had been raised by the sale of land in the year after the war and mortgages of £66,000 were paid off. It is clear that far-reaching decisions had been made regarding the duchy's future. The government's 'super-tax' (first introduced in 1909 by Lloyd George on incomes of more than £3,000 per year) was having a significant effect, some £11,500 being levied on the estate for the year ending 1920. It was not long after this that crisis meetings were being held to discuss a £25,000 deficit in the annual balance of accounts. Economies were yet again the order of the day and rent increases of between twenty and fifty per cent were imposed on tenant farmers and many other householders. However, it was not to be long before a nationwide agricultural depression led to rent rebates being forced on landowners, if farming tenants were to survive. By 1924 rent abatements totalled over £575 in respect of the estate farms, following: "several bad seasons and a fall in prices".

The end of military occupation at Ranby Hall had led to attempts to find a buyer. In July 1919, Joseph Harold Smith purchased the Hall (along with its four hundred and fifty acres of land) for £11,389. This ended the Newcastles' ownership of a property that had first been leased by the third duke back in the 1790's and then bought outright by his widow in 1828.

Figure 111 – Ranby Hall (circa 1932)
[Nottingham City Council, Leisure & Community Services, Local Studies Library]

Neighbouring Ranby House had been sold to Sir Albert E. Bingham during 1916 (he also paid £500 for annual shooting rights) and that property was later set up as a preparatory school for Worksop College.

***

To reduce the need to purchase from commercial suppliers, a new three-acre tree nursery was established near Cabin Hill [*see Figure 125*] and plans formulated to accelerate sales of timber. The intention was to raise '£2,500 from Clumber Park, plus £1,500 from outside in each year for the next seven to ten years'. In fact, over a nine-year period, the annual sales averaged only £2,511 although many new plantations were prepared, with around eighty per cent being softwood.

The new Head Forester had a much-reduced staff compared with his predecessor. The days of employing almost fifty woodsmen were over and the work was now done by just twenty-five men and one woman. The Head Gamekeeper's team currently comprised himself and four assistants. Expenditure at the Clumber Stables was giving concern, as costs had almost doubled in the four years 1918 to 1921. The total bill in the last of these years was £2,190, of which over half was on foodstuffs for the horses. The expense of liveries for the grooms had risen, and their annual wage bill was up from £363 to £600.

Head Gardener, Samuel Barker had just nine men plus two boys and two women left in his empire, meaning that numbers were at around half their pre-war levels. He was now under instructions to 'charge market prices' for any produce sold (his accounts for 1922 show a deficit of £764 on an expenditure of £1,944). This led to an intriguing tussle between himself and the duchess. Her Grace had been reconsidering the arrangement known as 'board wages'. These were costing almost £1,000 per year and included such items as beer, vegetables, milk, butter and other foodstuffs. It was decreed that this feature would be stopped for an experimental period, in order to check the practicability of the nineteen 'indoor' servants purchasing their own food as required. It is clear that this change was very unpopular and that Mrs Agnes Kidd, the Housekeeper, was leading the opposition, causing the duchess to comment that she was: "disgusted by the very unpleasant line you [Mrs Kidd] are taking".

It seems that the quantity of vegetables purportedly supplied for the use of the duchess and other members of the 'upstairs' nobility then increased dramatically! The duchess noted this and wrote to Mr Barker, complaining that: "it appears that I and the two Miss Hopes [Lady Doria and Lady Mary] have consumed a stone of potatoes a day during the month of March, which is of course absurd!" Mr Barker was upset by this whole matter (especially so as he was probably blameless) and amongst his responses was the comment that at least he had fixed his prices at some 15% to 20% less than Harrods!

HOME FARM

Cost cutting was applied as stringently at Hardwick Farm. Rarely a profitable enterprise, the ancient Hardwick Grange farm (with acreage of around 165 of grassland, 330 of arable and 5 of buildings) had been losing an average of one thousand pounds a year since well before the recent war. William Beattie, farm bailiff and much-respected judge of horseflesh, had retired to live in Bothamsall.

Much was expected of his replacement, William Davey. With a staff of fourteen (including dairymaid Miss Elsie Beattie, daughter of the recently-retired bailiff), he had responsibility for the eighty-nine Highland and Shorthorn cattle, one hundred and eighty-three sheep, thirty-eight pigs, nine horses and uncounted poultry. In addition, he was charged with managing the arable aspects of the farm and instructed to reverse the fortunes of this loss-making venture. If he achieved this aim, he would have been the first since the 1770's to do so! Sales of horses and cattle were hastened, but hopes of a healthy financial recovery were never to be realised. A first-year loss of £2,325 was followed by a second of over £1,500 and Mr Davey's tenure was to be short-lived.

In 1922 the new farming staff at Hardwick included one George William (known as 'Bill') Sissons, who started work there as a horseman. Bill had moved from the duke's farm at Haughton Hall, where he had been living in the ruins of that once fine dwelling, now long gone. The Sissons' family had been involved on the estates since at least the days of the fourth duke, when woods' labourer John Sissons (born 1806) was based firstly at Haughton, then at Bevercotes. John died aged eighty-five and having served four generations of the ducal family was buried at the Newcastle's Markham-Clinton Mausoleum. Another member of the Sissons' clan, namely George Pagdin Sissons, was born at Bevercotes in 1863. George became daily delivery boy at Hardwick Farm and took dairy produce from the farm to the mansion in a pony and trap. In his old age, he enjoyed regaling the family with the story of being given two 'love apples' by the Head Gardener. He recalled tossing away these strange red fruits, later coming to understand that they were the newly-introduced tomatoes!

The arrival of senior horseman, Bill Sissons, was a proud moment for the family. They noted that he was the first of them to have risen above the general labourer level. His family

Figure 112 –
Bill Sissons, winning yet another ploughing prize.

still recall that he won ten prizes in ploughing competitions (out of the eleven he entered). He later moved smoothly from horses to motor tractors and onto a senior position at the Hardwick Farm where he nursed a variety of new bailiffs through some twenty years or so.

NO MORE COALS FOR NEWCASTLE?

Despite the widespread disquiet amongst landowners about nationalisation of mineral royalties, exploratory diggings were authorised in the Bothamsall area, to establish the feasibility of sinking a new colliery on land close to the village road towards Thoresby. The first boreholes were dug some one third of a mile outside Bothamsall, just before the turning to Clumber Park. Another was tried two fields away and others at Checker House and Morton Hill. The results were not encouraging and no further action was taken, the engineer's report stating that: 'no important seams have been found above the Top Hard (or Barnsley Bed) Coal'.

THE DUKE AND DUCHESS

Never robust since the accident he suffered as a babe-in-arms, the duke's health was giving even greater cause for concern. Heart troubles had been diagnosed and his activities restricted. His visits to North America, so frequent during the twenty-five years prior to the war, had now ceased. In 1922 his holidays included a stay at the Manor House, Folkestone. The duke's occasional visits to Clumber were usually accompanied by apologies for previous absences! He managed a trip or two to Europe, his camera still very much to the fore. During the early 1920's he was in Paris but it is clear that he was neither well nor particularly mobile. It was not going to be long before the purchase of 'an electric wheelchair' was added to his expense account.

Back at Clumber, his Grace no doubt was shocked by the £1,489 cost of electric light battery plates that were required to replace the originals purchased only fifteen years before! Amongst the economies made were those outlined in the instructions: "all family/guest bedrooms should be dismantled and lights taken down (except for four) plus nurseries and state reception rooms to be dismantled. Only four guests to be allowed at Clumber – no large house parties for Doncaster [Races] ... Cars – limit expenditure to £900 per annum".

Figure 113 – Clumber House staff in the early 1920's
Agnes Kidd, housekeeper (3rd from left on the front row) surrounded by the house steward, cook, valet, footmen,
maids, houseman and others

The duke and duchess were living less and less in Clumber House. More than ever, the Forest Farm estate on the outskirts of Windsor Great Park, and the Berkeley House flat in London were becoming their regular abodes. The mortgage on Forest Farm had been cleared at the end of the war. The duchess (apparently as active as ever) was spending some £1,500 per year on her stables at both Clumber and Forest Farm, and continued judging duties at local and national dog shows. Press reports commented that she was still enjoying the occasional 'lawn hunts' in North Nottinghamshire. They also reported that, in 1920, she had been awarded the Order of an Officer of the British Empire for her war efforts in raising monies and comforts for the armed forces.

A small act of kindness to a servant of the estate has come to light that is well worth recording. It will serve as an example that the duke and duchess had adhered to the bishop's specific exhortations to remember their responsibilities to those who were in their service. In this instance, the duchess had, in May 1925, visited the cottage of the seriously-ill John Adcock. John (aged 73) having served as blacksmith for 48 years, had played his part in estate life as both Chapel banner-bearer and cricket captain. A few days after the duchess's visit, 'Old John' died and the duchess wrote to his widow:

I must write to tell you how much the Duke & myself sympathise with you and your children in your great loss. I little thought when I came to see you the other day, that it would be the last time I should see Old John in this world. Both the Duke & myself feel we have lost a good friend as well as a very devoted servant.

For you our sympathy, as for him we cannot grieve, after such a well lived life we know he is at rest, safe in his Master's keeping, where the troubles and sorrows of this world can touch him no more.

May we all be as ready to go when our time comes as he was.

With deep sympathy, K. Newcastle

Mrs Elizabeth Adcock wrote back to the duchess saying that her husband had loved Clumber and that it gave the family great pleasure to know that his services had been so much appreciated. Copies of both letters have been saved by the family and are much treasured. The funeral service was held at Clumber Chapel and John was then buried in the cemetery at Worksop. Mrs Adcock was granted a widow's pension of £26 per annum (one half of her late-husband's earnings).

Figure 114 – John Adcock (blacksmith)

Figure 115 – Kathleen (duchess), riding 'Kitty'.

***

Kathleen's own mother, the Hon. Mrs Candy, also died in 1925, aged 78, and was interred in the Candy family mausoleum at Rossmore Park, Co. Monaghan. A Requiem Mass was then held at Clumber Chapel, the duke being amongst the congregation.

MORE CHANGES IN SCHOOL ARRANGEMENTS

The Nottinghamshire Education Committee took control of the village school from January 1920 and the twelve boys of the duke's choir were permanently separated from the village children at this stage. From then, the choristers were to be educated in a 'voluntary' school and to have their classes in the 'Reading Room' at Hardwick. Fred Leeson, back from his army service, became the choirboys' sole teacher and was soon being praised for having enhanced educational standards. They were even blessed by the provision of a 'science laboratory' – actually a small wooden shed behind the Reading Room.

A boy who joined the new Choir School at this time, Michael Colston, later wrote of Mr Leeson that he was: "the best teacher I have ever come into contact with". He also mentioned the love and commitment shown to them by the Matron and the 'saintliness' of the disabled duke. He commented on the kindness proffered them in the form of presents of money 'usually a 10/- note' (50p) and the cameras, silver wristwatches, silver pencils and pens which came their way at the Dedication Festival time. Mr Colston went out of his way to dispel any suspicions that the modern reader may harbour, in respect of the possibility that 'abuse' took place in this remote spot. The food is remembered with affection but, says Mr Colston: "would no doubt frighten a dietician. I don't know why. It cannot have done me any harm because I am 86...!" He explained that the jam tart and custard offset the lead shot found in the rabbit! Another choirboy from the mid-1920's, Frank Ffoukes, remembered the fairly free rein which they had been on – despite the 6 or 7 a.m. rising – the cricket matches with the Rev. Hawkins and the rota for boys to act as server for the weekday communion services at the Oratory. Mr Ffoukes also recalls the duke as: "bowed, tiny and crippled ... a kind gentle man with a grey bushy moustache".

From June 1921, all children of the Park had use of the new open-air swimming pool. Completed at a cost of £500 and surrounded by a five-foot wooden fence, the pool measured some sixty-six-foot by fifteen and was deep enough for the swimmers to dive in from a diving board. They had eight changing rooms alongside and the water supply arrived via a culvert from the main lake (just above the waterfall near Hardwick Grange) – the temperature of the water is said to have been 'always cold'!

SALES AND OTHER MONEY MATTERS

Sales of the ducal family's gold and silver items were held at Christies in June 1921 and July 1922 and raised over £32,600. Amongst the pieces on auction were some once owned by John Holles, Duke of Newcastle in the 1790's. Of special interest was a two-handled cup presented to that duke by Queen Anne to reward him for his role as a Commissioner for the Union of England with Scotland. The cup was manufactured from the melted-down metal of the old Seal of England and was inscribed: "The last privey [sic] seal which belonged to England before the Union of Great Britain which took place the first of May, 1707". Regrettably, no record as to its sale price or new owner has been traced during the preparation of this narrative.

During 1927 and 1928 more land was sold at Newark, Nottingham and Worksop, raising over £13,000. There was a small offset to this when the duke purchased a sliver of Welbeck estate land near Truman's Lodge. This was to allow the attractive approach into the Park from the Worksop road to maintain its character.

Clumber's pre-war Country Shows had not been reintroduced after the war but the public was still visiting the Park in large numbers. Garden Fetes were held at Clumber in 1923 and 1924. The first was in aid of the 'Nottinghamshire Nursing Federation's Hospital for Women' on Castle Gate, Nottingham. The entrance fee to the Park was one shilling and three pence, with one shilling being charged as admission price for a tour of the House. Tea was served in the Stableyard and cost one shilling and sixpence [71/2p]. The Worksop Silver Band provided the musical entertainment and the expense of hiring them (£24 plus tea) was blamed for the eventual donation to the Federation of 'only' £237. In the second year, a fete held at August Bank Holiday raised £264 in aid of the 'Southwell Diocesan Rescue and Preventative Work'.

It was noted that the adverse consequences of army vehicles using the roads had now been worsened by increased motor charabanc traffic. This was causing surface problems particularly over the three-plus miles of Lime Tree Avenue, the one public road in the Park. Thus far, Worksop Urban District Council had being paying only fifty pounds per annum towards the upkeep of this highway, but, from the end of September 1921 they accepted complete responsibility for costs and repairs.

Estate accounts indicate that despite all efforts to balance the books, there was still an overall loss in income. Although investments were just about holding their own, rents, mineral royalties and timber receipts had dropped steadily. Rent receipts now totalled £29,000, which was around seventy-five per cent of the estate's rent roll at the time of the duke's accession. This is a further measure of the selling-off of duchy land. Nationally, arable farming was still in an unsatisfactory position and requiring whatever assistance could be offered. In the case of the Newcastle estates, rent abatements had continued for several years, although, in 1926, at a lesser rate than previous. Larger farms caused some difficulties in re-letting and this led to rents being abated for the first three or four years of new tenancies.

Many of the perceived necessities of a ducal estate were listed under 'Personal Expenses'. They all caused concern. Annually, the Household Staff bill was £8,500 at Clumber and £1,800 at Forest Farm. The Stables cost £1,500, Motor Cars and Vans £1,400. Clumber Gardens and Park expenditure was around £2,400. Clumber Chapel and the Choir Hostel required over £2,000 for their maintenance. It is also recorded that the duke had 'for many years' made an annual allowance of £1,200 for the duchess from the 'Newark rent monies'. It is not clear whether this latter entry was a hint by the Agent that this might be reviewed and adjusted either up or (heaven forbid) down!

Amongst the smaller investments, the Worksop Golf Club had leased enough of the duke's land alongside the old Coach Road (now known as Windmill Lane) for them to construct a nine-hole course. The duke had bought twenty-five £1 shares in this 1914 venture and became President of the Club four years later, although no record has been found of him playing golf there or elsewhere. Then, in 1922, a new lease was signed, allowing a further nine holes to be constructed. Soon afterwards, the President made a loan of £1,250 (at five per cent over 15 years) to help fund the construction of a new clubhouse and he also agreed a new 50-year lease for the Club.

Whilst on the subject of loans, amongst others made by the duke during this period were two substantial ones to members of his family. Firstly a £12,000 mortgage to his brother-in-law, Sir Lister-Kaye, with 20,000 shares in Denby Colliery being offered as security. Secondly, to his own brother, the ever cash-strapped Lord Francis, he loaned £18,000. As collateral for this he accepted the 'Hope Settled Estates', no doubt including property in Ireland.

Also at this time, it was noted that the duke's father had (in 1868) purchased ten £10 shares in the 'Ascot Hotel and Stables Company'. These had never been redeemed by the executors of the turf-obsessed sixth duke, but this painful reminder of those dark days which had led to bankruptcy and disgrace was quickly consigned to the waste bin, the solicitors advising that the expense of pursuing the matter would be prohibitive.

THE LONDON & FORT GEORGE LAND COMPANY

Following two years of discussions and examination of all the options, it was in 1927 that a major change was introduced in the financial arrangements for the Newcastle duchy. It was decided that the London & Fort George Land Company (L.F.G.) should take over almost all the duke's estates – he had recently purchased a further 6,000 shares in the business. With the exception of Forest Farm, all the duke's properties were sold to the L.F.G. for £965,000. As with so many other landowners, this action was taken with a view to reducing the burden of taxation. The duke's current annual tax bill stood at £33,000. This transfer arrangement provided for a £6,050 deposit to be made to him, followed by annual payments of £12,000 until the whole amount was paid – an eighty-year commitment! Fifteen thousand, five hundred and eighty-one acres were involved in this transaction which included Clumber House and Chapel plus the surrounding buildings, Gardens, Pleasure Grounds and so much outside the Park boundaries. It did not include the treasures of the house, either in storage or on exhibition elsewhere. Obviously, heirlooms were exempt, as were contents of the famous Library and other valuables. The duke was now to be tenant of the mansion and obligated to pay £500 rent per annum.

Figure 116 – Forest Farm, Winkfield, near Windsor.

THE DUKE'S LAST WILL AND TESTAMENT

The duke had now become very frail and an electric wheelchair and a 'Waygood' electric lift were installed in Clumber House by 1926. Possibly because of his increasingly unhealthy condition, and coupled with the new ownership arrangements for the estate, it was in July 1927 that he and his solicitors drew up his last will and testament. In this document he particularly remembered the duchess; his two remaining sisters, Lady Beatrice and Lady Florence; his brother and heir, Lord Francis; Lord Francis's three children, Henry, Doria and Mary; Arthur Elliott, the land agent; Agnes Kidd, housekeeper; George Cook, head coachman and Albert Johnson, chauffeur. Also mentioned were the Provost and Fellows of Eton College, who were to receive pictures, prints, engravings and books from the Forest Farm residence.

There is an intriguing entry made in the will regarding: "my uncle Lord Arthur Pelham Clinton (a person reputed to be dead and as to the proof of whose death some question might arise) ...". Lord Arthur, brother of the sixth duke, was said to have died in June 1870. The facts of the case have never been satisfactorily resolved, but the police were not convinced by reports of his death, and some said that Lord Arthur had fled to America or Canada to escape trial on charges involving homosexual activities (involving transvestites 'Franny and Stella'). If alive at the time the duke's latest will was prepared, Lord Arthur would have been eighty-eight years old. The stipulation in the document could not have been clearer – neither Arthur nor any of his heirs were to receive even a penny-piece!

Figure 117 – Lord Arthur Pelham-Clinton, a 'person reported to be dead'!

DEATH OF THE 7th DUKE

After a lengthy period of heart troubles, the duke spent time recuperating in the South of France before returning to Clumber in April, 1928. Once home, he became seriously ill and was visited by many concerned friends, including Adeline Genée. He then moved to his Berkeley House flat in Hay Hill Road, London where he suffered a major heart attack. Soon afterwards he was reported to be rallying a little. However, it was a false dawn and he died on Wednesday, 30 May 1928.

His body was taken to the small mortuary chapel at All Saint's Home. It was accompanied by the duchess, the duke's sisters and his valet, Mr J. Green. On Friday night, the body was moved to All Saint's Church, Margaret Street, to prepare for the following day's services. The senior choirboys then turned the space round the bier into 'a glorious garden', with over 120 wreaths and crosses on display. The duchess had chosen a huge cross of dark red carnations and this was laid at the head of the coffin, the one at the foot being from the new duke, comprising roses and lilies of the valley.

Starting at seven o'clock on Saturday morning, clergy of All Saint's, together with Father Hawkins from Clumber, began the day's services with a Low Mass. At nine o'clock, the Solemn Mass was sung in the presence of members of the duke's family and numerous friends. Many old boys of the choir were present (including the actor Laurence Olivier, mentioned in Chapter Five above). The duchess had selected the hymns and: "the choir never sang more beautifully" wrote the Vicar in the Parish Paper.

After the church service, the body was removed to Eton where the duke had chosen his burial plot in a quiet corner of the cemetery. The grave was lined with moss and ferns from Forest Farm, Windsor and covered with white flowers. The Provost, Vice Provost and Head Master were amongst those

Figure 118 – In the autumn of 2003, the author discovered the duke's neglected grave at Eton. Constructed of granite it displays the 'simplicity' mentioned at the funeral in 1928. The inscription reads: 'FLOREAT ETON –
HENRY PELHAM ARCHIBALD DOUGLAS PELHAM-CLINTON
7TH DUKE OF NEWCASTLE
BORN 28TH SEPTEMBER 1864 – DIED 30TH MAY 1928'

present. Captains of the School and of Oppidans represented the boys of the College. "In the Church he loved grandeur, for himself he loved simplicity and Eton ..." said the priest, who would also have noted that, very recently, the duke had given £1,300 to All Saint's for the purchase of a 'Suspended Tabernacle in Silver'. It was a simple ceremony on a sunny day, with a backcloth of blue sky, green elms and colourful flower tributes to uplift the sad occasion. Boys of All Saint's choir led the unaccompanied singing of 'Jesu, Lover of my Soul', after which the party dispersed.

On the following Monday morning, special services were held at both Clumber Chapel and Worksop Priory. The Requiem Mass at Clumber was led by the Chaplain and attended by a large congregation, including the Duke of Portland (Welbeck), Lady Robinson (Worksop Manor), Captain Foljambe (Osberton), Mr Elliott (Agent), Mrs Kidd (Housekeeper) and Mr Headland (tenant farmer at Elkesley). During a short address the Chaplain said that the Clumber Chapel: "would ever remain an abiding and magnificent witness of a great and good noble man." At Worksop Priory, the Rev. Canon d'Arcy paid an eloquent and touching tribute to the duke, quoting scripture to proclaim: "There is a Prince and a great man fallen this day". He also said: "... we owe him more than we can tell ... we will miss him at every turn". Rev. Canon Hayward, speaking at the Roman Catholic Church on Park Street, remarked: "By his death, Worksop has lost a great nobleman, a sincere and earnest Christian, and we at St. Mary's a very generous and consistent benefactor to our schools ..."

Figure 119 – Memorial Services card.

HENRY PELHAM ARCHIBALD DOUGLAS PELHAM-CLINTON,

7TH DUKE OF NEWCASTLE, 1879 TO 1928.

BORN 28TH SEPTEMBER, 1864;
DIED 30TH MAY, 1928.

MEMORIAL SERVICES,

MONDAY, JUNE 4TH, 1928.

CLUMBER.	WORKSOP PRIORY.
SOLEMN REQUIEM 10 A.M.	SOLEMN REQUIEM 11.30 A.M.

It seems that the duke's youthful wish to be 'a good man' had been achieved. His death marked the end of an era, and life for those around his much-reduced Nottinghamshire duchy was about to change as comprehensively as it had ever done.

Figure 120 – Clumber House and Terraces.
[One of Richard Alcock's photographs taken on glass plate negatives (circa 1930)]

CHAPTER SEVEN

1928 to 1936

The 8th Duke of Newcastle – Probate – '... the Park will have to be broken up' – 'Utmost Economy' – Chapel, Choir School & Worksop College – Lord Lincoln & his sisters – An American influence – More leisure activities in the Park – Well-foundered rumours & a new interest – Clumber Chapel, a casualty of the mid-1930's – Miscellaneous happenings – Moving towards the final decade as a ducal estate..

THE 8th DUKE OF NEWCASTLE

O N THE DEATH of the 'little Duke', his brother, Lord Henry Francis Hope Pelham-Clinton-Hope, became the eighth Duke of Newcastle-under-Lyme. Hitherto, Lord Francis's precarious financial standing had been centred on the value of his: "life interest in the Hope properties and several insurance policies". As we have noted, there had been many hiccups in his affairs and he had sold off various heirlooms held in his trust.

The 62-year-old duke decided against a move of home, stating that the palatial Clumber House did not appeal to him and declaring that there was a: "ducal atmosphere which pervades the place". He continued to live at Harrowlands in Surrey, which had been substantially rebuilt just two years before his brother's death. The Deepdene property near Dorking (amongst the assets he had received from his mother's 'Hope' family) had been leased out since 1893 and was requisitioned for the army's use during the Great War. It had then been turned into a hotel. His lands had included

Figure 121 – 8th Duke
[National Portrait Gallery, London]

those around Deepdene, together with a large part of the nearby Box Hill, which he had sold in 1914. In 1928, when he inherited the ducal title, he gave the area known as 'Glory Woods' to the Dorking Urban Council.

Born on 3 February 1866, the duke was educated at Eton College and Trinity Hall, Cambridge. As previously mentioned [*see Figure 44*] he married the colourful Mary 'May' Augusta Yohe in 1891. A budding theatrical star of America and London, 'May' had been born in Bethlehem, Philadelphia, and educated in Dresden, Germany. Lord Francis was not ungenerous in support of his beautiful young bride and May was able to continue her stage work after their wedding. He also lavished substantial amounts of cash into her productions at the Lyric and Court Theatres in London. Bankruptcy had followed and, in 1898, after successful pleas to the court, he raised £121,000 by selling Hope family heirlooms, in which he had held a life interest. Lady Francis (May) found another admirer at this time and deserted her husband for him. She was later to tell the press of her deep regrets at having deserted her 'English lord'. Lord Francis obtained a divorce in 1902.

Lord Francis then travelled to Australia, where he met and, in 1904, married Olive Muriel Owen, previously Shaw – née Thompson – who already had one daughter. Lord and Lady Francis had three children, one son (who was baptised in Clumber Chapel) and two daughters. With the

Ficgure 122 – Lady Olive Muriel.

Newcastle's tendency for misfortune, it was only eight years into their marriage that Olive died of leukaemia on 30 August 1912, aged only thirty-five. Lord Francis did not remarry. After his second wife's death, Lord Francis moved to the Hope's family home at Castle Blaney, in County Monaghan (some twenty-five years earlier, he had been appointed High Sheriff of that County). Returning to England in 1916, he had the 'Harrowlands' property built at Dorking, Surrey. During the nineteen-twenties, his main occupation was connected with dairy farming, where he traded as Messrs. Hope and Co.

Following his late brother's example, Lord Francis supported the Waifs and Strays Society and encouraged the use of his grounds for money-raising functions for them and also for local hospitals. However, unlike his brother, he was not a regular churchman, and this was to be an important factor in the next phase of Clumber's history. Incidentally, the late duke – undoubtedly knowing of his brother's lack of interest in matters ecclesiastical – had turned over to the Society for the Maintenance of the Faith rights of presenting the church livings of his six remaining Nottinghamshire parishes.

The eighth duke's three children spent their earliest childhood living with their parents in Surrey and at Castle Blaney. Since their mother's death they had spent increasing amounts of time at Clumber and Forest Farm with their uncle and aunt – the seventh duke and duchess. Popular with the tenants of the Clumber estate, they attended their parties and joined them in various events during school holidays. On reaching their mid-teens, they had been involved in assisting the Boy Scouts, Girl Guides and Brownie activities at Hardwick.

PROBATE

Valuations for Probate documents relating to the death of the seventh duke indicate a 'Provisional Value' of one million pounds for the Newcastle unsettled properties. All settled property had previously been held jointly with the duchess. Matters were extremely complex due to the transfer of the duke's estate to the 'L.F.G.' and, in preparing the accounts for Probate, great efforts were made to discover how other large landowners, such as the Duke of Rutland, had managed (allegedly): "to evade the necessity for a Valuation". Annual income from the Clumber and Worksop Estates for the year ending Lady Day 1928 was recorded as slightly under £14,000 from rents, plus just over that figure for royalties on minerals and around £750 from investments and woods. Nottingham and Newark rents produced around £15,000, which brought the total annual income to £43,800. Against this was set expenditure of £22,000, leaving £21,800 before tax.

Undeveloped land property in Canada was said to be: "worth very little indeed" and brought no income. Some $3,000 was held at the National Bank of Commerce, New York. The late duke had held around 20,000 shares in the L.F.G., which were valued at five pounds per share. The contents of Clumber House are recorded at £139,500 (including almost £34,000 of this being based on items of value in the Library and over £41,000 in pictures). Items at Forest Farm, Windsor and in the flat at Berkeley House, London were listed at around £7,000. Forest Farm's valuation for Probate was £9,540, although the probable offer price for sale appears to have been £14,000. 'All Minerals' value was entered as £194,000, with Basford land and other property at around £61,000.

'... THE PARK WILL HAVE TO BE BROKEN UP'

As early as July 1929, the eighth duke was expressing the view that: "sooner or later, the Park will have to be broken up".   He considered that a new boundary: "along the line of the public road known as Lime Tree Avenue" should form the northern line of Clumber.   There was a confidence that the new breed of commuter would be willing to travel from Doncaster, Nottingham or Sheffield to lease properties in the vicinity of the smaller Park.

The Clumber Estate residents had noted the changes of the previous two years with concern. Most of the House staff had been dismissed.   A few had taken retirement terms, including the Housekeeper, Agnes Kidd, and the long-serving chauffeur, Albert Johnson, who had coped with the

Figure 123 – Chauffeur Billy Pratchett went to Forest Farm with the Dowager Duchess.

Figure 124 – Kathleen, Dowager Duchess at Forest Farm, Winkfield.

duke's mostly second-hand cars for around thirty years.   Some employees (including James Kerse, head kennelman) had moved with the dowager duchess to Forest Farm, near Cranbourne and within Windsor Forest.

Many of the Clumber House contents had been transferred there, and some cattle and other livestock had been taken from the Hardwick Farm.

Clumber House was already proving difficult to let and was being used as: "a warehouse for the family heirlooms ... it will be difficult to find another tenant".   Whenever the duke travelled north to visit Clumber, he took lodgings at 'Ye Olde Bell Hotel', Barnby Moor.

'UTMOST ECONOMY'

There was mounting concern over the finances and 'Utmost Economy' were the watchwords. The guns of the late duke were sold. Shooting rights at Clumber and Bothamsall were again leased out. One of the early decisions was to offer the lease of Hardwick farm at a low rent if necessary – although this aim was not achieved until 1936. Clumber Stables were emptied and closed.

Clumber Gardens were to be maintained: "in skeleton form on a commercial basis". It is appropriate here to turn to the writings of a gardener, Sydney Brown – born in October 1900 – who late in life jotted down his memories of the Gardens organisation at the beginning of the 1930's. He described how, east from the Palm House and pot fruit house, the peach ranges with nectarines were on the back walls. To the west there stood four grape houses and one fig house. Looking south from the Palm House was a twelve-foot wide herbaceous border, with apple trees flanking either side. This led to the first east-west wall which was known as the peach wall, with a small fruit orchard close by. Within this orchard were eight asparagus beds and four watercress beds, the latter supplied with constant running water and shaded by bamboo grass. The walls of the most southerly garden area were known as the 'apricot walls' and these also sheltered two more grape houses. Running north to south were three carnation houses, to the west of which were other greenhouses for pot plants, including various species of orchids. There were sunken pits within the glasshouses and melon tomatoes grown, also one area – known as 'back-break frames' – used for carnation layering and other cuttings. The outhouses – to the rear and west – of the Palm House included the artificial manure shed, onion house, workmen's mess house, storage room for beet, carrot, seakale plus a potting shed. To the east were two large boilers for heating the greenhouses containing the vines and peaches. Then came the head gardener's and the foreman's offices, a mushroom house, three stores for tubs and plants from the terraces and pleasure ground walkways. Finally, there was the shed for barrows and tools.

Single gardeners - including those who were designated to work on the Pleasure Grounds – lived in the 'bottom bothy' and next door was housed the horseman who had two horses to fetch coke from Checker House station for the garden boilers. These animals were also used to cut the grass on the Pleasure Ground and on Cedar Walk. There was a third horse for the use of the head gardener. Behind the two houses were rose gardens, the plants grown in Bothamsall clay and

Bevercotes red clay, this material also having been carted from these nearby villages that had been a part of the Newcastle estate for so long.

The sense of purpose for this previously highly-rated aspect of the estate had been almost lost now that the duke was an absentee. Whilst he continued to live in Surrey, and Clumber's mansion stood empty, there was never again going to be that buzz and motivation that came from the 'walkabout' of a resident duke or duchess. The latest 'economy' plans were that the older greenhouses should be taken down and the House terraces sown with grass. It was a close-run thing that the Kitchen Gardens were not also turned to grass, however the new duke gave his opinion that, if they were, it might prevent their eventual sale. In the meantime, he ordered twice-weekly deliveries of: "three dozen items of choice fruit" to be sent to him at Harrowlands. He was soon expressing dissatisfaction with the quality of the figs and grapes supplied – "over-ripe and badly packed" was his opinion. Fortunately, the peaches were said to be satisfactory!

A tree nursery was established next to Cabin Hill House and was in the charge of Billy Milton, previously foreman at the kitchen gardens. The nursery certainly reduced the costs of providing sturdy saplings for planting around the estate's woodlands and included a succession of ornamental trees and shrubs.

Figure 125 – A rare picture of the tree and shrub nursery near Cabin Hill.
Billy Milton is shown in this location, which was his responsibility for much of the 1920's and 1930s.

Efforts to sell more Newcastle properties were accelerated. Outstanding mortgages were called in and initial attempts to re-let the late duke's Berkeley House flat were unsuccessful. A farm sale was held in July 1928. This raised £2,259 for the duchess's herd of forty-seven Red Poll cattle (introduced at Clumber in 1913), and included ninety-seven guineas for the final six of her Welsh Ponies. The late duke's Fiat motor car was taken to Harrowlands for the use of the new duke. The Morris and the Crossley cars were kept at Clumber.

Trustees, Messrs. H.M. Crookenden, Frank Isitt, Nigel Campbell and Colonel Colin Campbell (all of whom were also Executors), along with Mr Arthur Elliott, the co-opted Agent, had their regular London meetings to keep a tight rein on the finances. The duke and his son were often present. It was not long before the press made a confident announcement that Clumber House would remain unoccupied for at least nine years. This was more than a death duties matter – it was just too big and too expensive to run. There was also another aspect connected with the duke's will. He had linked certain bequests regarding the estate to the thirtieth birthday of Lord Lincoln – and that was nine year's hence!

In July 1928, just a few weeks after the duke's death, Arthur Elliott (Estate Agent since 1904), prepared a special Report for the Directors of the London and Fort George Land Company. Mr Elliott was already of the opinion that the Clumber Estate would be sold piecemeal, as opportunity arose, over a period of about sixty to seventy years. In his 1928 Report he outlined the state of each department of the Estate and, where appropriate, the economies which he planned or recommended should be taken.

CHAPEL, CHOIR SCHOOL & WORKSOP COLLEGE

The late duke had made known his wishes in respect of the Chapel, also the Choir School and their Hostel. He desired – no doubt sensing that major changes would follow his death – that they would continue and that the: "customary services be held". Acknowledging the spiritual needs of those who lived within the boundaries of the Park, the 'L.F.G.', agreed that the Chapel should remain open. However, they were more than slightly reluctant to finance the Chaplain's stipend.

Decisions on the fate of the duke's Choir School were equally disturbing to the residents, their parents and the staff. Ten year-old 'Jack' Pike (a nephew of the choirmaster) wrote cheerfully to his parents: "I do not think that the Duke, being dead, will stop us from carrying on with the school"! However, by October, Jack and the other boys were sent to their homes in Barrow-in-Furness, Cricklewood, Ealing, Ilford, Nottingham, Osterley Park, Sheffield, Wallington, Wath-on-Dearne and Westcliffe-on-Sea. Some of them took the offer of a place at Doctor Nicholson's new choir school at Chislehurst in Kent. Legal opinion was sought regarding the continuation of the bursaries from the late duke's funds for the ex-choir boys who were still at Worksop College. Eventually it was decided that they should complete their studies there if they so wished.

Hardwick's Hostel-cum-School furniture was sold and the building was converted to become a family house occupied by, firstly, the Farm Bailiff and later, the Estate Agent. The Choir's schoolmaster, Mr Fred Leeson, moved to a new post at Grantham Church of England School. The abandoned swimming pool eventually became a farm silo.

Around this period, Worksop College benefited from the gift of a grand piano and the loan of church vestments. 'Pelham' House and the 'Newcastle Scholarship' are amongst the College reminders of their ducal benefactor. In 1930, the headmaster suggested that the college be renamed 'Clumber College'. The directors of the L.F.G. put that suggestion on hold, but in the event, there was said to be: "family feeling" against the suggestion and the matter was dropped.

LORD LINCOLN AND HIS SISTERS

The eighth duke's only son, Henry Edward Hugh Pelham-Clinton-Hope, now took the title of Earl of Lincoln. His claim to fame so far was as Captain of the Eton College cricket team of 1926 during: "a year of unbroken success". At Magdalene College, Cambridge, his main interests lay in sport and he was said by some to have been of County or even Test match standard if he had chosen to channel his talents further in that direction. He had already scored impressive hundreds off the adult bowling of 'Gubby' Allen and Adrian Gore. Rugby and Ice Hockey were added to his cricketing interests and injury from a strain sustained at hockey affected his final year at university although he achieved his goal of earning his arts degree in history.

In 1930, press reporters had spotted the twenty-three-year-old noble-man playing the drums in London's Café de Paris. Whilst at Cambridge, he

Figure 126 –
The soon-to-be Earl of
Lincoln – captain of the
Eton cricket team 1926.

and a group of fellow students had formed a band and subsequently played the Mayfair nightclub. It seems unlikely he was doing this from necessity, although his father's continuing financial problems may be significant here. The earl was receiving £5,121 per year from the Newcastle Estate and had further income as a newly-appointed director of the L.F.G..

Lord Lincoln was to make his home at Clumber – but not in the 'Mansion'. Clumber Cottage (close by Truman's Lodge) was modernised for his use, initially as a 'Shooting Box' and then into a more substantial home. The cottage, known as 'Park Cottage' in earlier days, was a modestly-sized dwelling with two earth closets. In 1929, some £1550 was allocated for the improvements (including electric lighting) and by the following spring, the residence was ready for occupation.

Figure 127 – South face of Clumber Cottage .

At the same time, neighbouring stables were converted by the Worksop firm of Leverton and Brown into a small cottage for the use of a caretaker. A new and noisy water pump provided a supply from the nearby well and plans had been made to deepen the well. The lease of the late duke's Berkeley House flat was surrendered in October 1929 and furniture brought by rail from London to Worksop for use in Clumber Cottage. Liberty's provided the curtains and blinds. Silver items, such as cutlery, were loaned from stored items in Clumber House.

The cottage having been prepared, it was never occupied by Lord Lincoln. Invariably, whenever he was at Clumber prior to his marriage, he lodged with the Agent, Mr Elliott and his family, at Sparken House in Worksop. From June 1930, Elliott moved to a new job. Lord Lincoln was then able to offer the Clumber Cottage to his eldest sister, Lady Doria Lois, when she married Mr Frederick Baldwin Childe in that year. The duke described this arrangement as: "keeping the house warm for her brother". Their servant lived in the adjoining cottage. Two years later, Mr Childe decided that he would manage a piggery at Hardwick Grange and he and Lady Doria then moved into the Hardwick Grange accommodation. Clumber Cottage eventually became the home of the new Chief Agent, Major Kenneth Murray-Walker and his family. The Childe's marriage was annulled in 1935 and Lady Doria went on to marry Mr Stefan Neumann the following year but they had separated by the time of the birth of their daughter Roxanne in 1938.

Lord Lincoln's youngest sister also married in 1930. Lady Mary's bridegroom was Charles Kenneth Horne. Newspapers reported Mary to be a: "twenty-year-old, vivacious and very popular girl". Mr Horne, grandson of the first Lord Cozens Hardy, later became famous as a radio entertainer from the late nineteen-thirties to the late sixties. He was particularly noted for the comedy programme 'Round the Horne'. Their marriage was annulled in 1933 and Mary married twice more (secondly in 1939 and thirdly in 1947).

The young earl and his sisters became occasional participants in London's nightlife. It was on one very memorable evening that Lady Doria met the world-renowned Fred Astaire, whilst she was dining with friends at the Savoy hotel. When Astaire, arguably the most well-known male dancer of the cinema age, noted Doria's beauty and dancing prowess he asked her to partner him, and she was only too happy to oblige! Her big brother was also pleased to tell the tale for many a year!

Figure 128 – Lady Doria, eldest daughter of the 8th duke.

ANOTHER AMERICAN INFLUENCE

It was on 24 March 1931 that Lord Lincoln followed in his father's footsteps and married an American girl. He had met her whilst on holiday in the U.S.A. following the completion of his university studies. She was the recently divorced, twenty-five-year-old Jean Banks Gimbernat, slim and elegant, adopted step-daughter of David Banks who lived in Park Avenue, New York. The couple married in New York – in the flat of a friend of Jean's – just six months after their first meeting and one month after her divorce proceedings were concluded.

On arrival at Clumber, the earl and countess moved into Clumber Cottage. Soon after, they transferred to rooms in the mansion. They lived in the Red Drawing Room and the Duchess Suite, Lady Lincoln wrote "which I made cosy with flowers and a big fire'. By 1933 they had moved from the decaying Clumber House into the nearby Parsonage, after major improvements had been made there. Their rent was set at £150 a year and they employed a housekeeper, Miss Margaret Robinson, and a butler-cum-valet, Charles Bond. Also engaged were a cook (James Burden, who had served as Chapel Sacristan for many years), a parlourmaid, whose life experience was enhanced when she discovered that a married couple were content to use twin-beds!), a kitchen maid, housemaid, a chauffeur – Charlie Read, plus the odd job man, Jim Howard.

To help celebrate their marriage, the Lincoln's provided estate dwellers with a wedding party in a field at Hardwick. The consensus on the new Lady Lincoln was that she appeared to be: "a very nice American lady". Lord Lincoln, as heir to the dukedom, was in demand to grace local events with his presence. In particular, he followed his late uncle's lead in supporting Worksop College activities. Lincoln and his new wife attended the College Sports Day in 1932 and presented the prizes. He then raised a cricket team, 'The Earl of Lincoln's XI', and challenged the College to annual matches over the next few years. He also arranged for an Eton side to play a game there. The earl and countess attended the College performance of 'Hamlet' and awarded a prize for the best English verse of the year. This was the year of Lady Lincoln's presentation at Court, where she wore jewellery from the family heirlooms – and was proposed by the Dowager Duchess.

Lady Lincoln was soon playing her part in the local social scene. Estate tenants remember her with affection. Childless – although certainly not by choice – she is said to have always stopped her car to enquire after their family's welfare. One young girl of that time, Miss Constance Hile, daughter of the Clerk of Works, recalls that she and other schoolgirls were invited by Lady Lincoln to enter the Pleasure Ground and assist in picking daffodils, which were then sent to local hospitals. She also remembers that she and the other girls were allowed to take some of the flowers home as a present for their mothers. In November 1932 the countess was instrumental in the setting up of a Clumber branch of the Women's Institute, whose monthly meetings were normally held in the Reading Room at Hardwick. She became their President and the branch was well supported during her seven-year tenure.

Life should have been idyllic for the Lord and Lady Lincoln, with so much to entertain them at Clumber, whether boating, fishing, shooting or even golfing on the short practice course that chauffeur Charlie Read and the earl designed and constructed in the Pleasure Grounds. The Parsonage was large enough to give them room to entertain well and to have their own apartments for relaxation. They each had their own vehicles and sufficient money to travel within Britain or overseas whenever they wished.

But there were problems from the start of their relationship. Lady Lincoln recorded that her husband was soon displaying a melancholy side to his nature. He was said to be lacking in confidence and unwilling to face up to the responsibilities of his position as heir to the dukedom. As a consequence, his wife became distressed and very lonely. Their attempts to produce children were unfruitful and their future together seemed so uncertain. She admits that she had not been in love with him when they wed – indeed, they had made a pact that she would only agree to marry him if she could be released from the union if at any time she did fall in love. Lincoln had said that he hoped that she would come to love him.

The young men of the estate were especially envious of the cars belonging to Lord and Lady Lincoln. At this stage he had two cars, a dual-grey Bentley and a black Buick, whilst the countess drove a red M.G. sports car. Those who were young boys during this time also have memories of ''Nero and 'Rita', the two Great Danes owned by the Lincoln's. The dogs were bigger than most of the lads and terrified some of them. Massive, and over-friendly, Nero frequently knocked them to the ground in his enthusiasm. Some recall being licked by his huge tongue: "more like an army blanket!"

Figure 129a – Lady Lincoln & 'Nero', [Howard Barrett photo – 'Nottinghamshire Magazine', January 1933.]

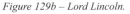

Figure 129b – Lord Lincoln.

A feature of Clumber in the 1930's was the Christmas parties, held at the Village Hall in Hardwick. These were less formal than those held during the times of the late duke. The countess displayed her un-Englishness by insisting that the adults call her 'Jean' and joining in the games with the youngsters, even crawling around the floor with them if the game required! The earl and countess also provided the children with presents – "invariably from Harrods"!

Figure 130 – The Earl of Lincoln leads out the Clumber Park cricket team of 1935.

MORE LEISURE ACTIVITIES AT CLUMBER

Lord Lincoln was very interested in, and supportive of the progress of, the regular Clumber cricket team and sporadically played there himself. A captain of the team recalls: "Whenever 'Lordy' (as all of the men called him behind his back) telephoned to ask if there was a vacancy in the team, we welcomed him with open arms – as if we'd dare do otherwise!" As a talented ice-hockey player he also promoted this sport at Clumber. He had a supply of hockey sticks prepared in the Hardwick workshops and his team played matches on the lake whenever the weather was suitable. They enjoyed seeing him skate at speed from the mansion terrace site to the lake arm at Hardwick for these matches. Several reports from estate tenants of the 1920's to the 1950's insist that it was the norm for the lake to freeze each year. It is said to have been the focal point for many winter sports, including 'cricket-on-ice'!

***

Uncorroborated stories are told of parties, hosted by the earl and countess – also by his sisters – being held in the uninhabited Clumber House during the mid-nineteen thirties. Attended by eminent personages, including royals, the guests are said to have arrived in streams of cars, some with blinds covering the windows. It is a fact that the nearby country club at Firbeck was a northern entertainment Mecca (boasting the famous Charlie Kunz as house pianist) for the young aristocracy, with lords and their ladies flying in there to enjoy Yorkshire and Nottinghamshire hospitality. Allowing for exaggeration – and wishful thinking – it is a fact that members of the earl's social set would call at Clumber. It is less likely that they would be entertained in the mothballed, unheated and uninviting mansion – its decaying grandeur emphasised by a lack of new paint since 1920. Now, there was only a caretaker present and it was declared by the L.F.G. directors as: "not available for visitors or hospitality".

WELL-FOUNDERED RUMOURS & A NEW INTEREST

In June 1936, Lord and Lady Lincoln sailed to America for a holiday on board the Cunard White Star liner 'Franconia'. On their return, some servants and tenants became perturbed when well-founded rumours of matrimonial friction abounded. There was also major concern that the countess had referred to Clumber House as: "that Victorian Mausoleum!"

It was soon after this that Lord Lincoln joined the newly-formed 609 Squadron of the Auxiliary Air Force at Yeadon. The squadron's first commanding officer was Harald Peake (later, Air Commodore Sir Harald, Director of the Auxiliary Air Force) a friend of the Lincoln's and leaseholder of the Newcastle property at Lound Hall from March 1935. Flight Lieutenant Lord Lincoln was almost immediately installed as Peake's Auxiliary Adjutant. He rapidly earned a reputation for administrative skills and hard-working habits.

CLUMBER CHAPEL, A CASUALTY OF THE MID-1930's

The Chapel had been the cause of much time-consuming paperwork since the seventh duke died. The problems occupied the attentions of the long-serving Chaplain, Father Hawkins; the Vicar of Worksop, Canon d'Arcy; the eighth duke; Lord Lincoln and the solicitors of the Trustees. It was decided that the Chaplaincy should be abolished and Father Hawkins was given three months notice in February 1931. This action came as a major blow to him, as he believed that he had the job for life. A pension of £200 a year was offered and he protested that this would not be enough to live on.

Figure 131 –
Father Hawkins, in happier days, enjoying the sunshine in Clumber Park's Parsonage garden.

With no increase in salary during his thirty years at Clumber, nor any entitlement to fees for weddings etc., he had no other income and few savings. The pension offer was later augmented by £50. This was not a big drain on the estate, as Father Hawkins – having taken a chaplaincy in Scotland – died in September 1934. Kathleen, Dowager Duchess attended his funeral along with twenty-nine other old friends from the Park.

Canon d'Arcy's chief concern was that he did not believe that anyone had the right to exclude him, as Vicar of Worksop Parish, from decisions relating to the recruitment or removal of clergy at any of the places of worship under his care. There was also the question of finance. There had been a workable compromise on the subject of distribution of the Chapel collections whilst the seventh duke was alive. In lieu of collections and fees, an initial figure of £30 a year towards the 'Curates Fund' had been agreed in the early 1890's. This had been increased to £150 over the intervening forty years. With only £48 in the Chapel collections in the full year June 1928 to May 1929, there was hardly enough monies to warrant a further increase. Nevertheless it became a bone of contention. The solicitors to the Trustees indicated that, with up to £40,000 death duties to concern them, they had little time to spare for the Vicar's protests. It was acknowledged that the Chapel lay in the Parish of Worksop and – as a private House Chapel – was described as a 'Chapel of Ease' – but the Trustees pointed out that the Chapel had never been consecrated, merely 'dedicated'. This distinction was claimed to have prevented it coming under the usual ecclesiastical jurisdiction – and the dreadful possibility of it being a: "public right of way"!

As a temporary arrangement, the Rev. Cowgill from Shireoaks conducted services from the winter of 1931. He shared the duties with curates from the Worksop Priory: "who are young enough to use bicycles to travel the eight miles round trip and should not require taxis"! Also to be considered was the Sacristan, James Burden, who had lodged at the Parsonage for twenty-seven years – he was eventually housed in one of the Stableyard cottages.

There then followed greater (albeit abortive) attempts to fill the chaplaincy. These efforts were floundering on the problem of: "small stipend [and] insecurity of tenure" – respectively £300 a year and based on a six months' contract. In an attempt to solve the problems, the duke travelled north from Surrey to meet Canon d'Arcy and agreed an additional £200 contribution towards the cost of a curate. This assistance was increased to £400 from October 1934 when the Rev. G. L. Woodhouse took over as chaplain. He was housed in Hardwick Grange – where Sunday School classes were also held – and stayed there until his retirement in April 1936.

Almost inevitably, other problems involved 'high' and 'low' church arguments, including the style and content of hymn books to be used, as well as queries over the use of vestments and other ceremonial features which had long been the pride and joy of services at the Chapel. The 'Clumber Hymnal', having been in use since 1896, was now exchanged for 'Hymns Ancient and Modern'. This apparently innocuous change caused considerable upset, as the High Church tradition of Clumber's own hymnal was thought by traditionalists to be a prerequisite for their worship. Father Hawkins, 'high' priest-in-charge since the mid-1890's, had departed and there was no other local champion found to forcibly lead the protest. "Lean neither to the Presbyterian nor to Rome" was the optimistic advice of Major Kenneth Murray-Walker, Chief Agent of the estate since 1931.

During 1933 electricity was provided at Clumber from the Worksop mains supply. The Mansion and Parsonage having now been fitted with this new utility and the old lighting plant dismantled, an extension of the supply to the Chapel was a major enhancement in the following year. Prior to this, only the vestry had been supplied with electricity from the estate's private plant. Estate families raised £41.10s towards the cost of extending illumination to the body of the chapel and the L.F.G. directors accepted Lord Lincoln's proposal that the exterior of the Chapel should be lit by: "hidden flood lights". Repairs to the Chapel's heating apparatus followed, having been operating fitfully since its installation in 1889.

The organist, Leslie Rupert Pike, was still in charge of music at the Chapel, as he had been for sixteen years. He had married Ivy Beattie, daughter of a previous farm bailiff, and they and their daughter lived in the cottage of the late Mr Tredaway. Mr Pike carried out all minor repairs to the forty-year-old organ, and nursed his choir of estate residents – how times had changed! Annual outings to Skegness continued and the choir sent their grateful thanks to the Newcastle Trustees for the financial assistance given, but by early 1936 Mr Pike was having trouble filling choir vacancies. The numbers of men and boys living in the Park had dwindled and it was also the time when the latest chaplain left and the L.F.G. directors made the major decision to close the Chapel. It is thought provoking that this magnificent place of worship then became a furniture store – although many art treasures were also housed at the Nottingham Castle Museum. Lord Lincoln arranged that a bus would be available each Sunday morning to take estate residents to Worksop, where they attended St. Anne's or the Priory Church services on alternate weeks.

MISCELLANEOUS HAPPENINGS

The Village School was destroyed by fire in 1936 and following this the children under eleven years were taught in the 'Oratory'. Their teachers were Miss Violet C. Havelock and Miss Winifred Turfit. Miss Havelock lived in the cottage on the north end of the Schoolmaster's House and the Turfit's at Manton Lodge. At eleven years some of the children went to school in Worksop.

Figure 132 – The final days for Hardwick's fire-damaged village school.

A Memorial Plaque to the memory of the seventh duke was placed in the Chapel in February 1935. By June of the same year, two of the duke's sisters had died – Lady Beatrice Lister-Kaye and Lady Florence Pelham-Clinton. Agnes Kidd, the retired Housekeeper, and Randolph Hile, Clerk of Works for fourteen years were amongst the estate staff who died in that year. Mr Hile was succeeded by Mr William J. Love. Clumber's postmistress, Mrs Mary Alcock, mentioned earlier as the first to fill this position in Clumber Park, died in 1940 and the widowed Mrs Emily Hile (now fifty years old and on a weekly pension of thirty shillings [£1.50p]) agreed to be in charge of the village Post Office. Estate workmen built an extension onto an end-terrace cottage at Hardwick and Mrs Hile and her children moved in there. Little did she realise that she would be in that job until the 1980's!

***

It was in the mid-1930's that the lakeside flagpole was taken down. A feature of Clumber over many generations, some seventy feet high and almost three feet thick, it was floated down to the Hardwick workshops where woodsmen sawed it up as useful timber.

Also cut were the numbers of gardening staff. Samuel Barker, the long-serving Head Gardener, was retired from full-time duties at the end of 1935. His thirty-six years at Clumber had not been without incident. An independent spirit had not endeared Sammy to the Agent, whose attitude can be deduced by the wording of his 1928 Report to the duke. In this, Mr Elliott described Mr Barker as a: "first rate gardener" but made it clear that he would be strongly against the gardener taking the Gardens over as a commercial undertaking. Elliott hinted at Barker's unwillingness to follow instructions – such as a marked reluctance to stop showing the garden's produce for cash prizes, which for around ten years had appreciably supplemented his annual wages of £180. Just three years after this report, the Agent was probably less than amused to receive an enquiry from the Royal Horticultural Society about Mr Barker. This was in connection with their 'Lennox Cup' award of October 1931. Awarded for: "the most meritorious display of fruit staged by an *amateur*", it had been won by Clumber's Head Gardener! Some suspicion must have lurked in the mind of the R.H.S. administrators when they sent this enquiry, which merely asked for an explanation of Mr Barker's status on the estate. The Agent was not able to bend the truth and the gardener was no doubt informed that (as a professional gardener) his hopes of receiving the cash prize and the trophy had been dashed!

Tenants were now commenting that the once glorious gardens were no longer being maintained to their previous high standards. It was proposed to reduce the area of gardens and number of glasshouses. A suggestion that two tennis courts be provided on land at the Gardens indicates the changed circumstances. Scotsman William 'Bill' Taylor moved into the head gardener vacancy but transferred to the Marquis of Tweesdale's estate after just two years. He was replaced by greenhouse foreman Fred McLeod who was to stay until the start of the Second World War.

The turbines of the Clumber House water supply – and consequently, those of the Parsonage – were reluctantly renewed, at a cost of £2,100. Apart from the normal requirements of any residence of this size, the two hydraulic lifts within the house were both water-powered, as were the Chapel organ bellows. Since the 1880's, the water had come from a shallow well, about twenty-four foot deep, and situated near Clumber Bridge. A pump-driven turbine – possibly built on the site of an old grotto – had raised the water to a 60,000-gallon brick reservoir near to the Paddocks. There had been constant complaints about the fluctuating water pressure and a plan to pipe water from the Elkesley pumping station was instigated. It was when estimates had been obtained that the absentee eighth duke was moved to ask why the supply should have: "so suddenly" proved deficient! In his view, un-necessary improvements in connection with the mansion were not in line with his longer-term intentions for the Estate.

The Hardwick village water supply was condemned at this time. The thirty-foot well in front of Hardwick Grange had supplied the village for around fifty years. Generated by a turbine from the lake, an electric motor had pumped the supply to a 4,500 gallon elevated water tower situated near the old kennels. From there the pipes fed through to the twenty-five room Grange, the farm buildings and fields as well as to the kennels. The cottages Sawmill and School had also depended on this facility. From the early 1930's, Clumber House's reservoir was linked to the estate village piping and the old system disbanded. Outlining dwellings, such as South Lodge, The Avairies, Truman's Lodge, Manton Lodge and Clumber Cottage continued to obtain water from their own wells. Carburton Lodge was supplied from the Welbeck Estate.

Farm Bailiff Padget left Hardwick farm in July 1932, and was replaced by Mr J. R. Cobb who (on a wage of £3.10s per week) became Clumber's last bailiff. Four years later Mr Cobb moved to Grove, near Retford. He was followed at Hardwick by William Pringle from Macmerry, in East Lothian, Scotland. Making a big impression when he arrived at Clumber Park in his brown coloured Rolls Royce – registration number UL 78 – Mr Pringle was to be the Park's tenant farmer at a rent of £275 per annum. The days of a ducal Home Farm complete with bailiff were well and truly over for Clumber.

Figure 133 – Helen and William Pringle with their son, William (who had recently been released from a Prisoner of War camp) – 1945

MOVING TOWARDS THE FINAL DECADE AS A DUCAL ESTATE

The end of this unsettled period in the life of the duchy is marked by a general lack of direction. There is no sign of any commitment to a plan of recovery. No records have been found as to meetings of heads of departments, a feature of the days of the seventh duke. All evidence points to liquidation intentions for the whole of the Nottinghamshire properties – other than mineral rights. The eighth duke was becoming increasingly unwell, his only visits to Clumber being to see his son and daughters. There is no indication that he took a lead in re-establishing the Newcastle's fortunes and he appears to have been content to leave all monetary matters to the Trustees and Directors of the L.F.G. His son's marriage was coming under increasing tension and a suitable location for a smaller 'Clumber House' was not being enthusiastically pursued.

Figure 134a (below) –
Charlie Read – chauffeur – with 'Rita'.

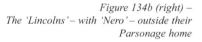
Figure 134b (right) –
The 'Lincolns' – with 'Nero' – outside their
Parsonage home

The cold and empty shell of the mansion was a reminder of better days. Gone were almost all the House servants. The art treasures, furniture and library contents had been stored away. Although the terraces and parterres were still tended and several of their flower beds trimly cut out in the shape of the Maltese Cross, their glory days were over. The three fountains that had added sparkle to the terraces for over one hundred years were switched off. Public visits had ceased. Gone was the noise and bustle associated with the vast stableyard. The fate of the estate was soon to be sealed and the Earl of Lincoln's thirtieth birthday was to be a crucial milestone in this story of the House of Clumber.

Figure 135 –
Clumber House, Terraces, Chapel, Stableblock and Kitchen Gardens– circa 1936.

CHAPTER EIGHT

1937–1946

A smaller Clumber House to be built? – Coronation 1937 – Clumber Sales – The 'Chantry' – Preparations for War – Clumber House came tumbling down – Lord Lincoln's Tenancy Agreement – Plans for a new sawmill and workshops – The sale of the Nottingham Park estate – War declared, access to Clumber Park restricted – The arrival of the Military – 'Colonel Warden' meets 'Nellie' – Lord Lincoln became the last duke to live at Clumber – Clumber residents join the war effort – A few of the ninth duke's exploits – Clumber Park saw action from the air – The gates were definitely opened! – The final party provided by a duke a Clumber – A Crucial Decision and a few of the Consequences.

A SMALLER CLUMBER HOUSE TO BE BUILT?

AS PREVIOUSLY NOTED, neither the eighth duke nor his son had any desire to live in the Mansion. Lady Lincoln undoubtedly did not wish to occupy the huge residence and, as a childless couple, the Lincoln's did not need the space! The market had already been tested and only one tentative enquiry had been received as to a short-term lease period for Clumber House – this from the Earl of Southampton. The initial query was not followed up by the enquirer and no other prospective tenants or buyers were found, even when the mansion was offered along with its associated cottages at Hardwick.

In 1931 the duke had written that it was: "unlikely that Clumber would ever be a private residence again". Despite their snug arrangement at Clumber's Parsonage, the Lincoln's were keen to have a completely new house built. Favoured sites were therefore short-listed – consisting of those near Woodcock Hill, Cow Pasture field, Cabin Hill, Ash Tree Hill Wood and Ice House Hill. All sites had their merits but the first, between Woodcock Hill and Coronation Plantation, was the one that the eighth duke recommended to his son. Its chief attraction was that it lay in a part of the Park northwest of Lime Tree Avenue. At that time, the duke was of the opinion that a new boundary of a smaller park might be set along the line of the Avenue and the northern area sold off. The plan for this new house – £15,000 was the decreed maximum – was short-lived. It was doomed when a discovery was made that the chosen site was on a line of possible subsidence from the Manton Colliery workings.

The London and Fort Land Company then took a decision to allocate an 'absolute maximum' of £30,000 for a replacement house at Ash Tree Hill Wood, near the Lake arm. The Ash Tree Hill position overlooks the Lake roughly halfway between the Chapel and Hardwick village. Trees were cleared and the area pegged out but nothing came of this either. Other sites were also explored and discarded. The costs of providing utilities to these isolated sites were a main factor in the repeated postponement of a decision.

The search for the ideal site went on for several years and, in October 1937 – when the sales of the art treasures and library contents of Clumber House were well underway – the duke wrote:

> My son has been staying with me for a few days and I have had the opportunity of talking over his proposals as to the future of Clumber, **and the question of where he is going to live now that the House is [to be] dismantled**. His scheme is comprehensive and I think that the conclusions that he has arrived at are thoroughly sound. I have all along suggested that an effort should be made to get away from what I call the ducal atmosphere which pervades the place, and I think that his suggestion that the House and its surroundings should be left [evacuated] entirely will materially help to attain that end. There is a good deal to be said in favour of the site of Cabin Hill for a new house, but it will not matter if this is left over for future consideration.

Figure 136 – Lord Lincoln (on the left) with the Clerk of Works and others. They are seen here examining the Ash Tree Hill site, one of the proposed locations for a new Clumber House.

Four months later, at a meeting of Executors and Trustees, the minute writer noted:

> Proposed new house for the Earl of Lincoln – The Earl of Lincoln to report that he had, after
> careful consideration, decided that the site of the proposed new house Cabin Hill was not
> suitable and that he had definitely selected a site at Ice House Wood and to produce sketch
> plans for the proposed new house and give approximate figures as to the probable cost.

Ice House Hill lies to the west of the Mansion site and, with the felling of certain trees to the south, would enjoy a magnificent view of the Lake, the Bridge and the Cascade. In May 1938, Lord and Lady Lincoln were involved with the planning on this project and had sketch plans drawn. Agreement had been reached that a 'pillar' would be left under the new house site for when, and if, the coal workings extended there from Manton Colliery.

The earl confirmed to the Trustees that the building of the new house would mean that the planned demolition of the Clumber mansion should go ahead. However, this was to be the year when his marriage problems reached crisis point and the subject of a new house took a poor second place.

<h2 style="text-align:center">CORONATION 1937</h2>

Figures 137 & 138 – Lord Lincoln (in his A.A.F. uniform) stands alongside the Throne, awaiting his moment to present the Worksop Glove to the monarch, King George VI.

During the spring of 1937, in the midst of all the insecurity of the Lincoln's marriage and the future of the estate, the earl and countess received an invitation to the Coronation of George VI. Lord Lincoln, recently appointed as a Deputy Lieutenant of Nottinghamshire, was present on the 12th of May close to the centre of the ceremony in Westminster Abbey wearing his Auxiliary Air Force uniform. In the absence of his father due to ill-health, he was there to represent the Trustees of the estate, who were now, strictly, Lords of the Manor of Worksop. As mentioned in earlier chapters, for almost four hundred years this title had carried with it the privilege of presenting a glove for the new monarch's right hand. The Court of Claims had spent much time in considering the matter but had finally ruled in favour of the Trustee's claim. An urgent search was then made at Clumber for the glove used at the previous coronation in 1911, before it was realised that King George V – not unreasonably – had retained it. A new one was commissioned from Messrs Harborows of New Bond Street, London, glove makers to the Queen, at the cost of £36.15s. This was unfortunate for the mayor of Woodstock, a town with a tradition for glove manufacture, who had written to the trustees just too late, requesting that his celebrated local craftsmen be allowed to create such a glove for the presentation.

The 166 residents of the Clumber estate were not to be deprived of a coronation party! Saturday, 15th May 1937 saw a cricket match between the Clumber team and a police team. A sandwich lunch was provided for all and the festivities centred on a marquee erected close to the cricket ground.

Figure 139 – Charlie Favill maintained high standards at the cricket ground.

The events – including a fancy dress parade for the children – were enjoyed by all and the highlight of the entertainment was a rendition of 'Home, Home on the Range', with Lord Lincoln playing firstly the ukulele and secondly, the guitar. Tenant Gilbert Holdsworth led the singing and each of the estate families received an engraved glass ashtray to mark the occasion.

CLUMBER SALES

Overlapping with the search for a new house, Lord Lincoln was very uneasy that government legislation relating to the nationalisation of royalties on minerals was certain to diminish estate income by some £6,000 a year.

Another echo of his father's situation some forty years earlier was that Lincoln proposed that the executors and trustees allow him to sell family treasures. The minutes of the meeting in November 1936 give little sign of demur. Provided that he waited until his thirtieth birthday in the following April, and he left untouched the pictures which were at the Nottingham Castle Museum – or were at Clumber but of family interest, and that he did not sell the family jewels! – this proposal was accepted.

Following this decision little time was wasted! From June 1937 – three months after the earl's thirtieth birthday – he was formally granted a tenancy agreement on Clumber House. Christie's and Sotheby's personnel began to hold auction sales in London and at Clumber. Christie's sold the art treasures and furniture, and Sotheby's the Library contents. Sales went on over several days and, from the vantage of upper galleries around the Grand Hall, servants and estate staff watched the auctions sadly and silently. There were many similar events being organised throughout the country at this time, those at Rufford Park being the closest example, which meant that (apart from the general economic situation) it was not to be a good time to hold such dispersals of assets. Nevertheless, buyers from several continents attended, bid and bought items.

Christie's records indicate that several pieces did go more locally. A number of them found their way to the home of socialist millionaire, Mrs Violet Van der Elst, newly-established at Harlaxton Manor, near Grantham. Amongst her purchases were two marble lions – from the eastern steps of Clumber's terraces – to flank the fountain at her new home. A Mr Manvers bought several pieces of statuary, including the Westmacott statue of 'Euphrosyne' (£115). Thomas Bank's exquisite 'Thetis dipping the infant Achilles in the River Styx' was bought for just £80 and later gifted to the Victoria and Albert Museum (where it can still be viewed). The pairs of 'Dancing Children' were relocated at Harewood House to embellish the terraces there. Other precious objects went to museums around England and Europe. The highest price paid for any single item was a stunning £13,500 for a particularly fine French Illuminated Book. Hogarth's painting, 'Southwark Fair', sold for £3,045 and Gainsborough's 'A Woodland Scene' for £3,150.

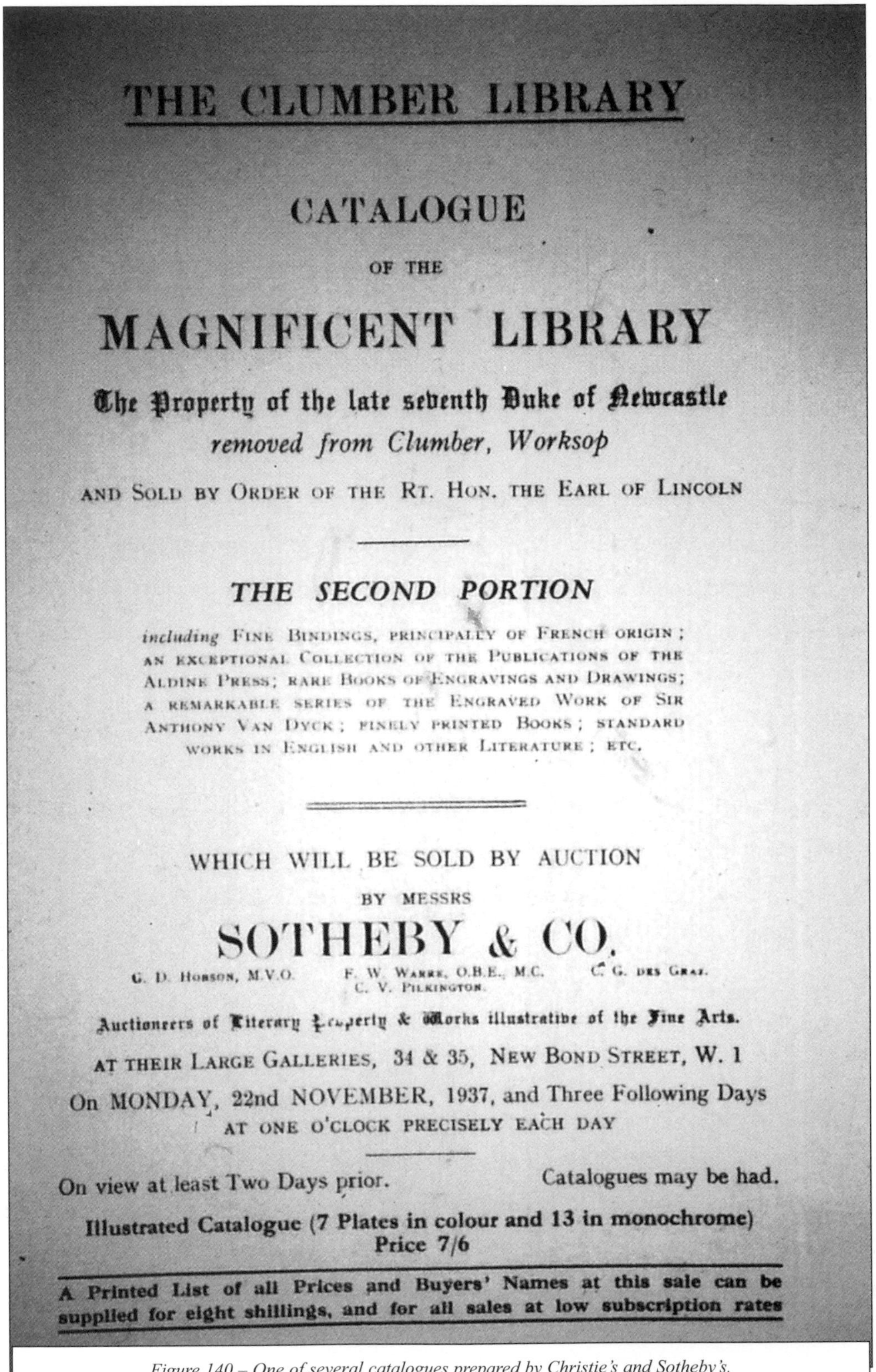

THE CLUMBER LIBRARY

CATALOGUE

OF THE

MAGNIFICENT LIBRARY

The Property of the late seventh Duke of Newcastle

removed from Clumber, Worksop

AND SOLD BY ORDER OF THE RT. HON. THE EARL OF LINCOLN

THE SECOND PORTION

including FINE BINDINGS, PRINCIPALLY OF FRENCH ORIGIN ;
AN EXCEPTIONAL COLLECTION OF THE PUBLICATIONS OF THE
ALDINE PRESS ; RARE BOOKS OF ENGRAVINGS AND DRAWINGS ;
A REMARKABLE SERIES OF THE ENGRAVED WORK OF SIR
ANTHONY VAN DYCK ; FINELY PRINTED BOOKS ; STANDARD
WORKS IN ENGLISH AND OTHER LITERATURE ; ETC.

WHICH WILL BE SOLD BY AUCTION

BY MESSRS

SOTHEBY & CO.

G. D. HOBSON, M.V.O.   F. W. WARRE, O.B.E., M.C.   C. G. DES GRAZ
C. V. PILKINGTON.

Auctioneers of Literary Property & Works illustrative of the Fine Arts.

AT THEIR LARGE GALLERIES, 34 & 35, NEW BOND STREET, W. 1

On MONDAY, 22nd NOVEMBER, 1937, and Three Following Days
AT ONE O'CLOCK PRECISELY EACH DAY

On view at least Two Days prior.   Catalogues may be had.

Illustrated Catalogue (7 Plates in colour and 13 in monochrome)
Price 7/6

A Printed List of all Prices and Buyers' Names at this sale can be
supplied for eight shillings, and for all sales at low subscription rates

Figure 140 – One of several catalogues prepared by Christie's and Sotheby's.

On offer at a later date were fifty lots of residual furniture and works of art, plus statues and mantelpieces. The latter proved to be the chief attraction, especially the chimneypiece from the Red Drawing Room, which fetched £250. A marble mantelpiece by Thomas Banks also reached almost the same sum, this one from the Yellow Drawing Room, displaying two male figures playing musical instruments, connected by a frieze of foliage and a bas-relief running across the lintel.

The fourth duke's notable Carrera copy of (reputedly) Franzoni's statue of Napoleon, depicting him as a Roman Emperor, attracted the non-too-princely sum of £220, £42 less than it cost in 1823! Magnificent cut-glass chandeliers were sold, the large one from the State Drawing Room attracting £410. Twenty-six bronze model cannon – plus cannon balls – from the 'Lincoln' frigate and lakeside Battery fetched just £72. [*In May 2003 two of these guns sold for £7,000 at a sale in Salisbury, Wiltshire!*] In all, the net proceeds from the Clumber sales were reported as £106,566.14s.2d. Many pieces of the Clumber House furniture and carpeting, which had not been offered for sale, were stored in the Chapel and the Duke's Study and remained there throughout the war. The most valuable pieces – including six crates of porcelain – were hidden from view by piling lesser quality items on top. Other hideaways included the staff billiard room (now better known as the Clumber Park Clocktower Shop) – and even R.A.F. Cranwell!

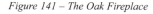
Figure 141 – The Oak Fireplace

Another impressive item was a notable oak chimneypiece, which was bought by the Nottinghamshire County Council with the intention of it being installed in the new County Hall at West Bridgford. This was decorated with the coats of arms of all the schools, colleges and universities attended by many generations of the Newcastle dynasty. The war having delayed the construction of the County Hall, the fireplace was put into storage. On inspection at the end of the nineteen-forties it was found to be infested with woodworm and was declared un-usable for its intended purpose.

Figures 142 & 143 – Two of the many items sold in the 1937 sales.

THE CHANTRY

Since the Chapel choir had been disbanded in 1928, the 'Hostel' had been used to house the Hardwick farm baliff. The baliff had then returned to the Grange Farmhouse and the 'Hostel' stood empty for some time. During late 1937 the building was used as a store for those items that had not reached their reserve price in the year's sales. In the winter of 1938, the 'Hostel' was splendidly refurbished and nostalgically re-named as 'The Chantry'.

In the winter of 1938, over £2,000 was spent on improvements, under the direction of the new tenants, Major and Mrs Kenneth Murray-Walker, who had moved there after living for several years in Clumber Cottage. Almost every room underwent a refit and a new garage was provided on land where the Village School had once stood. Major Murray-Walker (born in South Africa in 1894) was both Chief Estate Agent and Secretary to the Trustees. He had previously worked on the Duchy of Cornwall estate and the Inverlochy estate in Scotland. It was an example of the continuing high standing of this

Figure 144 – Major Kenneth Murray-Walker.

senior member of staff that he was allocated a car, with a chauffeur/handyman, 'Reggie' Weeks. His other staff included Mrs Richardson the cook, her daughter, 'Cissy', who was employed as the parlourmaid and Janet Storrs of Tank Cottage, the nurserymaid.

PREPARATIONS FOR WAR

Early in 1938, when the national preliminaries to war were being orchestrated, Clumber householders were assembled in the Oratory-cum-Village Hall at Hardwick and addressed by Lord Lincoln on the topic of 'Air Raid Precautions'. Following the meeting, arrangements moved on apace for recruitment into the wartime voluntary sector. A schedule was drawn up of the one hundred and sixty-six adults living on the Estate. Wardens, Fire Service personnel, First Aiders, Special Constables, Patrolmen and Drivers were required.

A supplement to the 'Worksop Guardian' newspaper records appointments including the Head Air-Raid Warden as William Pringle, farmer at Hardwick with other qualified Wardens such as Messrs. Charles Bond, the Butler/Valet who was living at Cricket Ground Cottages. Also listed are H. Harding, of Hardwick Terrace; Fred McLeod, the new head gardener; Barratt Stanhope who lived at the Aviaries and George Thompson of New Cottages, Hardwick. Sydney Brown of Tank Cottages became a Special Constable. They were all issued with their registration cards, rattles, whistles, eye-shields, respirators, armlets, gloves, boots, trousers and jackets, curtains, lamps, stirrup-pumps and hand bells.

Several men of the estate volunteered to set up the Clumber Park Auxiliary Wartime Fire Service. Their duties were: "to deal with forest and other fires which may be caused by enemy action" and the training was provided by professionals at Worksop Fire Station. The latter were able to contact the Clumber volunteers by means of a specially-installed telephone, fixed in the home of Leading Fireman Harold Storrs at Tank Cottages. At long last the estate was provided with a fire engine, which was housed in a specially erected garage near the Hardwick Terrace cottages – how delighted the seventh duke would have been that his duchy did not have to finance it!

On-site training for first-aid volunteers was provided by the school-mistress, Miss Violet C. Havelock. For the Wardens and their deputies, early morning secret film shows were on offer at the Regal Cinema in Worksop.

CLUMBER HOUSE CAME TUMBLING DOWN!

Whilst the worries of another war brought gloom to all inhabitants of the Park, the redundant yet magnificent Clumber House stood empty and forlorn. The die had been cast and its fate was irrevocably sealed. On 25th May 1938, the readers of the 'Manchester Guardian' were amongst the first members of the general public to learn of: "the End of a Famous Mansion". The newspaper report stated that an authoritative source had informed them that it was all due to 'heavy taxation'. They had also heard of the plans to erect an alternative dwelling: "two or three hundred yards from the site of the present house" (on Ice House Hill). Whether or not 'taxation' was the sole reason and whether or not a new, smaller, house was to be built, the Parsonage was considered capable of being extended and improved for Lord Lincoln's foreseeable needs.

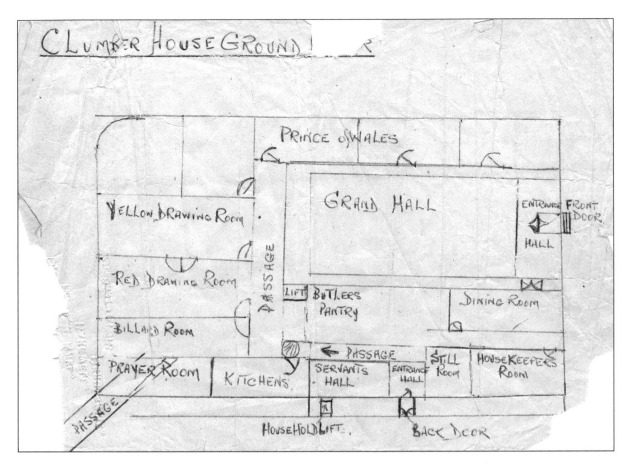

Figure 145 – Plan of the Clumber mansion's ground floor in the mid-1930's.
Sketch prepared by Thomas William Barratt Stanhope, the last of the 'House Joiners' to work at Clumber.
Son of a Clerk of Works, 'Barratt' was born in Clumber in February 1905 and died in February 2001

Two days prior to the 'Manchester Guardian's item, one of the most dramatic moments of the Clumber story began. Foreman George Easter and a handful of his men arrived from Norwich, in the green lorries of Harry Pointer's firm, to begin the final stages of demolishing the House. The firm's business was in purchasing buildings for demolition and then selling off the materials to achieve their profit. They had first been to the site in early March, carefully removing some of the most saleable items. After a few weeks the Clumber Agent had asked them why it was taking them so long. In reply, Pointer's men remarked that they had found at least twenty-five per cent more material than had been anticipated. They reported: "very thick walls, of extraordinary proportions, the majority averaging three feet in thickness – twice as thick as ever expected".

Figure 146 –
Clumber's Grand Hall standing empty, awaiting the
demolition men.

Figure 147 –
In the Library, the cupboards are bare.

Charles Boot of Thornbridge Hall, near Ashford-in-the-Water, Derbyshire (and partner of J. Arthur Rank in the development of Pinewood Studios, Buckinghamshire) had spotted the potential of much of the House material and arranged for his selected items to be removed first. He hired specialist shot-firers from the Manton colliery to supplement Pointer's men and they used minute explosive charges to separate the most valuable pieces. Estate tenants noted the care with which Mr Boot's men worked: "they even put down rubber tyres to protect items when they fell". He purchased much of the terrace statuary as well as the famous Italian white marble fountain (with the twelve feet six inch diameter lower basin and a column decorated with four dolphins that supported the four feet diameter upper bowl). The fountain had graced the lower terraces for just short of one hundred years. Mr Boot also bought a vast quantity of the balustrade from Clumber House roof and terraces. Magnificent panelling from the library, plus four Corinthian pilasters, marble fluted and jasmine coloured, all made their way to his Derbyshire home. One particularly distinctive item was the 'frontispiece' from the south-facing wall of the mansion. This was a large depiction of the ducal coat of arms, which had embellished the lakeside face of the House since the 1760's. Why Mr Boot wanted a 'Pelham-Clinton' crest remains a mystery.

***

Ten weeks after their first visit, Pointer's firm hired men from the labour exchange at Worksop and issued them with large sledgehammers. Starting on the north wing, they commenced reducing the House to its component, saleable parts, until the mansion was reduced to sad piles of materials and rubble. Eyewitness recollections of the event are vivid – particularly when describing the unwanted woodwork of the stately home being burnt on a beautiful summer's evening.

What the 1830's Reform Act rioters and the fires of 1879 and 1912 had failed to do was eventually achieved by October 1938 – the mansion's demolition was complete. Unfortunately for Pointers, this meant that the original time-scale for the demolition job had not been met and they were required to forfeit £85 of their agreed fees.

Figure 148 – The Demolition of Clumber House in progress, during the summer of 1938.

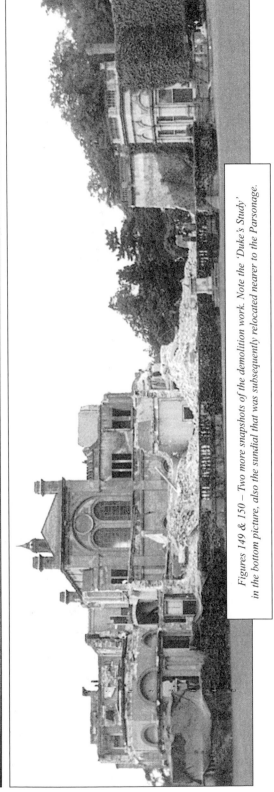

Figures 149 & 150 – Two more snapshots of the demolition work. Note the 'Duke's Study' in the bottom picture, also the sundial that was subsequently relocated nearer to the Parsonage.

Saleable materials had been stacked up outside the site of the West Door entrance and the firm of Henry Spencer's, Auctioneers, of Retford, were engaged to conduct sales, which began some four months before the demolition was finished.

Figure 151 – Wood, bricks and cladding stone awaiting the auction sales of 1938.
Figure 152 – Cover of Spencer's catalogue.

In his autobiography 'Drama at the Sale', Rupert Spencer mentioned that several electric lifts, architraves, elegant staircases and ceiling mouldings were on offer. The much envied sienna-rouge marble pilasters with Corinthian capitals from the Great Hall proved popular items, as did the magnificent mahogany panelling from the Library. Representatives of London buyers skilfully scraped off gold-leaf from the ceilings of the State Drawing Room and the boudoirs. At the lower end of the market, staircase treads, which led from the splendid Grand Salon to the Galleries, were sold at prices as small as 1/6d (7^{1}/2p) each. Five thousand tons of the white cladding stone (magnesium limestone from the Steetley quarries) was also for sale, in addition to half a million bricks. Brick maker, Mr J. McCarthy, of Thames Street, Bulwell, Nottingham, bought one thousand tons of the Steetley stone and some of the same material also went to a farm at Walkeringham.

One of the most recurrent 'Clumber' anecdotes heard in the North Nottinghamshire area over the last five decades has been that the demise of the House was due to a major fire. This is clearly incorrect and is probably due to exaggerations built on the factual reports of the burning of surplus wood, following the Spencer's sales. Another persistent fable is the one that proclaims Clumber House to have been dismantled stone by stone (each piece being numbered) and shipped to America. Those who have read this far will know better. The belief in the American rebuild may be connected to the reports that some of the cladding stone from the house was to be transported to the Liverpool Docks for shipment to America for purposes unknown. Some who remember these reports also recall that the stone did not in fact leave England, and that it was used to line the base of new or reconditioned waterways on Merseyside. The American dimension could relate to purchases from the various auctions of treasures, when transatlantic buyers acquired certain fixtures and fittings in addition to items from the Christies and Sotheby's sales. But, in connection with the sales of the house materials, the Retford auctioneers have been unable to assist with the details of any buyers. Relevant documents perished in a fire at their premises in the 1970's.

Newspaper reports and local historians in the Sheffield area have assisted in piecing together some details of the purchase of cladding stone and house bricks from the sales. The bricks, mostly manufactured at Bothamsall and Gamston brickworks in the 1760's, were identified as being ideal for a new purpose.

Parishioners of St Bernard's Anglican Mission Church, at Parson Cross, Sheffield were encouraged by their priest to purchase some 300,000 of Clumber's hand-made bricks, at one penny per brick. These were required in readiness for the building of a substantial new church, intended to replace their: "wood-and-paper" mission hut. Incidentally, the boys of the Clumber-connected Worksop College were at this time enthusiastically supporting the work of the mission at Parson Cross with money-raising events.

Canon Roseveare (one of the Kelham Fathers of the 'Society of the Sacred Mission') and his team planned to save over one thousand pounds by cleaning the bricks themselves on site. They undertook this task, but the bricks were never used for their intended project as the outbreak of the Second World War thwarted this plan. The bricks lay in ever-diminishing piles near the mission church throughout the war and, eventually, the remnants were used for hardcore.

LORD LINCOLN'S TENANCY AGREEMENT

From the 4th November 1937 a formal tenancy agreement had been drawn up to permit Lord Lincoln to lease and maintain some twenty-five acres of the Clumber estate at £225 per annum. The 'book value' of the property was £8,000 and included the parsonage, with the adjoining buildings, chapel, pleasure grounds (where the earl had constructed a golf practice hole with several sand bunkers), kitchen gardens, vinery, glass houses and frames, the head gardener's house, two cottages and seven lodges.

Situated in the melancholy shadow of the doomed mansion, the parsonage was less than an ideal place to live for most of the year 1938. The records are blurred as to where the earl and countess stayed whilst the dust settled. As the Agent had just moved into the 'Chantry', Clumber Cottage was vacant but (taking account of the unhappy state of the Lincoln's marriage) staying at his air force base would have been an obvious and attractive alternative for Lord Lincoln. At this time, the plan was that the demolition of the mansion and the building of the new house on Ice House Hill would be timed to coincide. This, it was thought, would limit the amount of construction traffic and general disturbance to the estate. The plan was doomed!

The Lincoln's moved back to the Parsonage in September 1938. Three months later, plans were drawn up for its enlargement, with the provision of five en-suite bedrooms, a study and new billiard room. In the event, no further alterations took place – their personal relationship was in terminal decline. Lady Lincoln recorded that 'I being utterly miserable; the situation was becoming unbearable and I decided I would leave … terribly lonely with no companionship with [my husband] and after seven years, I have become very nervous also, and on the verge of a breakdown'. She went to live in a penthouse flat in Westminster.

These marital difficulties led to divorce proceedings in October 1939 and during the following year a decree absolute was granted on the grounds of Lady Lincoln's misconduct. She married again at Easter, 1940 having been the latest to miss the opportunity of becoming a 'Duchess of Newcastle'.

***

Squadron Leader, the Earl of Lincoln, was appointed commanding officer of the newly formed Doncaster-based Number 616 (South Yorkshire) Squadron of the Auxiliary Air Force in November 1938. He had served with Number 609 (West Riding) Squadron at Yeadon since February 1936. With his first marriage dissolved and in the aftermath of the demolition of Clumber House, he spent most of his time living and working at the base, gaining a reputation for commitment to duty. He wrote to the vice-chancellor of Sheffield University soon after his new appointment to seek volunteer officers for his unit.

Lincoln (or 'Pelham' as he preferred to be called by his friends) then applied for his petrol-coupon rationing book, in order that he could travel to his wartime air force duties, driving his new 9HP Hillman Minx – registration FAU 59. In April 1939, following certification as qualified by a civilian flying club, he was awarded his flying badge. At the commencement of war, being an auxiliary officer, he was transferred to the General Duties Branch, posted firstly to Doncaster and later Hucknall, near Nottingham.

PLANS FOR A NEW SAWMILL AND WORKSHOPS

Clumber residents had gone about their business with only a passing interest in the matrimonial escapades of their noble landlord. Of greater significance to them was the provision of new sawmills and workshops at Hardwick in the spring of 1938. Almost two thousand acres of the Park had been leased to the Forestry Commission on a 999 years lease from Lady Day (25th March) of that year.

It was obvious that yet again the timber of the Park (still under the command of head forester Mr H. Palfrey) would be a highly-prized commodity during the forthcoming war. Joinery and other workshops had been in use since the mid-eighteen hundreds, and similar work had probably gone on for much longer around the Park. Detailed plans were drawn up for the new buildings. At a cost of £658.10s, these included integral cottages, garages and stables with lofts, creosoting and drying sheds, with a lock-up shed to enclose a stokehole for the creosoting tank. In addition to the sawmill unit, an office, mess room and two privies, several lean-to sheds and a garage for the steamroller were included. The Park was again poised for another war effort, but it was to be mainly local firms, rather than direct Newcastle employees, who would be involved in the work.

THE SALE OF THE NOTTINGHAM PARK ESTATE

In what can now be recognised as one of the most significant developments in the 'wind-down' of the Newcastle's presence in Nottinghamshire, the Nottingham Park Estate was sold for £297,500 on 8th March 1939.

It had been part of the Newcastle dukedom's properties since the seventeenth century. Always linked to the famous Castle, the land had moved from use as a deer park, cavalry barracks, bowling green and allotment gardens before its transformation to a prestigious (and mostly leasehold) housing development under the direction of the fourth and fifth dukes of the present title. Nottingham Park had been a consistent money-maker for the House of Clumber, frequently bailing them out when other holdings stumbled or fell.

The eighth duke encouraged this sale by his land company, and it was completed via the Nuffield Medical Trust and the Curators of the 'Oxford University Chest'. The purchase was part of one million pounds gifted by Nuffield for the development of medical education at Oxford University. It was to be the estate's last major land transfer for several years.

WAR DECLARED –
ACCESS TO CLUMBER PARK RESTRICTED

Shortly after the beginning of the Second World War in September 1939, special passes were issued to Park residents. A few months later a military presence was established there – at an initial annual rent of £400 – and army checkpoints were set up near the Lodges, Gatehouses and Clumber Bridge, where strict control was maintained on admissions.

***

Several people who have encouraged the writing of this story insist that we should not omit two memorable characters from this period. Herbert and Florence Fletcher – known to many as 'Ned and Flo' (and to others as 'Ebb and Flo') – were not easily deterred from wandering through Clumber Park during the war. No special passes were issued to them, but they pushed their precious belongings in a rickety old

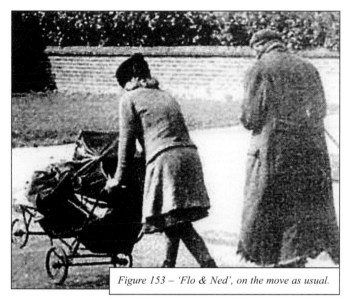

Figure 153 – 'Flo & Ned', on the move as usual.

pram wherever the mood took them. Florence had been a maid in the Fletcher household at Manton and she and Ned were married following his discharge from the forces at the end of the Great War. They had taken to tramping the roads – travelling as faraway as the London area – but always returning to the 'Dukeries' district of their home county. From a safe distance, children loved to make fun of them as they passed and were fascinated by the obscenities that were screamed back in their direction! Following Ned's death, Florence was befriended by the landlord of the King William public house in Worksop, who provided her with a room until her death in the mid-1970's.

***

Bus travel was arranged on two days each week for estate dwellers to be taken out of the Park. Wednesday was a special day, as it was market day in Worksop and the bus arrived to take the ladies shopping there. The return journey was timed to allow the shoppers to take lunch at the Cooperative Stores café. A bus was also provided on Sundays, to convey churchgoers to and from services at either St Anne's or Worksop Priory. With Clumber Chapel being closed, this catered for both 'low' and 'high' church preferences.

THE ARRIVAL OF THE MILITARY

For anyone who has served in the armed forces, or watched British wartime films, the following anecdote will come as no surprise! During the first months of the war, some 400 men of the Cheshire Yeomanry arrived at Clumber with instructions to use 'Clumber House' as their barracks. Astute readers will realise that this was a difficult order to obey! Evidently no one had updated the army records regarding the mansion's demolition and it caused more than a little derision from the soldiers concerned. Accommodation was ultimately found for them in the nearby village of Whitwell.

It was not going to be long before the residents of the estate were to find Clumber turned upside down as it took on its role of Number 24 Ammunition Sub-Depot ('A.S.D.'), Royal Army Ordnance Corps for the duration of the Second World War. Anti-aircraft gun bases and searchlight platforms were erected at Hardwick and vast quantities of deadly shells and other weapons of war were stored in Clumber Park. Each stack of 400 cubic feet was housed in an iron shelter constructed of 21 sheets of curved corrugated iron bolted together. Groups of these were situated around the Park (in particular along Lime Tree Avenue), where hundreds of these

Figure 154 – Unloading ammunition in Lime Tree Avenue, Clumber Park – where no unauthorised photography was allowed!

shelters filled peacetime picnic areas. Safety distances between each group of huts had been decreed by the War Office. The railway halt at Checker House, near Ranby, was enlarged to accommodate the needs of the supply trains, which carried the lethal stores to and from Clumber.

The Park was divided into the Northern and Southern zones. The North Zone ('Area Number 1') being administered from a temporary office base situated on the corner of Windmill Lane, just a hundred yards from Manton Lodge. The first nissen hut which housed this control unit proved too flimsy as it was blown down in high winds – with consequential panic as the papers containing details of the Park's secrets were scattered amongst the gorse and bracken! A second office was erected a few yards away but suffered the same fate! The third attempt incorporated the building of a four-foot high brick base on to which the hut was then lifted. This seems to have been a more successful project, although the facilities were rural in all senses. When a new Auxiliary Territorial Service (A.T.S.) clerk asked where the toilets were, she was directed: "out of the hut door, turn left, then right after fifty yards – then find the nearest tree!"

Various sectors of the Park held different ammunition. Deadly phosgene gas is said to have been stored in Clinton Wood, near Manton Lodge. A de-contamination unit was built close by, in Manton Wood. At the time of writing, the dilapidated building is still just about standing and (for several years) was inhabited by 'Albert', a man who was so much at home there that he had a clearly marked 'letter box'! Albert (who died early in 2003) told the author that the structure was the 'Canada Army Barracks'. Although no record has been found of the Canadians being at Clumber during the Second World War, readers will recall the comments made in Chapter Five regarding the presence of Canadian lumber-jacks during the Great War of two decades earlier.

A rail track was laid just a hundred yards from Manton Lodge on the road to Hardwick. This formed a semi-circle, which penetrated the depths of the woodlands called Clinton Wood. Low, flatbed type trucks were used to transport the ammunition to the separate storage areas, hidden from view. Trucks were pushed by hand, providing a task for members of the Pioneer Corps as well as prisoners of war. Other tracks were laid near Drayton Gate, alongside Clumber's border with the Thoresby estate, where there were large storage huts for newly-arrived ammunition.

Elsewhere there were other supplies of naval ammunition: "including some shells at least a metre high". Nissen huts abounded throughout the Park, some for living accommodation and others for mess huts. Women of the A.T.S. were billeted in the northwest rooms of the Stableyard quadrangle and drove trucks which carried ammunition and supplies to and from the railway stations. By 1943 British troops were being supplemented by German and Italian prisoners of war, brought in from their camps in Boughton; Carburton; Carlton Hall at Carlton-in-Lindrick; Nether Headon, near Retford; Norton Camp at Cuckney and the Proteus Camp in Thoresby Park.

Dispatch riders and army headquarters office staff were also based in the Stableyard accommodation. The 'Turning Circle' area in front of the west face of the Stableblock (where midsummer theatre performances now take place) was the site of two Nissen huts. These were the Park's central kitchen and dining mess areas. The Cricket Pavilion became the Medical Hut, where service personnel saw the Army doctor if they wished to 'report sick'.

Members of the Women's Land Army worked at the Grange Farm and in the Gardens. Some of them were provided with accommodation in the Garden's House, where a new bathroom and hot water supply were installed. Later, young people from Worksop College and the Doctor Barnardo's organisation also assisted with work on the estate, especially in the potato-picking times. By this time, efforts had been made to put the gardens on a purely commercial basis – in fact they made what was probably their first-ever annual profit in the year ending March 1942, when the accounts show a modest plus balance of £174!

The Village Hall at Hardwick became the venue for home-spun concerts. Mrs Ada Stanhope, ex-laundry maid, was a leading light in keeping spirits high with sketches and songs. Wednesday evening film shows at the Normanton Inn were an added wartime feature, with estate tenants as well as servicemen attending. The duke's garage (now the bike-hire centre) was adapted to use as a general meeting room. This was invariably cigarette-smoke filled when used for entertainment, such as concerts provided by the ENSA units (the 'Entertainments National Service Association' – affectionately distorted by the troops to: "Every Night Something Awful"!). Similar morale-boosting events were also held in a marquee alongside the Normanton Inn, these usually being Sunday night affairs attended by estate dwellers in addition to the armed forces personnel.

'COLONEL WARDEN' MEETS 'NELLIE'

A Company of Royal Engineers was also present in Clumber. Under the command of Major T. Whitehouse, and at their secluded camp west of Tank Cottages, secret experimental work was their responsibility. One of their foremost projects led to a very low-profile visit by a very high-profile personage.

Winston Churchill, under the alias 'Colonel Warden', paid a hush-hush visit to Clumber in November 1941 (there is a photographic record of this event in the Imperial War Museum, two of whose pictures are shown below). The Prime Minister's presence was to allow him to witness the trials of a prototype trench-digging tank, which he had championed. Built by the Lincoln firm of Ruston Bucyrus (with another three hundred and fifty firms involved in design and manufacture of various parts) the vehicle was initially called 'White Rabbit No.6' and later 'Cultivator No.6'. As the Ministry of Supply's N.L.E. (Naval Land Equipment) department controlled the design work, it was perhaps inevitable that the machine should become known as 'NELLIE'!

This formidable machine weighed some 130 tons, was 77 feet long and said to be capable of churning out 100 tons of earth per minute. The trench measurements were five feet deep and seven feet wide at the bottom. Although the trials went well, the War Cabinet's decision to have 240 of these monsters built was never implemented. Initial plans to power them with Merlin-Marine type engines were shelved when the needs of the Royal Air Force for these engines took priority. Alternative engines, adaptations and further trials took place at Clumber and elsewhere but the expensive project was finally jettisoned in May 1943. [*See Appendix Three*]

Figures 155 & 156 –
The Prime Minister, Winston Churchill,
inspecting 'Nellie', the trench-digging tank
that was being trialled in Clumber Park
during 1941.

Figure 157 – Major T. Whitehouse and his No. 2 Section of the 796 ME Company of Royal Engineers.
Several men of this Company were stationed close to Tank Wood in Clumber Park during 'Nellie's' secret trials.

LORD LINCOLN BECAME
THE LAST DUKE TO LIVE AT CLUMBER

Seven months prior to the Prime Minister's visit, the eighth duke died at Clumber. He had been staying at the Parsonage with his eldest daughter, Lady Doria, who had acted as his hostess since her second marriage had, in effect, ended in 1939. On 20th April 1941, the eight duke's body was placed in his coffin by men of the estate, including Charlie Favill, and Barratt Stanhope. These men thereafter enjoyed telling the tale of how they got a big surprise when the duke's foot 'fell off' whilst they were performing this last act for him! As he had lived away from Clumber since he inherited the title in 1928, the late duke was not well known to them and the amputation was not common knowledge.

He was buried at the Hope mausoleum in Surrey and his only son, Lord Lincoln, became ninth (and penultimate) Duke of Newcastle-under-Lyme. The new duke was away on operational duties in the Middle East at the time and could not attend his father's funeral. He was apparently indifferent to his elevated status, and never bothered to have his own Coat of Arms prepared.

Neither did he have any noble robes, nor attend the House of Lords. Inheriting the balance of his father's estate, including what was left of the Hope properties; he was able to live in comfort for the rest of his life.

As we have seen, his childless marriage had ended in divorce during 1940. His distant cousin, Edward [*Ted*] Charles Pelham-Clinton – descended on a family line from Lord Charles, son of the 4th Duke – became heir to the title, by accident of the death of Edward's elder brother. That was unless and until the new duke was blessed with a son and heir.

Figure 158 – the 9th duke in R.A.F. dress uniform

Whilst away, the new duke was firming up on a plan that would lead to the end of the Newcastle's duchy in the 'Dukeries' area. Personal factors, such as his recently ended childless marriage and his father's death – which was closely followed by the demise of Doria, his devoted sister, at the early age of thirty-four – were no doubt taken into account when reaching his major decision to move to a new life when the war ended.

Since the death of the seventh duke in 1928, it had been an open secret in the higher echelons of the estate that Clumber Park would not remain unchanged. The ninth duke was now making a crucial decision to move his duchy not only away from Clumber but also many miles from Nottinghamshire.

CLUMBER RESIDENTS JOIN THE WAR EFFORT

We noted earlier that nineteen out of fifty-seven men from the estate had died in combat during the Great War of 1914-1918 – now sons (and daughters) of Clumber Park families had again joined the armed forces. Unlike the situation at the beginning of the First World War there was not a large pool of trained volunteers ready and waiting for the call. As conscription laws were gradually being brought in, all the suitable under 27-year-olds had been registered by May 1940. Clumber's bothies were now sparsely populated, as many able-bodied single men, especially farm hands and gardeners, had received their call-up papers. In Mr Palfrey's Woods Department there were now only seven men employed in 'agricultural or woodlands' work, with just two sawyers and five others in a 'general labour pool'. The Repairs Department boasted twenty-five men, including drainers, building tradesmen and labourers, plus one lorry driver – remember those sixty men of 1904? Game Department staffing was down to three men, under the control of Mr W. Hawkins.

As we know, Lord Lincoln was one of the auxiliary airmen who had spent some years in training. At the beginning of hostilities he had been on hand to encourage the estate's young men to select the particular branch of the armed forces in which they would prefer to be conscripted. The earl was enthusiastically assisted in this task by his Agent, Major Murray-Walker. Jack Allison, David Harrington, Philip Hile, Reginald Pole and Arthur Simpson enlisted in the Royal Air Force. Allison and Harrington (both air-gunners) were shot down and killed. Reginald Pole also died. Army recruits included farm worker George Cobb who later died in a Japanese prisoner of war camp. George Read was killed in a bombing raid on London, his mother and sister then travelled by rail to the capital to escort his remains (which were wrapped only in a body bag, due to a lack of coffins) back to Worksop for burial. Royal Marine Cyril Tideswell (who had worked in the dowager duchess's kitchen at Forest Farm, near Windsor) was another fatality. Having been rescued after the sinking of H.M.S. Repulse, he died during the evacuation of Singapore, aged just nineteen. Cyril's brother, Norman, was luckier, although his missions were equally hazardous. Norman had joined the Territorial Army before the war, and had been enlisted in the 11th Scottish Commando and served in North Africa. From there he was selected to join the newly-formed Special Air Service (S.A.S.). One week before D-Day, he was behind enemy lines in Central Europe, assisting in wreaking havoc wherever the opportunity arose. Norman completed his war service unscathed.

Figure 159 – Norman & Cyril Tideswell

Others who served included Bob Allison, from the 'Aviaries', Kelly Howard, whose family lived in a Clumber Stableyard cottage, also Frank, Ralph and Ron Sissons. They and Ron Stanhope had many fascinating stories to tell.

Tales of war service by the Clumber ladies are perhaps less dramatic but no less poignant. Women with young children and those that were pregnant were exempt from war service under the 1941 conscription laws. They were busy enough with their enforced loneliness and separation from their husbands, enduring the tribulations of rationing systems and other deprivations. In other instances, many of the Clumber women were either too old or too young for military duties – some continued to work at home or on the land.

Two particular examples of women who were 'called up' were Janet Storrs and Veronica Sissons. Janet, a nurserymaid whose home was at one of the Tank Cottages, joined the Women's Auxiliary Air Force.

Veronica, of New Cottages, had married gardener Ron (shown below in his Royal Engineer's garb) and had then followed him into uniform. She served firstly as a Land Army worker on the Hardwick Farm and later as a policewoman in the Auxiliary Territorial Service.

Figures 160 & 161 – Ron and Veronica Sissons. After the war, Ron became Head Gardener at the Duke of Devonshire's property, Compton Place, Eastbourne.

'Cissy' Kelk (born in 1911), parlourmaid at the Agent's house, had to leave these duties and start work in the offices of a scrap firm in Sheffield. There, she was rather close to the action when a feared German 'dooglebug' passed overhead and landed in a nearby street with devastating results. Fortunately, 'Cissy' (now better known as Mrs Hilda Mary Favill) escaped injury and is still able to tell the tale.

Figure162 – 'Cissy' (second from the right) with family and friends. Ethel Jackson (wearing hat), is in the centre.
Ethel was famous at Clumber for her expertise in carnation propagation.
[This photograph was taken in Clumber's Walled Gardens – c.1932]

A FEW OF THE NINTH DUKE'S EXPLOITS

Following the duke's posting to duties in the Middle East in the early days of the war, he had returned to England and served at Digby, in Lincolnshire, where the legendary Guy Gibson recorded their first meeting: "The controller that night was the Duke of Newcastle, a Squadron Leader and a very likeable man. He was a good-looking man and I noticed that all the girls had quite an eye on him ..."

One young lady who certainly had her eye on him was Lady (Mary) Diana Montagu-Stuart-Wortley, second daughter of the 3rd Earl of Wharncliffe whose family home was Wortley Hall, South Yorkshire. Lady Diana was serving as a driver and dispatch rider with the Mechanised Transport Service. She had been engaged to famed fighter pilot and journalist (later 'Sir') Henry Dundas, who was a cousin of Newcastle's senior colleague, Air Commander Harald Peake, but this romance had ceased.

Figure 163 – Lady Diana
[National Portrait Gallery, London.]

Figure 164 – Wing Commander, His Grace, the 9th Duke.

The duke and Diana became engaged during the final years of the war and, whilst enjoying periods of leave from their respective duties, they often met at Clumber and took pleasure in the idyllic surroundings of the Park and its Lake, where boating was one of their favoured pastimes. At this time they were both moved on to other wartime postings. In the duke's case, he was firstly with Number 2 Group, Fighter Command and then sector controller at Henley and Biggin Hill, subsequently moving on to interception control at North Weald. Lady Diana was based in Yorkshire and later in the Cambridge area.

One of the duke's most noteworthy duties was as a Sector Commander during the Normandy landings. It was from a naval vessel in the English Channel that he had controlled his flight sector on 'D. Day' (6th June 1944). One month after that adventure he was the senior RAF officer on board a Signals and Radar Control Unit off Barfleur, when a torpedo blew up the craft from which he was operating. He was: "fished out of the Channel, dressed in an ordinary seaman's gear and very dirty ... was taken to Naval H.Q. in Portsmouth, where the C.-in-C., observing a figure resting in the sunshine on the grass outside his office, said ... : "What is that filthy object? Bring it in!" ... The "filthy object" was presented to him with the introduction: "[*Acting*] Wing-Commander His Grace the Duke of Newcastle, Sir"! Although his other 'special duties' have proved difficult to uncover, it is known that he was also a member of the liberating force in Norway during May 1945.

His contribution to the war effort was acknowledged in the form of a military OBE, which was awarded in the New Year honours list of January 1945. The recommendation for this award read:

> Squadron Leader [his substantive rank] The Duke of Newcastle proceeded, as Officer Commanding, Air Section, with the Assault Forces during the landings in Normandy on 'D' Day, in Fighter Direction Tender No. 216. By hard work and personal example, this officer welded the Royal Air Force personnel on board into a most efficient team, controlling British and American Fighter aircraft engaged in the Assault Area. The efforts of this team contributed largely to the success of the operation 'NEPTUNE'. Later, when this craft was torpedoed, it was due to Squadron Leader The Duke of Newcastle's splendid discipline and personal effort, that only small loss of life was sustained.

CLUMBER PARK SAW ACTION FROM THE AIR

The Park was the location for wartime incidents involving aircraft. Manned by volunteers from the estate, the Clumber Auxiliary Wartime Fire Service was called into action when a stray German plane dropped two firebombs on the area known as 'no-mans land', adjacent to the Normanton Inn. Fortunately, no ammunition pile was in the vicinity and the Park's secrets appear to have escaped discovery.

An incident arising from this chance bombing is recalled by one of the volunteer firemen, estate plumber George Merrills. Mr Merrills arrived at the scene to be met by a couple who had, without permission, been caravanning some short distance from the point where the bombs landed. They met him and his colleagues with the question: "could you tell us where the nearest air-raid shelter is please?" The answer – which may or may not have been offered to the trespassers! – was that there were three or four shelters around the Park, having been provided at a cost of some £260. One was in the sandstone area close to the 'Oratory'. This was a cave-like excavation, hung with hessian and crudely covered over with lengths of tree-trunks. Another was a more elaborate construction, a brick-built affair with a concrete base, close by 'New Cottages'. Clumber Cottage and the Paddocks also boasted similar structures. Locals recall the dank smells of these shelters and the wearing of gas masks whilst practising their air-raid drill.

More sombre aircraft incidents involved at least four crashes in the Park and several others nearby. In August 1943, a Wellington bomber took off from RAF Ingham, Lincolnshire, for operations on Hamburg but developed engine trouble, which resulted in a forced landing near to Truman's Lodge. The Polish crew were all injured and the aircraft burnt out. Anecdotal evidence states that the crew were pulled away from the burning wreckage by a group of poachers who were in the vicinity, but when the police and wardens appeared the poachers were arrested and the late-comers claimed credit for the rescue – this cannot possibly be true, or can it?!

Early in December there was a crash some two hundred yards south of the Newcastle Mausoleum near Milton which involved a Lancaster from 9 Squadron, RAF Bardney. Returning from a mission over Berlin, with fog and limited fuel adding to the urgency of landing, the pilot attempted to land firstly at RAF Ossington but overshot the runway. He flew on the short distance to RAF Gamston, near Retford, but was again unsuccessful in landing. All four engines then failed, the aircraft crashed and was completely destroyed, with at least five of the crew being killed and two seriously injured.

One evening in January 1944, a Wellington from RAF Worksop took off on a training flight and crashed at Forest Cottage, close by the farm lane north of Truman's Lodge. All five crew members were killed. The following April, another Wellington, whilst on a training run from RAF Ingham, carried out a forced landing near the Worksop-Ollerton Road entrance to the Park, causing injuries to five members of the crew. Just four months later, a Stirling EF200, from RAF Swinderby, near Lincoln, crashed into large trees at Double Clump near Hardwick due to engine failure when attempting to land at RAF Gamston. Five of the Canadian crew were killed and three injured. Yet three more lives were lost in February 1945 when a North American Mitchell bomber from RAF Fersfield, sixteen miles from Norwich, crashed near Clumber Cottage.

THE GATES WERE DEFINITELY OPENED!

On a lighter note, George Merrills – whose story of the caravanners and the air raid shelter was mentioned above – also recalled an incident that occurred near Truman's Lodge. A well-known sergeant-major stationed at Clumber (and known as 'Fire Jack') was taken by army truck into Worksop one night to visit his favourite public houses. On return, having enjoyed an 'elegant sufficiency' of the local ale, not only was the driver's vision impaired and the night dark, but the masked lights of the vehicle were barely adequate. 'Fire Jack' and the driver then had a friendly disagreement as to whether the Truman's Lodge gates were opened or closed, the senior man declaring that they were absolutely, definitely and positively open. He was mistaken! At least the driver could plead that he was only following his senior's order when the truck smashed the gates away from the archway pillars! Then, having hastily placed the wrecked ironwork onto the vehicle, they continued on their unsteady drive to Hardwick. Miss Emma Gilbert, the elderly lady living at Truman's Lodge at this time came running out crying: "Where did it land? Where did it land?" She was apparently of the opinion that an aircraft or a bomb had come to earth close by! The army supplied new gates and the old ones were disposed of as scrap. Whether the soldiers were disciplined for this expensive adventure is not recorded!

THE FINAL PARTY PROVIDED BY A DUKE AT CLUMBER

Combined V.E. ('Victory in Europe') and V.J. ('Victory in Japan') Days were celebrated on Saturday 25 August 1945, the duke financing the festivities. An afternoon tea-party was arranged for the children at Hardwick, with a conjuror and ventriloquist being provided for their entertainment. In the evening, 'The Vivacities' (an eleven-strong Concert Party from Manchester) presented cabaret-style interludes between the dancing, the revelries finishing at midnight. This was to be the final estate party to be provided by a member of the Newcastle family at Clumber.

A CRUCIAL DECISION
AND A FEW OF THE CONSEQUENCES

By the time of the decision that Clumber Park was to be sold in its entirety, many acres had already been leased to Worksop timber firms. From mid-1940, the local businesses of Tomlinson and Smiths, also Messrs Oates (who had some sixty years involvement at Clumber) had secured rights to fell and sell timber. Their involvement was linked to the War Office's requisitioning of the Park for military purposes.

The duke addressed the L.F.G. directors in November 1942, stating that he had concluded that it would be: "beyond his means" to ever make Clumber his permanent residence. He believed that the extraction of so much war timber and the problems caused by coal mining in the area would lead to further: "inevitable industrialisation and deterioration of the Estate" and make it an undesirable location for his duchy. He requested that the L.F.G. liquidate the Clumber and Worksop Estate and stated his intention to settle in a more 'rural area' once the war ended.

***

This is our final opportunity to record the financial state of the Estate as outlined in the documents of the L.F.G.:

Year ending 25 March 1941

Income –			Expenditure –		
Worksop	£51,385		Worksop	£45,354
Nottingham	£	612	Nottingham	£	372
Newark	£	1,953.	Newark	£	964
Total	£53,950		Total	£46,690

The above sums include Rents totalling £13,946; Royalties on Minerals, £16,833, and Income on Investments £7,772. Whilst it is interesting to compare these figures with those given in the earlier chapters of this book, it is essential to allow for the changing value of currency and other costs over that extended period.

***

The result of the decision to move away was to mean much work for the Estate office staff based at Park Street premises in Worksop. There, the Agent's team were now the hub of the 'House of Clumber' empire. They included a tax adviser, chief accountant and cashier, draughtsman, a secretary and two general office workers. It was to be many years before the bulk of the Nottinghamshire lands were disposed of and careful record-keeping was essential. The Muniments Room, alongside the Duke's Study, already overflowed with the titles and deeds of the Newcastle Estate. A new safe was installed at the Park Street office to supplement the mansion's strongroom.

On the specific matter as to the sale of Clumber Park, there was much debate and paper work about how the estate should be sold, either in parts or in one package. Somewhat surprisingly, Worksop College was invited to purchase the Chapel, Stableblock, Pleasure Grounds, Gardens (including the Garden House, Garden Bothy and two cottages), the Paddocks house and the

Figure 165 –
The Newcastle Estate Office,
Park Street, Worksop.

Cricket Ground Cottages, together with fifty-four acres of other land. The asking price was £11,000, which included £2,500 for standing timber. In December 1943 the L.F.G. recorded that the College offer had been put on hold: "whilst the war lasts". Two years later it was decided by the Estate Management Committee that the invitation to purchase should be withdrawn.

The saleable value of the Park's standing timber was estimated at £25,000 and local firms were showing interest – especially Oates Timber Merchants of Worksop, who offered to purchase the whole Park for £75,000. However, another aspect of the proposed sale was as to how much cognizance there should be of the Government's intentions to move towards increased availability of National Parks for its citizens. By June 1944, advisors Messrs. Whatley, Hill and Co. were urging the L.F.G. to resist the temptation to sell more rights to the Forestry Commission. The same advisors also believed that it would be a: "mistake to offer the property for sale except in one Lot ... and that the offer price should be around ten pounds an acre, excluding marketable timber".

The National Trust had already responded favourably to an approach that they consider purchasing the Park and, in October, the Trust went public, declaring their intentions to raise sufficient monies for the purchase. Their letters to the press invited readers to help raise (within less than three months) a sum of £45,000, explaining that this was the largest appeal they had made for twenty years and recognized that they had: "undertaken no light task". The Pilgrim Trust was amongst the earliest donors, promising £3,800. Messrs. Boots pledged £1,000 and the Bairnswear clothing factory's employees sent £105. Several individuals offered £100 each, thereby entitling them to be Honorary Members of The National Trust. News of these donations was soon followed by an announcement that fourteen local authorities had been represented at a conference convened by Nottinghamshire County Council, and that all present had promised to recommend their respective authorities contribute towards The National Trust's appeal. In December, this proved sufficiently encouraging for the L.F.G. to agree to the Trust's securing of an option to purchase, matching the earlier bid of £75,000 by the local timber firm. The L.F.G. also agreed to an extension of the previous deadline of December 1944.

Matters dragged on, with the several local authorities holding public meetings to enlist support in money-raising efforts – including those of the towns and cities of Derby, Doncaster, Nottingham, Rotherham and Sheffield, also the county councils of Derbyshire, Leicestershire, Lincolnshire, Nottinghamshire and the West Riding of Yorkshire. 'Flag days' were held at various football grounds and a variety of other fund-raising events were organised. Between them, the local authorities raised £24,000 and offered this, plus an annual contribution towards maintenance costs. One elderly lady was so moved by all this 'scrimping and saving' that she sent a one pound note to the duke at Clumber, hoping that if sufficient numbers did so, then he would have no need to sell the Park after all!

CHAPTER NINE

POSTSCRIPT

The Dukedom headed towards extinction – A New Life: Clumber Park's Third Creation – Clumber Chapel – Army Out, Public In – Clumber Gardens – Clumber's Stableyard and other buildings – Goodbye to the 'Lincoln' frigate – Goodbye to land and titles – The first of two Duchesses returned to Clumber – A duke (and later a duchess) revisited.

THE DUKEDOM HEADED TOWARDS EXTINCTION

BY MID-1946 THE NINTH DUKE had completed the move to his new duchy at Boyton, in the Wylye Valley, Wiltshire. Several of his estate employees from North Nottinghamshire accompanied him there. These included the Agent, Major Murray-Walker, who never forgot the advice given to him at his 1931 appointment interview: "put not your trust in princes"! Several office staff, tradesmen and their families also went to a new life on the duke's new lands. Others (such as Barratt Stanhope and Gilbert Holdsworth) accepted invitations to visit and consider working on the duke's new 2,275 acre estate, but declined the opportunity of service so far from their roots. The relocation of those who did transfer mirrored the actions of the families who, back in the mid-eighteenth century, had made the journey north from Surrey to Nottinghamshire with the Henry Fiennes Clinton who became the second Duke of Newcastle-under-Lyme.

In April 1946, the duke reached his thirty-ninth year and was heading towards a new life, following some ten years with the Auxiliary Air Force. He married twice more. The marriage to Diana Montagu-Stuart-Wortley took place during November 1946 at Caxton Hall, London. This union produced two daughters, Patricia and Kathleen. During 1948 the couple moved to a 1,200 acre tobacco farm near Salisbury, Rhodesia, but Diana soon realised that she would rather be back in England. She returned to Wiltshire in 1950 (where she received the surprise news that the duke would not be joining her) whilst pregnant with her second child, and the marriage was eventually dissolved after several years of separation.

The duke's third wife was Sally [formerly Williams, née Anstice], whom in 1956 he snatched from her second husband, Fikhret Jamal, the harbourmaster at Kyrenia, Cyprus. Sally's elopement with the duke made the national headlines when they hastily fled from the island in his 153 ton yacht. The duke and his new duchess married in October 1959, having settled in Jamaica for a while before returning to England to live at Shockerwick, near Bath in Somerset. By then, he had sold the Rhodesian property and was soon to dispose of the Boyton estate.

Although the third duchess had sons by her previous husbands, her third marriage was childless and, as a result, meant that the ducal title was hanging on by a slender thread. From its earliest days, there had always been a blood-line son, brother or nephew to succeed to the title and coronet on the death of the holder. By late-1988 there would be no male relatives closer than a several-times-removed cousin to take up the reins. Following his third divorce, the duke ended his days in Hampshire. His younger sister, Mary, lived in an adjacent cottage. The duke died at his Lymington home on the 4th of November 1988.

As mentioned earlier, the sole candidate for the title of tenth and final Duke of Newcastle-under-Lyme was Edward ('Ted') Pelham-Clinton, a retired curator of the Royal Scottish Museum in Edinburgh. Distinguished for his excellence as a microlepidopterist, 'Ted' was a sixty-eight year-old bachelor when he inherited the ducal coronet. Regrettably, he did not live long to enjoy the status and privileges that his new title should have afforded him. His untimely demise on Christmas Day, 1988 brought to an abrupt end the ducal dynasty that had begun in 1756. The secondary (but earlier) title of

Figure 166 –
The 10th (and last) Duke
of Newcastle-under-Lyme.

'Earl of Lincoln' was to endure for a while longer, being claimed by an Australian-based 'Fiennes-Clinton'.

A NEW LIFE – CLUMBER PARK'S THIRD CREATION

Whilst the ducal title had little or no chance of being re-created, Clumber Park's future was much more promising. Having been formed around 1709 as a deer park from what were desolate wastelands, Clumber's second coming had been built – during the final third of the eighteenth century – on the costly projects of the seventh Earl of Lincoln, Henry Fiennes Clinton. He described his handiwork as being: "An Ornament of Sherwood Forest". During those times of huge spending, the Park was set up as a ducal country estate for that Clinton, who became second Duke of Newcastle-under-Lyme on the death of his uncle in 1768. With a change of surname to Pelham-Clinton, the family line had ensured that the estate survived into the mid-twentieth century, through several decades of largely self-inflicted tribulation on the way.

The Park's 'third creation' was to be a major challenge for the National Trust. The purchase of Clumber in mid-1946 was at a time when the Army still occupied 1,239 acres. Returning this land to civilian control took almost nine years. A National Trust Land Agent of the 1980's, Mr P. H. Pearce, no doubt understated the daunting task that had faced his colleagues in those early days: "When the Trust acquired the property, it was in a badly neglected state after wartime occupation by the army. The woods were derelict, the park landscape disappearing, the farm reverting to scrub and the lake becoming silted".

The Estate Management Committee diligently undertook their duties, supported by almost £5,000 a year from the interested local authorities towards 'maintenance and preservation costs' (varying contributions from a reducing number of authorities continued until 1980). From July 1948, and under the watchful eyes of volunteer wardens, 300 acres of the South Lawns area of the Park were opened to the public. The Drayton Gate was the only entry and exit point available at this early stage. Lavatories and refreshment facilities were soon provided and the growing number of visitors began to claim at least part of Clumber as their own. In the spring of 1952, the Army's occupation was reduced to 319 acres. By this time some 860 acres of the Park were available as a public amenity, including the old Mansion site and the Pleasure Ground area around the Chapel.

CLUMBER CHAPEL

Many thousands of pounds needed to be spent on restoring the fabric of the Chapel, its roof and the organ. During the late-1940's, the previous organist, Leslie Rupert Pike, had endeavoured to raise monies towards the required repairs for the organ, but much more cash was needed. A Chapel Committee was set up, chaired by the National Trust's agent for the Park, Mr John Trayner, who lived in the Parsonage. There were a succession of secretaries, the first three of whom had lived in the Park for something over one hundred years between them, firstly estate resident, Ralph Sissons, a printer at Richard Martin's in Worksop; then the long-serving joiner, Barratt Stanhope and thirdly, Miss Violet Havelock, Hardwick's retired schoolmistress. Through the efforts of the Committee, supplemented by more cash and expertise from the National Trust, the organ was sufficiently repaired and cleaned for the re-opening service of the Chapel held on 25 May 1952. Hymn books, Communion plate, vestments, candlesticks and an altar cross had to be found, as all these items had been taken away following the closure of the Chapel in 1936. Clergy from churches at Newark, Shireoaks and Worksop were invited to conduct services, and contact with various local concerns brought the attention of many to Clumber Chapel's restoration. Worksop Hospital received donations of fruit and flowers from the Harvest Festival service and the Edwinstowe 'Toc H' group were prominent on Remembrance Day. The efforts of visiting choirs and organists were appreciated, and the occasional presence of the Bishop of Southwell and other church dignitaries attracted positive publicity. A 'Friends of Clumber' group was formed to assist with regular improvement work in the Chapel. Over a three-year period the members of the group renovated the wrought-iron work, cleaned the statuary and repaired the war memorial. A new life was being brought to this imposing place of worship.

It was in 1956 that Lord Rosse and his mother, Lady de Vesci, called to examine the Chapel and were greatly impressed by the renovation work that had been done. Lady de Vesci was a niece of the seventh duke and as reported in an earlier chapter (she was known then as Lois Lister-Kaye), had been at Clumber for her 'coming out' celebrations in November 1898.

ARMY OUT – PUBLIC IN

In April 1955 the Park was finally de-requisitioned by the War Office and the residual acres were made available as a public amenity. As might be expected, the many interested parties that had assisted in raising funds to help purchase Clumber Park for the nation now required their rewards for so doing! Canoeing, cycling, fishing, hacking, a water bus, sailing, swimming, golf course or golf practice range and a zoo were on the list of demands. The leading money-raiser, Nottinghamshire County Council, had requested permission to use Clumber Chapel as non-denominational County and City War Memorial, but this suggestion was rejected as the Chapel had clearly been designated as a Church of England place of worship. The Nottinghamshire Youth Hostels Association – having raised £500 towards the National Trust's appeal for funds – sought to have one of their hostels erected within the Park boundaries. They too were unsuccessful. Over several decades many visitor facilities were introduced. Scout camps and orienteering were eventually allowed, as were caravan sites, a day room for visiting school parties, car rallies, horse trials, garden exhibitions, plant sales, a shop, restaurant, information centre, lakeside concerts and midsummer theatrical performances. However, in the records of those days, the Trust's concerns regarding the possibility of hidden stocks of ammunition featured large.

Figure 167 – Headline from the 'Worksop Guardian' dated 5 September 1947

Deadly finds had repeatedly been made and were reported in local newspapers. Late in August 1947 a multiple explosion of ammunition devastated woodland of over one square mile and was loud enough to be heard in the outskirts of Nottingham, some twenty-seven miles away.

This incident was started by a spark from a fire that ignited some thirty tons of mines stored in corrugated iron shelters and was threatening to reach many more tons of anti-tank mines. Shrapnel flew as far as one mile from the centre of the explosion. All this mayhem required the attendance of the largest number of fire appliances ever assembled in the Park. Sixteen appliances and their crews were sent from Arnold, Carlton, Edwinstowe, Harworth, Hucknall, Langold, Mansfield, Newark, Nottingham, Retford, Shirebrook, Sutton-in-Ashfield, Tuxford, Warsop, West Bridgford and Worksop. As the water supply from a static tank dried up, more had to be pumped from the Lake, almost a mile from the scene of the conflagration. It was considered miraculous that no fireman, resident, soldier (or the still-to-be-freed prisoners of war) was injured or killed by the great quantity of shrapnel that was flying about. However, four fire-fighters were sent for hospital treatment after their lorry was in collision with another vehicle.

Some time later, a regular clearance programme was introduced to trace and remove remaining ammunition supplies. Villagers at Bothamsall, just two miles to the southeast of Clumber Park, recall the white acrid smoke which drifted towards their homes as a result of at least one of these 'clearances'. They were relieved that the smoke cloud had, to some extent, thinned by the time it passed over and around them. In the mid-1970's, divers investigating the area near Clumber Bridge brought up two anti-tank mines and a box of .303 rifle ammunition. Allegedly, the waters near the Bridge had been a favourite area for discarding surplus boxes of bullets which had somehow been 'missed' from a delivery. The consequences of admitting this oversight to a senior non-commissioned officer were said to be too serious to contemplate! As recently as the late 1980's, a volunteer discovered remnants of the deadly examples of the Park's long-lost explosives. At that time the lake had been drained due to subsidence problems, and whilst a team from Worksop College were involved in a bottle-clearing working party near the 'duck walk' below Clumber Bridge, it was discovered that at least one of the discarded bottles contained a phosphorus substance. Providentially, the young lady who had found this item only suffered damage to her footwear, which was replaced by the National Trust's Head Warden.

CLUMBER GARDENS

Up to the time of the handover to the National Trust, the London and Fort George Company had run Clumber Gardens as though it were still a private estate department, with only modest efforts being made to achieve good profits. The Trust initially approved its continuation, although on 'slightly modified' lines. The produce was made available for sale within the Park and also in one retail shop outlet in Worksop. It soon became apparent that the difference between income and expenditure was such that a new approach was required. The old Head Gardener, Charlie Frankish, who had served many years in a wide variety of private estates, was retired and a tenant gardener sought. The plan was that the new man would stand or fall by his own efforts and the Trust would be relieved of the nuisance of financing what had never been intended to be a commercial venture.

Mr Peter J. Van Dyk was the first of the new-style tenant gardeners, arriving in 1950 and staying for seven years. He was followed by Mr Bruce Pugh who held the position until 1971. On his departure the Trust discontinued the use of the Gardens as a tenancy and reverted to the employment of their own staff, with selective outlets for the limited amounts of produce grown there.

Incidentally, the Trust agreed to the Meteorological Office's request that rain gauge measurements at Clumber Gardens should again be regularly supplied for national records. These readings had been made at Clumber from the early days of the seventh duke's arrival in the 1880's until Mr Van Dyk's arrival.

CLUMBER'S STABLEYARD AND OTHER BUILDINGS

The impressive stableyard had been the scene of much activity and excitement at the time of the 1832 Reform Riots and during the Second World War. Now, the goings-on there were related to its gradual transformation into a base for the Regional Office of the National Trust. The Agents of the late-1940's and 1950's had lived in the Parsonage and the various buildings that surrounded it. These premises were now being increasingly brought into use as administration offices and storerooms. Around the Park, many residences, including the old bothies, were converted into offices or revived as usable cottages, either to house employees or for lease to selected tenants.

GOODBYE TO THE 'LINCOLN' FRIGATE

The 'Lincoln' frigate's demise was a due to a combination of old age plus a helping hand from some youngsters. With many re-fits, the thirty-two feet vessel had stayed afloat since the early nineteenth century. For over ten years, it had not been serviceable enough to fulfil its intended role of noble plaything, its hull having been stuck fast in the shallows of the lake. Understandably, it had become a tempting attraction for the children of Park families. When there was no one around to deny them the pleasure, they borrowed a rowing boat and enjoyed the exciting activity of boarding the 'Lincoln'. However on one cold winter's day soon after the end of the war, Clumber Lake was frozen solid and several boys plus at least one girl reached the boat on foot, by sliding over the ice. One of the boys had a partiality for fires and – no doubt as a warming device rather than a mischievous prank – a fire

was lit which led to the end of the vessel's days as a unique adventure playground. When the youngsters went home, the smouldering embers were not properly extinguished and some damage was caused, the boat moving even more rapidly towards its closing days as an ornamental feature of the Lake.

Figure 168 – The final days of a unique adventure playground

In the late-1970's, members of the Newark Sub-Aqua Club went beneath the waters to investigate the possibility of raising the remains. They found this to be impractical but rescued several items (such as some remnants of the masts and a decorative water closet). These were handed over to the National Trust. At the time of writing this, the hull of the 'Lincoln' is still a recognisable profile, lying in the shallows opposite the old boathouse site at the east-end of the Pleasure Grounds. During more recent years, whenever the lake's water level drops sufficiently, the shell of the hull has re-appeared and numerous newspaper editors have sent a photographer to record the event and relate an account of the boat's history.

GOODBYE TO LANDS AND TITLES

Whilst the new custodians of Clumber Park were wrestling with a multitude of problems related to making their new purchase available to the public, the Trustees of the seventh duke's will were still active with various sales of land and assets. From the late 1940's, many sales were held and large numbers of new owners found for 'Newcastle' properties.

Amongst the other assets released were numerous 'Lord of the Manor' titles previously in the hands of the 'Little Duke'. In July 1994, the Manorial Society held a Sale at Newark Town Hall and the final thirty-one titles were put up for auction. Amongst those which fetched good prices were: Worksop £40,000; Newark £18,500; Clumber £12,500; Markham-Clinton £11,750; Hardwick £11,000; Brinsley £10,000; Elkesley £9,500; Hodsock £8,500; Carlton ['with'] Lindrick £8,250; Gateford £7,500; Manton £7,000 and Egmanton £6,500.

Some of the packages on offer were enhanced by the inclusion of items such as 'the Robes, Garter, Sash and Breast Star of the Order of the Garter' which had been awarded to the fourth duke in 1812. The Worksop package included ducal Coronation Robes and Coronet plus the 'Loyal Address' of many of the estate's tenancy in 1885 [*See Appendix Four*].

THE FIRST OF TWO DUCHESSES IS RETURNED TO CLUMBER

During the late 1960's, and due to a very unfortunate episode at the Markham-Clinton Mausoleum, a duchess was once again to be seen in Clumber Chapel. Previously, the only Newcastle duchesses to be found there had been Kathleen, the wife of the seventh duke and her mother-in-law, the dowager duchess, Henrietta. They had both been worshipping members of the congregation. Now, the chapel was to become the refuge for the outstanding memorial to Georgiana, the wife of the fourth duke.

Georgiana had lived at Clumber for around fifteen years from 1807 and was influential in providing monies for the Park's many improvements at that time. In 1822, having died in childbirth, she was buried in Bothamsall churchyard, alongside her dead twins, a stillborn girl and a ten-day-old son. Bothamsall had been the Newcastle family church from the late 1790's and there were two more of the duchess's children buried there, as well as Charlotte, sister of the fourth duke. In 1836, some two and a half years after the completion of the building of the Newcastle's mausoleum

249

between Milton and West Markham, Georgiana's remains and those of four of her children were removed from Bothamsall and interred in the new vaults of the Greek Doric design mausoleum.

Since the internment of the sixth duke there in 1879, and the opening of Clumber's new Chapel a decade later, family interest in the mausoleum had waned. The seventh, eighth and ninth dukes showed little or no interest in it and it had ceased to be a parish church for the Markham-Clinton villages of Bevercotes, Milton and West Markham. From 1949 it had become a 'redundant' church and a museum piece, in that it housed the much admired memorial to Georgiana, prepared by Sir Richard Westmacott and financed by the fourth duke to the tune of one thousand pounds – more than fifty thousand at current values!

Acts of vandalism at the mausoleum's vaults in the late-1960's led to the desecration of coffins (which included those of the fourth, fifth and sixth dukes). These were broken open and the contents scattered about, presumably with theft of valuables as the intention – although there were rumours of even more disturbing activities, such as satanic rituals. The mausoleum was described at this time as: "virtually gutted and the only thing of value inside the church is this monument. The left arm of the Duchess's effigy is broken off and lying on the mattress". There were also other memorials and plaques within the church, relating to various members of the 'House of Clumber' dynasty.

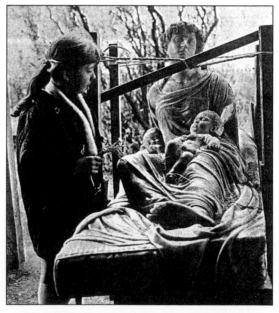

Figure 169 – The memorial to Georgiana, 4th Duchess...
Figure 170 – on the move to a temporary home in Clumber Chapel.

An approach was made to the Earl of Rosse, who was at that time Chairman of the Trust's Historic Building Committee. As a member of the Newcastle family, Lord Rosse was suitably moved by the matter to write to the Bishop of Southwell. He expressed the view that the Trust was: "certainly willing to accept guardianship of these memorials if that is the only means of safeguarding them", although they considered that there were more suitable sites in the county than Clumber Chapel.

Following these and many more consultations, the imposing memorial (all fifteen hundred-weight of it) was moved to Clumber. It went there along with the sculptured wall relief, incorporating the death mask of fourteen year-old Anna Maria, the fourth duke's eldest daughter, who had died some four months prior to the duchess's death. Once at Clumber, the structure was repaired and cleaned. Despite the clash of the: "romantic late classical school of the 1820's" origins, when set against the: "medieval gothic" of the Chapel, it made a striking addition to the Chapel's magnificence and remained for some years. There it was admired by many of the visitors who were then flocking to the Park. From the time that the disused Mausoleum was placed under the care of the Redundant Churches Fund (more latterly The Churches Conservation Trust) plans were made to return the memorial to its original site in the Markham-Clinton parish. This was achieved in the late-1980's and the unfortunate consequences of that decision are now plain to see in the deteriorating condition of Richard Westmacott's fine piece. At the time of writing, the fate of this monument to the duchess and her children is in under review and there is optimism that its restoration and cleaning may be followed by a more secure future.

A DUKE – AND LATER A DUCHESS – REVISITED

In the late 1970's – after an absence from Clumber of around twenty-five years, the ninth duke was on his way south to Hampshire from Yorkshire, accompanied by his personal agent, Charles Stableforth. They chose to detour from their route down the A.1 and call in at the duke's old Nottinghamshire home. Entering Clumber Park at the noble Apley Head gates and travelling almost two and a half miles to the crossroads north of the Paddocks, they were turning left towards the site of the demolished mansion when an unanticipated situation met them. From August 1967 the National Trust had introduced charges in respect of admission to the Park for the motor cars of non-members. Neither the duke nor his agent was a member of the Trust at that time and they paid the charge without comment.

***

In September 1997, Diana, second wife of the ninth duke and mother of his two daughters, died at her Wiltshire home and – a month later – her ashes were scattered on the waters alongside Clumber Bridge. Diana's affection for the Park had led to the request that her remains should be returned to this spot. She had special memories of pleasurable times spent there during the latter years of the Second World War. A small circular plaque commemorating this occurrence was incorporated into the centre of the bridge walling.

***

The above events that end our story occurred around one hundred years later than the matters examined in the first Chapter of this book. For very different reasons, there was no incumbent duke at Clumber in the 1870's, nor was there one living there a century later. From private ownership, the old Newcastle estate had now been widely dispersed and, due to the efforts of many organisations and individuals, an outstanding and very popular public amenity had been created in Clumber Park.

Figure 171 – Clumber Bridge – a view little changed since the 1760s

APPENDICIES

APPENDIX ONE   –   CLUMBER SPANIELS

– Pages 254 to 255

APPENDIX TWO   –   7TH DUKE'S WAR SPEECH

– Pages 256 to 257

APPENDIX THREE – 'NELLIE' – THE EVACUATING MACHINE

– Pages 258 to 259

APPENDIX FOUR   –   NEWCASTLE TENANTS of 1885
        SOME FAMILY NAMES   – Page 260

APPENDIX ONE

CLUMBER SPANIELS

During my delving over the past ten years, I have attempted to distance myself from the rough and tumble of debate on Clumber's canine matters. It has however proved impossible to ignore the mysteries surrounding them, as so many people have approached me about any relevant research items I may have uncovered that might explain those secrets.

"*The origins of the breed are untraceable*" – so wrote Jane Buckland in 'The Field' magazine of 23 April 1970 – and she may be correct! However, the time-consuming efforts of 'Clumber' enthusiasts to prove Ms Buckland wrong are impressive.

Alpine spaniels, St. Bernards and Basset hounds are amongst the breeds suggested as progenitors. Eighteenth century French noble estates – especially those containing the kennels of the Duc de Noailles (south of Limoges) – have been identified as the probable earliest whereabouts of these aristocratic gundogs.

The title and earliest recognised dating of the breed in England suggests that the first specimens here were acknowledged as being strongly linked to the time when the second Duke of Newcastle-under-Lyme was at Clumber Park – broadly spanning the years 1768 to 1794.

If folklore is believed, the Duc de Noailles gifted his entire kennels of prized spaniels to the Duke of Newcastle-under-Lyme at Clumber Park. If we look at the known facts, the Clumber duke did not move to Clumber House as his main residence until the late-1780's. Although he began to use this North Nottinghamshire estate as his hunting ground from the time of his first appearance there in September 1760, he continued to live at Oatlands in Surrey until 1788. When he was at Oatlands, two of his gamekeepers were William and John Mansell and it is clear that the Mansells moved to Haughton - part of the Clumber estate – by the early-1770's. In the well-renowned painting 'Return from Shooting' (1788) by Francis Wheatley R.A. (to be seen at Sheffield City Art Galleries), William Mansell is depicted near Clumber Bridge, alongside his noble master and four of the dogs. This is believed by many (but not all!) to be the first depiction of the breed.

The outbreak of the French Revolution in 1789 has been pointed to as the reason for the Duc de Noailles shipping his dogs to England. Perhaps he did, but no-one has yet found satisfactory evidence that this was so. What is indisputable is that gundogs which have been identify as early examples of the Clumber Spaniel breed are displayed in Wheatley's 1788 painting.

The 'Newcastle Manuscripts' housed in the Manuscripts and Special Collections Department of the University of Nottingham [*under the reference prefix 'NeA'*] contain estate accounts for the years 1775/1776. The following items from those accounts are relevant to the matter of dogs at Clumber. At least some of these were spaniels transported from Surrey to Nottinghamshire to be placed in the hands of Mr Mansell at Haughton:

NeA 290/25/1 – "John Mansell keeping dogs 1775"

NeA 290/25/3 – "Mansell keeping Pointers; Rabbit dogs and One Spaniel – from December 1775".

NeA 290/26/1 – "The Spaniel's Bill - William Mansell - £46.13.6d - 1775"

NeA 290/26/2 – "William Mansell's Bill for Spaniel's keeping -

12 Spaniels – January 1775 – January 1776

2 Spaniels – 'Jack' and ['Leo'?] – 48 weeks

1 Spaniel Bich – 'Jesey'

3 Spaniels that came from Oatlands – September 1775 – September 1776

The Mansells were based at Haughton Kennels Farm and gundogs were kept both there and at kennels at Budby Corner, prior to the building of the Hardwick kennels in the 1890's.

During the fourth duke's incumbency (1807 to 1851) the reputation of the Clumber Spaniel reached the ears of many of his neighbours (including the Foljambes at Osberton and the Manvers at Thoresby). Prince Albert, consort of Queen Victoria, had four Clumber's as early as 1840. In March 1851 – the fourth Duke of Newcastle-under-Lyme having died – the occupants of his kennels were sold at auction by Tattersall & Son at Hyde Park Corner. Some thirteen 'celebrated and pure-bred Clumber Spaniels' and ten 'young Clumber Spaniels' were amongst the forty dogs on offer.

The seventh duke's marriage in 1889 proved to be a turning point in the breed's history at Clumber. His duchess, Kathleen, was a real 'doggy' enthusiast and was instrumental in the building of the superior kennels complex at Hardwick. She had around 140 dogs on the estate. In addition to her main loves, Borzois and Fox Terriers, she kept some twenty Clumbers. Unfortunately, she reported that the breed – having undergone 'considerable modifications in the course of time' was 'dying out'. The cost of a Clumber puppy was £5 at that time (£750 is a sale figure quoted in September 2004!).

That the 'White Spaniel' has survived is obvious by the breed's current popularity and the existence of so many Clumber Spaniels clubs all around the world.

***

APPENDIX TWO

7TH DUKE'S WAR SPEECH [*See Chapter Five*]
[*as published in the 'Worksop Guardian' on 18 September 1914*]

This speech was delivered to the men of Tuxford, Nottinghamshire by the seventh Duke of Newcastle-under-Lyme. The occasion was a meeting held in the Newcastle Arms, Tuxford on 15 September 1914. The Chairman was Mr W.K. Hume-Williams K.C., M.P.

"I DO NOT SUPPOSE THERE IS A SINGLE PERSON in this place who has a shadow of doubt to the justice of our cause in the terrible war in which the greater part of Europe is now engaged. There are, I believe here and there a few eccentric individuals who are whining for peace, and slobbering a maudlin sympathy for the enemies of their country. Well, such creatures ought to be deported to Germany, they could probably get there by way of Holland – when they did, I fancy they would soon change their opinions as to the charms of their Teutonic friends. But we don't need to consider such freaks tonight. I know that I am talking to true English men and women and all that it is necessary for me to do is to urge with all my power, the vital, the deadly importance of rallying to Lord Kitchener's standard, and giving him the great army for which he asks.

It is not much use lamenting the 'might have been'; it is profitless to sigh over lost opportunities, but one cannot help thinking how different our position would have been today if the advice of Lord Roberts and others, urged over and over again in recent years, had been taken. We should have had the great army in being which we now have to build up in such haste. It is more than probable that the war would not have taken place at all. There is no doubt that the Kaiser fully believed that in the first place we would never fight, and if we did our little army was a negligible quantity. Well, he has been painfully undeceived on both points! We have shown him that our army, whatever else it may be, it is certainly not negligible; our soldiers have covered themselves with undying glory, and if their quantity had been equal to their quality can you doubt that the German army would have been utterly destroyed?

Gentlemen the war, I fear will be a long, a very long one. Germany is desperate. She knows full well that if she is beaten, which, please God, she will be, no mercy whatever will be shown her, and she will have to pay a terrible price for the infamies which her barbarian hordes have perpetrated. She is desperate I say, and is fighting for her existence as a nation. That is why the conflict must be prolonged, unless by some blessed chance and overwhelming catastrophe should shatter her forces. But we must not count on this. We must be prepared for the worst and build up such an army that in the end victory must rest with England and her gallant allies.

Perhaps there are still some people who say 'Oh, England is all right, her navy will never allow a German invasion'. Well I do not wish to be pessimistic, and if the matter were unimportant I should certainly say that the chances are against an invasion but we cannot afford to take these chances, and until the German navy is at the bottom of the sea we shall not be safe. And consider what such a thing would mean! An invasion by a foreign enemy would always be a disgrace, but if we were fighting a civilised and chivalrous foe, the disgrace, bad as it would be, would end there. But our foes are neither civilised nor chivalrous; they have proved themselves to be brutal and ruthless savages. Their deeds will make them infamous for all times. There is no doubt of the atrocities inflicted by these devils upon helpless men, women and children, they are vouched for by unimpeachable witnesses, and some of them could not be mentioned in public at all. But you have read, perhaps, of the baby who was dashed to the ground and killed because it had `France' on its cap; of the little boy in France, three years old, whose arms were cut off and who was bayoneted by German soldiers because he cheered for England? These are only samples which could be multiplied to a sickening extent.

Does anyone want these horrors to be repeated in England? Yet, they most certainly will be if these monsters ever set foot upon our shores. There is no reason whatever to suppose that they will be different here to what they have been elsewhere, and they have already displayed a special hatred of our people. No, they must never land, or if they do must be crushed instantly by overwhelming force, and it is to meet this real and terrible danger that we call upon our young men in their hundreds of thousands to rally to the defence of their country and their homes.

Before calling upon Mr Hume-Williams to address you, I wish to draw your attention to what I feel most strongly has been a defect in the country's magnificent attitude in this awful crisis. She has been fully conscious of what she owes to gallant little Belgium, who has covered herself with imperishable renown; there is no fault to be found with her behaviour to France, and it is pleasant to think we are forging a link of lasting friendship with that delightful country. But what about Russia? I fear that England as a whole, does not yet realise what she, what Europe owes to that great country in the hour of peril. Perhaps there are still people who fear Russia - a groundless fear it certainly is. Think what would have happened if she were neutral now! Millions of Austrians and Germans would have been set free to invade France, and could the latter have stood against them? As it is, by a rapidity of mobilisation and brilliant generalship, probably never surpassed, Russia has moved her mighty army against the common foes with such vigour that Austria is practically wiped out, and Germany is hurrying back to her eastern frontier. It is not too much to say that Russia is the saviour of Europe, of civilisation, and of religion. I say religion advisedly, because the triumph of Germany would mean the triumph of all that is Anti-Christian. The spirit which informs Prussia, and which is responsible for this war and the way in which it is conducted, is frankly materialistic and atheistic. This is most fully realised by the Russians, to whom this is a Holy war for the defence of Christianity. She entered upon her crusade with a great public service in the presence of the Emperor, humbly asking the blessing of God upon her armies. There was nothing of this of the blatant blasphemy of the Bully of Berlin, with his arrogant assumption of intimacy with the Almighty. Yes, Russia is magnificent, but let us do our share too, let us not relax our efforts until the enemy is crumpled up like a withered leaf, and Europe breathes freely once more."

APPENDIX THREE

'NELLIE' – THE EVACUATING MACHINE
[See Chapter Seven]

Trench warfare strategies of the First World War were still accepted as a necessary evil as the 'storm of war' again approached in the late-1930's.

In Sir Winston Churchill's book 'The Second World War', Volume One [published by Cassell and Co. Ltd.] he outlined his thoughts on this matter during the dark days that preceded the declaration of war in September 1939:

> I gave much thought and compelled much effort to the development of an idea which I thought might be helpful to the great battle when it began. For secrecy's sake this was called 'White Rabbit No.6', later changed to 'Cultivator No.6'.
>
> It was a means of imparting to our armies a means of advance up to and through hostile lines without undue or prohibited casualties. I believed that a machine could be made which would cut a groove in the earth sufficiently deep and broad through which assaulting infantry and presently assaulting tanks could advance in comparative safety across no-man's-land and wire entanglements, and come to grips with the enemy in his defences on equal terms and in superior strength.
>
> It was necessary that the machine cutting this trench should advance at sufficient speed to cross the distance between the two front lines during the hours of darkness. I hoped for a speed of three or four m.p.h.; but even half-a-mile would be enough. If this method could be applied upon a front of 20 or 30 miles, for which two or three hundred trench-cutters might suffice, dawn would find an overwhelming force of determined infantry established on and in the German defences, with hundreds of lines-of-communication trenches stretching back behind them, along which reinforcements and supplies could flow.
>
> Thus we should establish ourselves in the enemy's front line by surprise and with little loss. This process could be repeated indefinitely.

Churchill had ordered a prototype of this machine to be worked on during the First World War. Now, in late 1939 – and as First Lord of the Admiralty – he allocated funds for urgent work to begin again. Within six weeks, a three-feet-long working model was designed and manufactured by Messrs. Ruston-Bucyrus of Lincoln. It worked well when trialled in a sand-pit in the basement of the Admiralty.

After gaining the support of the Chief of the Imperial General Staff, Churchill proudly showed the model to the Prime Minister, Neville Chamberlain. He then took it over the Channel to show to the French generals. It soon gained the approval of the War Cabinet and agreement was reached that some 200 of these so-called 'infantry' machines would be put into production immediately and that they should be ready for operational use by March 1941. Under the central control of Ruston-Bucyrus's chief engineer, some 350 firms made the separate parts that were sent to his Lincoln factory. Despite the large number of people involved, it appears that utmost secrecy was maintained about the project.

During 1940 - by which time Churchill had been appointed as Prime Minister – the order was increased to allow for 40 larger machines to be provided, ensuring that certain trenches would be wide enough to allow for the movement through them of British tanks. These 'officer' machines would be able to cut ditches in loam of five feet depth, seven-and-a half feet width and travel at half-a-mile an hour. They were reckoned capable of moving 6,000 tons of soil during that time. Geological analysis of the soils in Northern France and Belgium helped to influence battle plans for the use of these monsters.

A hitch occurred when it was realised that the intended power source of the excavator – Merlin-Marine engines – were all desperately required by the Air Ministry. A heavier engine had to be accepted, bringing the machine's weight to over one hundred tons.

During 1941, the Prime Minister paid his visit to Clumber Park to witness the successful trials of the tank. By that time, factory workers and soldiers had re-christened the machine 'Nellie'. This was probably inevitable, as the secret Ministry of Supply Instruction Book regarding its construction was headed 'N.L.E. Trenching Machine' – 'N.L.E.' being the abbreviation for the 'Naval Land Equipment Department'.

***

Churchill's record concludes:

> But all this labour, requiring at every stage so many people to be convinced or persuaded, led to nothing. A very different form of warfare was soon to descend upon us like an avalanche, sweeping all before it ... A few specimens alone were finished and preserved for some special tactical problem or for cutting emergency anti-tank obstacles ... These survivors were kept in store until the summer of 1945, when the Siegfried line being pierced by other methods, all except one was dismantled. Such was the tale of 'Cultivator No.6'.
>
> I am responsible but impenitent.

APPENDIX FOUR

NEWCASTLE TENANTS OF 1885 – SOME FAMILY NAMES

Elaborate depictions [*see Colour Plate 4*] of the Newcastle-under-Lyme ducal coat of arms were included on two separate 'Loyal Addresses' that were commissioned by the 7th duke's tenants to commemorate his coming-of-age in 1885. The 'Addresses' were sold in 1994 as part of the Sale of 31 Lordship of the Manor titles. Tenants' names were recorded by the Manorial Society in the Sale prospectus and are copied here with the kind permission of that Society:

WORKSOP

Peter Allington, William Allen, John Appleton, Thomas Arthur, George Baines, George Barlow, Joseph Beard, Matthew Beard, Thomas Berry, Henry Bower, John Brammer, Edwin Brown, Martha Candlin, John Caudwell Snr., William Isaac Cookson, William Dennel, Kirk Dennis, Rosa Dyson, George Eddison, John Edeson, Christopher Fleming, Thomas James Flockton, Joseph Garside, William Gray, Francis Greaves, Samuel Hall, John Hardy, James Cobb Harris, James Harrison, Henry Sweet Hodding, William Hudson, Cavil Hunter, John Lillyman, Mary Hannah Mosley, Joseph Naylor, D.M. O'Connor, John Palmer, Samuel Pressley, James Preston, John Preston, M. Robinson, G. Rollit, Henry Simpson, Henry Skinner, H. Smedley, James Stubbings, G.W.Sudbury, R.L.Towne, William Traunter, Henry Watson, Charles Wilson, David W.Winks, Charles Tylden-Wright.

ELKESLEY

Joseph Allen, Walter Baguley, George Caudwell, George Cowley, Mary Doncaster, William Evison, Thomas Fell, John Fox, Tom Giles, Adam Kelly, George Kitchen, Samuel Lidgett, James Marshall, William Petch, George Richards, James Salmon, Samuel Scott, James Standing, William Wells, John Wyer.

MARKHAM

Hanna Alvey, Sarah Bacon, George Bagshaw, J.Billiard, Charles Boddy, H.P.Clark, John Cree, John Footitt, W. Fox, Fred Gilbert, Timothy Lamb, John Littlewood, Charlotte Nunn, John Peat, W.Pierrepont, David Staniland, John Taylor, Thomas Tindall, George Wilson, William Wood.

MARTIN

James G. Cameron, F.W. Cartwright, George Cartwright, J. Hibbert, George Taylor, William White.

WALESBY

Joseph Ashworth, John Belyard, Ann Brown, John Chambers, John Gilbert, Charles R. Gorton, Joseph Hall, Thomas Hardwick, Thomas Highfield, Joseph Kirkland, J.G.Laughton, Daniel Mills, Charles Nice, George Parsons, Henry Ratcliffe, Richard Ratcliffe, Thomas Robbins, John Searson, Samuel Swinscoe, Daniel Thompson, Jane Tissington, Richard Tong, Mark Whitworth, Richard Whitworth, John Wombell.

BRINSLEY

William Andrews, John Beardsley, Ann Chambers, Samuel Cooke, John Cresswell, Edward Crowder, Francis Dovey, William Foster, John Gascoyne, John Gregory, William Hallam, John Hicking, Matthew Hopkinson, William Housley, William Hutsby, Thomas Knighton, Robert Lacy, John Laurence, Mary Lygo, George Meakin, Henry Meakin, Mary Moore, Ann Naylor, John Naylor, William Naylor, John Norris, Ann Oates, Enock Onell, Percival Page, Alfred Pugh, Edward Riley, Isaac Riley, John Riley, Joseph Riley, William Saxton, William Scarson, John Severn, George Skelton, Samuel Smalley, Thomas Smalley, Samuel Smeeton, William Smith, George Smithurst, Ann Stevenson, William Swain, William Taylor, George Ward, Isaac Wardle, Thomas Williamson.

NEWARK AND SURROUNDING MANORS

Edward Bousfeld, John Howe, W.E. Knight, Robert Davey, Joseph F. Birtlett, W. E. Tallents, Godfrey Tallents, Robert Griffin, James Perfect, George Brown, James Wilson, John Pastill, John Mills, John McLeod, R.P. Layton, G.W.Charrington, George Sheppard, James Thorpe, Alfred J. Bishop, Henry Branston, Robert Bayliffe, William Hancock, Edward Jackson, Edward Castle, Henry Sand, Charles Elsow, George Hart, John Brown, Thomas Dabbs, John Ellwood, Charles Baines, George Duke, John Bell, Joseph Burgess Jr., William G. Love, Henry Morgan, John F. Loversidge, Sarah Hollis, Mary Maysfield, William Marriott, John Geary, Thomas Factwell, George Thorpe, William Paulson, William S. Kirkley, Harry Hollis, Henry Widdison, Sarah Middleton, Richard Smith, James Garnett, Susan Lockton, John Lineham, William Henry Selby, Elizabeth Tomblin, Sarah Franks, Samuel Frost, John James New, George Edward Rockliffe, Daniel Dyson, William Blyton, George Perfect, James Withington, Thomas William Alexander, Robert Chatterton, William Wallis, J. Dale, John Thomas Caffs, James Else, Henry Hemsley, Robert Mansfield, W. Butter, E. Doe, Frederick Duke, Thomas Alfred Hoe, Charles Taylor, Alfred John Smith, J. M. Walker.

***

ACKNOWLEDGEMENTS

After several years of research and dependence on so many kind folk for information and encouragement, the following are nominated as more than worthy of mention. I offer sincere apologies to anyone else who is aggrieved by the absence of their names from this list. They must remind me of the omission and may find that they appear in any subsequent edition!

Representing providers of dumber estate families and properties detail were: John & Ruth Alcock [Manton Lodge], Kevin Allbones [Budby Comer], Mac Bailey & Linda Milne [Lady Lincoln], Diana Bakel [Tomlinson], Patricia Brookes [Paddocks Cottage], Jean & Robert Bryant [Cabin Hill], David A. Chapman [Budby Corner], Cliff and Gillian Cowley [Alcock], Sally Fallon [Pike], Hilda Favill [Adcock], Brenda Finch [Storrs], Susan Garratt [Murray-Walker], Leslie & Margaret Hallam [Read & Thompson], Mervyn Headland, Nancy Hibbs [Tideswell], Constance, Philip & Richard Hile, Geoff Holdsworth; Alan Littlewood [Brown], Robin Murray-Walker, Ken Ollivant, Lady Kate Pelham-Clinton-Hope, Arthur Read, Richard and Gill Sheldon [Chantry], Frank Richard Smith M.B.E. [Rudolph Schmidt], Ron & Veronica Sissons, Charles Stableforth, Ailsa Pringle [Hardwick Grange], Roxanna Van Oss, John & Sybil Weth [Clumber Cottage], J. Timothy Woolley [Murray-Walker]

National Trust staff and volunteers who offered particular assistance included: Andrew Barber, Helen Bingham, Lynne Bower, Ron Burton, Stuart Chappell, Pauline Crawshaw, Ian Deans, Nigel Dorrington, Barbara Fox, Joanne Rawson, Leigh Rix, Andrea & Bob Salmon, Josephine Scott and the late David Wilson.

Invaluable information, depictions and encouragement were provided by Bemadette Ayton [Shireoaks], Sally Beer [Choir School], Peter Brammer ['Ned & Flo'], Joanne Bower [1869 Insolvency], Ron Burton [Royal Engineers], Wendy Caseldine, [Clumber Chapel], Anne Clough, Frank Friel [aircraft crash], Brenda Gee [Lound Hall], John Hammond [1885 'Coming-of-age' bannerettes], Neville Hoskins, Bill Ironside [Clumber Spaniels], Ernest Marshall [Manton Colliery], Tim O'Connor-Fenton, Dr Rawll [All Saints' Church, Margaret Street, London], Bill Rose, Doris & Peter Smith [Forest Farm], Mike Spurrier, Bill Taylor [aircraft crash records], Ruth Timbrell [Forest Farm, Winkfield], Frances Soubry, June Wilde [Women's Institute].

Numerous archival stores were involved, all were useful and some exceptionally so. Persons named here represent a few of those who 'went the extra mile' to provide material: Alice Blackford [Oxford University Archives - sale of the Nottingham Park estate]. Mark R. Shaw [National Museums of Scotland - detail on the 10th duke], Charles J. Stableforth, June M. Spong [Harrowlands], Evan Towle [Urban Archives, Temple University Libraries, Philadelphia - items regarding the 8th duke], also the Nottingham City and Nottinghamshire County Library Services (especially Tim Warner at Newark Library). Staff of the University of Nottingham Manuscripts & Special Collections Department deserve high praise for the thoroughness with which they carry out their custodial role of 'Newcastle Manuscripts^, under the direction of Dr. Dorothy Johnston.

Many thanks go to the readers and improvers of my draft scribblings: Vernon Brown, Nigel Dorrington, Sandra Fletcher, Constance Hile, Ailsa Pringle, Charles Stableforth, Joe Stainforth, and Phil Webster. Julie and Tim at the 'Dukeries Print Services' also deserve mention, as do all the supporters of my Illustrated Talks and Guided Walks over the past eight years. Finally, 'respect' to the inventors of that incredible research facility - the Internet!

BIBLIOGRAPHY
[This list does not profess to be an exhaustive list of the available material]

Bassett, A.T. (Ed.) (1936). Gladstone to his wife.:Methuen.

Beamish, H.J.H. (1986). Archaeological Survey, Clumber Park.:National Trust

Bradbury, D.J. (1988). Clumber.:Wheel Publications.

Brand, K.(1984). Park Estate, Nottingham. The development of a nineteenth century fashionable suburb:
    Transactions of the Thoroton Society 88, pp54-75

Cameron, L.C.R. (1907). Book of the Caravan.:L. Upcott Gill.

Chapman, D. A. (2000). Families of Late Victorian Clumber.; Millennium History Course project, North Notts College.

Clifton, M.C. (1979). Enchanted Palace, Clumber Park, the Newcastle family seat.
        :B.A. dissertation, University of Nottingham.

Dundas, H. (1988). Flying Start – A Fighter Pilot's War Years.: Stanley Paul.

Fernyhough, A.H. (undated). History of the R.A.O.C. 1920-1945.: R.A.O.C.

Firth, J.B. (1916). Highways and byways in Notts.: London, MacMillan.

Foster, V. (1993). Clumber Park.: National Trust.

Guest, I. (1958). Adeline Genee, A lifetime of Ballet under Six Reigns.: Adam & Charles Black.

Harris, J. (1998). No voice from the hall.: John Murray.

Hilton. K.L. (1989). Old Palace School (Croydon) Centenary History.: Private Publication.

Hine, T.C. (1876). Nottingham: its Castle; military fortress, a royal palace, ducal mansion, blackened ruin,
        museum and gallery of art.: London, Hamilton, Adams & Co.

Innes-Smith, R. (1984). Dukeries and Sherwood Forest.: English Life Publications.

Jacks, L. (1881). Great houses of Nottinghamshire and the county families.: W. & A.S. Bradshaw.

Jackson, M.J. (1992). Victorian Worksop.:Worksop Archaeological and Local Historical Society.

Jenkins, R. (1995). Gladstone.:Macmillan.

Magnus, P. (1964). King Edward the Seventh.: John Murray.

Masters, B. (1975). Dukes.: Blond & Bridges.

Matthews, H.C.G. (Ed) (1978). Gladstone Diaries (Vols. 5, 6 and 14). : Clarendon Press.

Patch, S.S. (1976). Blue mystery, the story of the Hope diamond.: Smithsonian Institution Press.

Pawle, G. (1963). War and Colonel Warden.: Harrop.

Ray, J. (1994). Pleasure Grounds and Terrace Gardens at Clumber Park. :Janette Ray Associates. York.

Redfern, R.A. (1974). Dukeries of Nottinghamshire.: Dalesman Book.

Reid, Wemyss. Sir (Ed.).(1899).Life of William Ewart Gladstone.: Cassell & Co.

Rodgers, J. (1908). Scenery of Sherwood Forest.: T.Fisher Unwin.

Sherwood Forest & the Dukeries. (Third Edition 1889/1900).: Ward Lock.

Spencer, R. (c1972). Drama at the sale.: Private Publication.

Stamp, G. & Symondson, A. (1982). Clumber Chapel.: National Trust.

Thomas, D. (1998). Victorian Underworld.: John Murray.

Tomlinson, W. (1878-1915). Diaries of a Head Forester at Clumber Park: unpublished – transcribed by Di Bakel (2002)]

Turner, J.T. (1988). Occasional Papers in Lincolnshire History and Archaeology (Number 7). 'Nellie' –
    The History of Churchill's Lincoln-Built Trenching Machine.: Society for Lincolnshire – History & Archaeology.

[Unnamed author] (1957). Wartime Evacuating Machine – from the 'Engineer' magazine 15 March 1957 (pgs 396-399).

White, R. (1903). Dukery records.: Robert White.

Williams, C.J. (Compiler). (1990) Handlist of the Glynn-Gladstone MSS in St. Deiniol's Library, Hawarden.

List and Index Society, Special Series, Number 24.

Ziegler, F.T. (1993). Story of 609 Squadron – Under the White Rose.: Crecy Books

Note also: 1) Newcastles of Clumber. A Pictorial and Documentary History of an Important Nottinghamshire Family
        – a guide to the exhibition held at the University of Nottingham – 1992.

2) All Saints, Margaret Street, London – 'Church and Parish Paper – Vol. XXXVI.

INDEX

Abercorn. Duke of, 95
Adcock. John (blacksmith), 45, 128, 171, 172
Alcock. Charles William (joiner), 120
Alcock. Gillian Mary, 121
Alcock. Mary (post mistress), 105, 198
Alcock. Richard (estate resident), 120
Alcock. Richard George (foreman joiner), 120
Alcock. Richard John, (estate resident), 119, 121
Alexandra. Queen, 49, 133
Allison. Jack (estate worker), 230
Allison. Robert (estate worker), 231
American Kennel Club Show, 49
Anderson. George (houseman), 65
Anne. Queen (1710), 125
Annesley. Lord, 95
Ardilaun. Lord, 79
Arthur. Sir George, 145
Arundel, Sussex, 138
Ascot, Berkshire, 175
Ashley. George F. (organist), 45
Astaire. Fred (dancer and film star), 190
Auxiliary Air Force
    609 (West Riding) Squadron, Yeadon
    and 616 Squadron, Doncaster, 194, 221
Aylesford. Lord, 74
Babbington, Nottingham 56, 116, 144
Babworth, Retford, 94, 101, 124,155
Baden-Powell. R.S.S. Lord, 132, 157
Bagthorpe, Notts., 56, 88, 100, 113
Bairnswear (clothing manufactures), 239
Balderton, Notts., 87
Banks. Thomas (sculptor), 207
Bardney, Lincolnshire, 236
Barker. Samuel (head gardener), 92, 118, 122, 127, 134,
    164, 167, 198
Barlborough, Derbyshire, 117
Barnby Moor, Notts., 36, 79, 184
Barrow-in-Furness, 188
Barry. Charles (Jnr.), 17, 18
Barry. Sir Charles, 17
Barsby, Leicestershire, 65
Basford, Nottingham, 87, 100, 113, 144, 183
Bassetlaw (cricket) League, 68
Beattie. William (farm bailiff), 104, 134
    Beattie. Elsie (dairymaid), 169
Belfit. Annie M. C. (head parlourmaid), 67
Bellicourt British Cemetery, 67
Belph, Derbyshire, 117
Belvoir, Leicestershire, 5, 16, 36
Bentley. Seymour Rev., 8
Beresford Hope. A.W.B. (uncle of the 7th duke), 43
Besthorpe, Notts., 87
Bethlehem, Pennsylvania, 73
Bevercotes, Notts., 77, 123, 168, 169, 170, 250

Blagg. Charles (woodsman), 16
Bloomfield. Mr (gamekeeper), 127
Blyth, Notts. 67
Bodley. George Frederick (architect), 35
Boer War, 99, 101
Bond. Charles (valet), 191,212
Boot. Charles of Thornbridge Hall,
    Ashford-in-the-Water, Derbyshire, 215
Boots (chemists), 239
Bothamsall, Notts., 5, 6, 64, 77, 87, 123, 185, 219, 246,
    249
Bourne H.S. (school teacher), 152
Bowler. Sergeant Major, 126
Boyton, Wiltshire, 241,242
Brinsley, Notts. 56, 70, 77, 85, 87, 249
Bradford. Earl of, 164
Bristol Wagon Works, 50
Brocklesby Park, Lincolnshire, 16, 104
Brookfield. George (house steward), 164
Brookwood Cemetery, nr. Woking, 114
Brown. Sydney (estate worker), 212
Buchanan Castle, Stirlingshire, 79
Budby, Notts. 68
Burden. James (Sacristan and cook), 191, 196
Burmuda (King's Palace), 19
Burnham Beeches, Buckinghamshire, 70
Burton. Baroness, 92
Campbell. Colin George, 70
Campbell. Colonel Colin, 187
Campbell. Nigel, 187
Canadian Forestry, 150
Candy. Frances Kathleen (7th duke's mother-in-law), 65
Candy. Kathleen Florence May. See Kathleen, duchess
Candy. Major Henry Augustus (father of Kathleen,
    duchess), 42, 78, 135
Carburton, Notts., 79, 140, 146, 150, 151
Carlton Ferry, Notts., 124
Carlton-in-Lindrick, Notts., 249
Carrera (artist), 209
Castle Blayney, Co. Monaghan, 2, 38, 42, 182
Caxton (manuscripts), 19
Chamberlain. Joseph (politician), 105
Chapman. '*Little Jimmy*' of Budby Comer, 129
Charlesworth. James, 36
Checker House, Ranby, 185, 224
Cheshire Yeomanry, 224
Chesterfield, Derbyshire, 41
Chewton Mendip, Somerset, 40
Childe. Frederick Baldwin, 189
Chislehurst, Kent, 188
Churches Conservation Trust, 251
Churchill. Winston - alias '*Colonel Warden*',
    226, Appendix 3
Clarence. Duke of, 69

Clay Cross, Derbyshire 41
Claypole, Notts. 113
Cleethorpes, Lincolnshire, 104
Clerkenwell (Church of the Holy Redeemer), 35
Clinton. Rev. Henry Fiennes, 36
Clowne, Derbyshire, 117

Clumber House, 10, 59, 110, 136, 138, 164, 175, 176, 183, 184, 185, 194, 199, 201, 203, 207; Grand Dining Room, 7; Grand Hall, 18, 25, Colour Plate 2; Dining Room, 18;   Smoking Room, 19; Oak Room, 19; Yellow Drawing Room, 19; Red Drawing Room, 19; State Drawing Room, 18, 209; 'Prince of Wales' suite, 108; .Housekeeper's room, 10; Billiard Room, 19, 131; Library, 11, 207, Colour Plate 8; Duke's Study, 40, 132, 238; Muniments Room, 238; Electrical installation, 110; Terrace plantings, 122, 201; Plans to build a new house, 204; Ice House Hill site, 205, 212; demolition of the mansion, 205, 212

'Clumber Hymnal', 78, 196

Clumber Park (residential properties):
Apleyhead, 26, 39, 113, 123, 124, 155;   Aviaries Cottage, 32, 127, 199; Bothies, 20, 185; Budby Comer, 48, 70, 129, 154; Cabin Hill, 4, 21, 36, 70, 143, 155, 165, 186, 203;   Carburton Lodge, 58, 112, 123; Chantry (previously 'Choir Hostel'), 141, 211; Choir School, 187, 188; Clumber Cottage, 68, 127, 189, 199, 211,236; Cricket Ground Cottages, 113, 165; Garden's House, 226; Gas House Cotts., 66; Hardwick Grange, 28, 151, 152, 168, 196;   Hardwick Cottages, 198; Hardwick Workshops Cottage, 105; Manton Lodge, 58, 116, 121, 197, 199, 225; New Cottages, 121, 236; Organist's Cottage, 40; Paddocks Cottage, 20, 89, 236; Parsonage, 46, 140, 191, 196, 203, 212, 228, 244; Schoolmaster's Cottage, 116; South Lodge, 32, 58, 199; Stableyard Cottages, 196, 225; Tank Cottages, 65, 66; Trumans' Lodge, 58, 62, 108, 174, 199, 236, 237

Clumber Park (non-residential properties):
Blacksmith's Shop, 20; Boathouse, 20; Chapel (1867-1886), 11, 14; Chapel (opened 1889), 41, 44, 47,63, 66, 67, 70, 120, 121, 140, 146, 164, 172, 176, 179, 182, 187, 195, 196, 197, 199, 223; 243, 245, 249, 250, 251; Drayton Gates, 58, 25, 243;   Gasometer, 20; Glasshouses, 87, 92, 118; Gun Battery, 29, 31, 32, 42, 209; Hardwick Workshops, 4, 20, 27,66, 123, 165, 221; Hardwick Village School, 39, 139, 197; Hardwick Village Hall (also known as 'The Oratory'), 63, 78, 173, 236; Hardwick's water tower, 48; Kennels, 20, 48, 79, 99; Normanton Gates, 58, 119; Sawmills, 4, 21, 150, 165, 221; Swimming pool, 173, 188; War Memorial at Hardwick, 67, 158, 162

Clumber Park (land and water areas)
Apleyhead Wood, 154; Ash Tree Field, 79; Ash Tree Hill, 123, 203; Beech Avenue, 79; Cabin Hill Tree and Shrub Nursery, 167, 186;   Cedar Avenue, 47; Coronation Plantation, 203; Cow Pasture Field, 148, 203; Clumber Old Wood, 155; 'Duke's Last Drive' 8; Gardens and Glasshouses, 20, 24, 47, 118, 122, 148, 161, 176, 185, 226, 247; Hardwick Wood Round, 41; Ice House Hill, 71, 203; Lady Garden, 32; Lake, 150; 'Lincoln' frigate, 39, 42, 130, 209, 248; Leeping Bar Wood, 129; Lime Tree Avenue, 32, 58, 92, 107, 116 124, 148, 154, 155, 174, 184, 203, 224 ; Lincoln Stables, 11, 20; Pleasure Ground, I, 29, 30, 47, 176, 191, 243, 244; Pinetum, I; River Poulter, 117, 150; Shooting rights, 185;   South Lawns, 104, 143; Woodcock Hill, 203

Clumber Park (events and organisations):
Annual Shows (1900-1914), 96, 143, 149; Boy Scouts, Girl Guides and Brownies, 183; Clothing Clubs, 64, 149; Coal Clubs, 64; Hardwick Village activities, 64; Sick Clubs, 64, 135; Coronation festivities (1902), 101, (1937), 206; Cricket Club, 66, 67, 128, 193; Fishery Club, 129;   Football Club, 66, 129;   'Friends of Clumber', 244; Women's Institute, 191

Clumber Park (wartime-related events):
aircraft crashes, 162, 235;   air-raid shelters, 236; appointment of wardens and special constables, 212; army check points, 222; Auxiliary Fire Service, 212, 235;   'Canadian Army Barracks', 150, 225; conscription, 230; ENSA concerts, 226; First World War declared, 149; 'Ned and Flo' (of no fixed abode), 223;   'Nellie' - trench-digging tank, 226, App. 3; timber, use of, 154; preparations for war (1938), 211; R.A.O.C. Ammunition Sub-Depot, 224;   Royal Engineers, 226; prisoners of war in, 225; servicemen from the Clumber Park estate (1914-1918), 150; stableyard, 225; 'V.E.' and 'V.J.' Days celebrations, 237; Women's Land Army, 226; decision to sell the Park, 237; National Trust efforts to raise monies to purchase, 240; Local authorities involved in providing financial assistance, 240;   de-requisitioning, 245; ammunition explosion, 245

Clumber. Lord of the Manor of, 249
Clumber Spaniels, Appendix 1; Colour Plate 7
Cobb. George (farm worker), 230
Cobb. J.R. (farm bailiff), 200
Cocked Hat Plantation, Elkesley Forest, 41
Coddington, Notts. 87, 126
Cole. Christine Mary, 121
Cole. William, 121
Condon. Eliza (housekeeper), 5, 11
Connault. Duke of, 86, 89
Cook. George (head groom), 87, 95, 137
Correggio (artist), 11

'*Country Life*' 122
County Hall, West Bridgford, Nottingham, 209
Court of Claims, 206
Cowgill. Rev. ofShireoaks, 196
Cowley Fathers, 77
Cranwell. R.A.F. Station, 209
Cromwell, Nottinghamshire, 8, 36, 77, 79, 124, 134,
　144,154
Crookenden. H.T. Mr (solicitor and Trustee), 187
Crookford, Notts. 79
Crowther. Mr. J.P., 108
Cuckson. William Isaac, 6
Czar's kennels at Catchnia, 49
Dallas-Yorke. Mrs, 119
d'Arcy. Rev. Canon, 129, 179, 195
de Jersey Morris. Miss Evelyn, 127
de Tabley. Lord (George Warren), 3, 9
de Vesci. Lady, 89, 108, 244
Deepdene, Dorking, 2, 135, 181
Denby Grange, Yorkshire 108
Derbyshire and Nottinghamshire Electric Power Bill, 86
Digby, Lincolnshire, 234
Ditton Park, Surrey, 92
Dogs (various breeds), 48, 49, 99, 112, Appendix I
　See also: 'Clumber Park Kennels'
Doncaster, 16, 30, 111, 170, 184
Drayton Avenue, Notts. 69, 93
Duchess's Garden.
　See Clumber Park - 'Aviaries'
Dufferin. Lord, 95
'*Dukeries*' 5, 70, 89, 108
Duncombe. G. Mr (band leader), 134
Durer (artist), 11
Duty and Discipline Movement, 157
East Markham, Notts. 8, 68, 76, 77, 88, 107
East Retford aerodrome, 156
Easter. George (demolition foreman), 213
Eaton, nr. Retford, Notts., 79, 124
Edward VII. King, 99, 100, 105, 108, 133
Edwinstowe, Notts. 23, 58, 89, 244
Egmanton, Notts. 8, 77, 113
Elkesley, 5, 6, 8, 23, 39, 77, 79, 87, 155, 199, 249
Elliott. Arthur (Agent), 107, 123, 128, 134, 137, 161,
　177,179, 187, 189, 198
English Arboricultural Society, 70
English Opera Singers, 69
'*ENSA*' concerts, 226
Eton College, 9, 24, 86,157,177, 182, 188, 191
Farndon, Notts. 87, 123
Famham Royal, Buckinghamshire, 100
Farnsworth. George (nurseryman) 47
Favill. Charles (estate worker), 206, 228
Favill. George (estate worker), 64
Favill. Hilda Mary (parlourmaid), 211, 233
Fernhill, Windsor Forest, 51
Fernie. Robert, 164
Fersfield, Norfolk, 236

Fiennes-Clinton. Rev. Henry, 8, 36
Firbeck, Yorkshire, 68, 194
FitzWilliam. Earl, 123
Fitzwilliam. Edward. Lord, 79
Flawborough, Notts., 87, 107, 134
Foley. Lord, 6
Foljambe. Captain, 179
Forest Farm, Winkfield, 87, 103, 112, 146, 171,176,
　183, 184,230,
Forestry Commission, 238
Ffoukes. Frank (choir boy) 173
Francis and Crookenden (solicitors), 104
Frankel. Simon (jeweller), 102
Franklin and Sons of Oxford, 35
Frankish. Charles (head gardener), 247
Frogmore Mausoleum, 98
Froissart ('*Chronicles*'), 19
Gabbitas. Joseph, 104, 127, 128, 155
Gainsborough (artist), 11, 138, 207
Gainsborough. Lincolnshire, 16
Galway. Lord, 32, 41, 126
Gamston, nr. Retford, Notts. 113, 123, 219, 236
'*Gardeners' Magazine*', 122
Garside. Joseph, 23
Geldart. Rev. Ernest, 44
Genée. Adeline. Dame (ballerina), 133, 157
George V. King, 69, 124, 133, 148
George VI. King, 205
German Imperial Automobile Club, 124
Gibson. Guy (airman), 234
Gimbernat. Jean Banks, see Pelham-Clinton-Hope. Jean,
Countess of Lincoln
Girton, Notts. 87
Gladstone. William Ewart, 3, 9, 24, 11, 15, 16, 17, 88
Gleeson. Michael (head gardener), 43
Gloucestershire estate, 134
Godley and Goulding (timber merchants) 23, 154
Gordon-Stables. Doctor William, 50
Gower (manuscripts), 19
Grace. Doctor William Gilbert (cricketer), 67
Grahame. Kenneth (author), 51, 94
Gray and Davison (organ builders), 45
Greasley, Notts., 77
Great Central and Great Northern Railway Company, 85
'*Great West Road*', Notts., 37
Grimsby, 67, 104
Grove and Rufford Hounds, 114
Grove, nr. Retford, 200
Guido (artist), 11
Hamilton. Duke of, 9
Hampstead Register Office, 73
Handsworth Nurseries, nr. Sheffield, 5, 107, 113
'*Hansard*', 86
Harborows of Bond Street, London (glove makers), 206
Harding. Mr. H. (estate worker), 212
Hardwick Hall, Derbyshire, 123
Hardwick (in Clumber). Lord of the Manor of, 249

Harewood House, Yorkshire, 207
Harlaxton House, Grantham, 207
Harrington. David (estate worker), 230
Harrington. Walter (head gamekeeper), 89
Harrowlands, Dorking, Surrey, 181, 182, 186, 187
Hartenstein. Miss (Choir School matron), 141
Harwarden Castle, Flintshire, 11, 89
Harwood. George (woodsman), 16
Haslam. Joel (Agent), 5, 29, 63, 107
Hastings. Lady Aileen, 70
Hatfield Farm, nr. Worksop, 56
Hatton. Rev. J.E., 46
Haughton, Notts., 5, 69, 88,100,116,123, 169
Havelock. Violet C. (school mistress), 197, 212, 244
Hawkins. Rev. Frank, 76, 108, 128, 134,140, 152, 178, 195
Hawkins. W. (gamekeeper), 230
Hawley. Rev. E., 8
Hawton, Notts., 79
Hayward. Rev. Canon, 179
Headland. Joseph (farmer at Elkesley) 179
Heanor, 85, 87
Henry of Prussia. Prince (brother of the Kaiser), 124
Hickson. William (wine merchant), 68, 127
Hile. Constance Miss (estate resident), 165 191
Hile. Emily (postmistress) 165, 198
Hile. Philip (estate worker), 165, 230
Hile. Randolph (clerk of works) 165, 198, 204
Hile. Richard (estate resident), 165
Hine. Thomas Chambers (architect), 14
Hodsock, Notts., 249
Hogarth (artist), 138, 207
Hohler. Thomas Theobald, 24, 142
Holbein (artist), 11, 19
Holdsworth. Gilbert (estate worker), 206, 241
Holles. John. Duke of Newcastle-upon-Tyne, 125
Holme, Notts., 41, 79, 134, 144, 154
Hood. Robin, 86
Hope Diamond, 73, 102, Colour Plate 5
Hope, Anne Adele (6th duke's mother-in-law), 2, 14, 17, 18, 29
Hope. Francis. Lord. 8, See Pelham-Clinton-Hope.
Henry Francis Hope (8th Duke of Newcastle-under-Lyme)
Horne. Charles Kenneth (radio entertainer), 190
House of Lords, 14, 86
Howard. Jim (odd-job man), 191
Howard. Kelly (estate resident), 231
Hubbard. Mrs (Choir School matron), 141
Hucknall,Notts.56,87,221
Huddersfield, Yorkshire, 104
Hull. Yorkshire, 162
Huntingdon. Earl of, 70
'Illustrated London News', 10, 58
Imperial War Museum, 226
Ingham, Lincolnshire, 236
Inverlochy estate, Scotland, 211

Isitt. Frank Seymour Nelsson (solicitor), 133, 139, 187
'Jack the Ripper' 145
Jackson. Lucy Ann (housekeeper), 50, 78
Jaggs. Mrs (Choir School deputy matron.), 141
Jamal. Fikhret (harbourmaster), 242
Johnson. Albert (chauffeur), 51, 94, 148, 177
Kaye. Rev. W.K. John, 44
Kelham, Notts., 220
Kempe. Charles Eamer (stained glass windows), 44
Kenmare. Earl of Meath, 79
Kerse. James (head kennelman), 184
Kidd. Agnes (housekeeper), 78, 168, 177, 179, 184, 198
Kilnton, Surrey ('Globe and Rainbow'), 51
King. James (head keeper), 36
Kirton, near Ollerton, Notts. 4, 8, 77, 113
Kneller (artist), 11
Knight. Alderman (Newark), 145
Kunz. Charlie (pianist), 194
Landermare. Mr (chef), 89
Langwith, Notts. 85, 126
Latham (family), 6, 8
Lauder. Harry (singer), 125
Laughton-en-le-Morthen, Yorkshire, 164
Leaver. Miss (school teacher), 39
Leeson. Fred (headmaster), 151, 152, 173, 188
Leinster. Duke of, 79
Lely (artist), 11
Leverton and Brown, Worksop (builders), 189
Lilleshall Hall, Shropshire, 124
Lincoln. Bishop of, 43
Lincoln. Earl of, 88, 242, 243
Lincolnshire Yeomanry, 16
Lind. Jenny, (the 'Swedish Nightingale'), 157
Lines. George (house steward), 144, 164
Lister-Kaye. Beatrice Adeline. Lady (sister of the 7th duke), 29, 108, 134, 177, 198
Lister-Kaye. Lois (7th duke's neice). See de Vesci.
Lister-Kaye. Mr (Osberton), 88
Little Morton, Notts., 36
Liverpool. Earl of, 50
London; Park Hotel, 7; Belgrave Square, 14; St Paul's Cathedral, 30; Carlton Club, 34, 86; Croydon, 35, 36; Colonial Exhibition, 36; Westminster Abbey, 36; Houses of Parliament, 36; Natural History Museum, 36; Royal Albert Hall, 36; St. Alban's, Holbom, 43; Regent Street, 44; South Audley Street, Mayfair, 44; Grovesnor Hotel, 70; Earls Court, 70; All Saints Church, Margaret Street, 43, 44, 76, 133, 156, 178; Garrick Club, 86; St James' Club, 86; White's Club, 86; Hayes Mews, 86; 11 Hill Street, 86, 103; Natural History Museum, 103; Metropole Hotel, 103; Lincoln's Inn, 104; Berkeley House, 112, 146, 178; 183, 189; St. Paul's Cathedral, 113; Coutts Bank, 117; Westminster Cathedral, 142, 205; Strand Theatre, 157; Sotheby's, 157, 207; Savoy Fair (1917), 157; Harrods, 168, 192; Christies, 174, 207; Ealing, 188: 'Café de Paris', 188; Liberty's, 189;Victoria and Albert Museum, 207

London and Fort George Land Company ['*L.F.G.*'], 139,176, 183, 204, 238, 247
Londonderry. Marquis of, 9
Longsdale. Lord, 123
Lound Hall, Notts., 23, 41, 79, 194
Love. William J. (clerk of works), 198
Lucas. Messrs (of London), 18
Lymington, Hampshire, 242
Lyttleton. Lord, 18
Macmerry, East Lothian, 200
Madison Square Gardens, 49
Magdalen College, Cambridge, 188
Magdalen College, Oxford, 26,29, 30, 38, 43
'*Manchester Guardian*', 212
Manchester Show, 112
Mansfield, Notts., 126
Manvers. Earl, 6, 32, 63
Maplebeck, Notts. 77
Markham Moor, Notts. 93
Markham-Clinton, 8, 77, 127, 236, 249
Marshall. George Henry (solicitor), 103
Martin nr. Bawtry, 4, 16, 56
Mary. Queen, 69
Massey. W.H.. *See* Clumber House (electrical installation 1906)
Mattersey, Notts. 79
McCarthy. J. of Thames Street, Bulwell, Nottingham, 219
McLeod. Fred (head gardener), 212
Melton Mowbray, Leicestershire, 62
Merrills. George (plumber), 235, 237
Middleton. Lord, 148
Middletons G.G. of Worksop (builders), 113
Miller. John (head gardener), 5
Milton, Notts. 8, 41, 236, 250
Milton. Billy (gardener), 186
Milton. Lord, 79
Mitchell. F. (forester), 123
Montague. Lord, 92
Montague-Stuart-Wortley. Lady Mary Diana. *See*: Pelham-Clinton-Hope. Diana, duchess (second wife of the 9th duke)
Montreux, Switzerland, 135
Montrose. Duke of, 79
Morton Grange, Notts., 36
Morton Hill Farm, Notts., 23
Murillo (artist), 11
Murray-Walker. Major Kenneth (agent). 190, 196, 211,241
Muskham, Notts. 113, 134, 154
National Insurance, 115, 135
National Telephone Company, 68
National Trust, 33, 240, 242, 244, 247, 251, 252
'*Ned and Flo*', 223
'*Nellie*' - trench-digging tank, 227, Appendix 3
Neumann. Stefan, 190

Newark, 5, 32, 34, 37, 41, 79, 87, 88, 105, 107, 113, 115,123,126,144,145,154,174, 176, 183, 244, 248, 249
'*Newark Advertiser*', 6
Norfolk. Duke of, 5, 6, 56, 85, 100
Normanton (including the Normanton Inn), 5, 6, 36, 37, 70,79,87, 93,119, 126, 146, 151, 158, 226, 235
Norton Hall, nr. Sheffield, 128

Nottingham, 5, 32, 70, 87, 115, 148, 154, 174, 176, 183, 184, 188; Castle Museum, 11; Basford Garden, 70; Haydn Road, 85; Dob Park, Basford, 85; Theatre Royal, 100; Assizes (1904), 103; Nottingham Castle, 197, 207; Nottingham Park, 70, 100, 113, 146, 222
Nottinghamshire County Council, 173, 209, 240, 245
Oakham Post Office, Leicestershire, 123
Oates of Worksop (timber merchants), 23, 238, 239
Odd. William (house steward), 50, 63
Olivant. Jane (milk maid), 116
Olivier. Lord Laurence Kerr. (actor), 156, 178
Ollerton, Notts., 89, 125
Ordsall, Retford, Notts., 67
Osberton, Notts., 18, 179
Ossington, Notts., 236
Ouvrey. Frederick (solicitor), 3
Owen. Olive Muriel (formerly Shaw, née Thompson) *See* Pelham-Clinton-Hope (née Owen). Olive Muriel
Oxford University, 222
Oxmanton. Lord, 108
Padget, Mr (farm bailiff), 200
Palfrey. H. (head forester), 164, 221
'*Pall Mall Gazette*' 9
'*Pall Mall Magazine*' 99
Paris, France, 9, 38, 65
Peake. Air Commodore Sir Harald, 194, 234
Pearce. Mr P.H. (National Trust Agent), 242
Peel. Sir Robert, 9

Pelham-Clinton. Thomas (**3rd Duke** of Newcastle-under- Lyme), 167

Pelham-Clinton. Henry Pelham Fiennes (**4th Duke** of Newcastle-under-Lyme), 32, 45, 88, 125,157, 229, 250
Pelham-Clinton (née Mundy) Georgiana, (duchess of the 4th duke), 84, 249
Pelham-Clinton. Lady Charlotte., 6, 8, 32, 36
Pelham-Clinton. Lord Charles., 8
Pelham-Clinton. Lord Thomas., 8
Pelham-Clinton. Lady Georgiana., 32
Pelham-Clinton. Lady Anna-Maria, 251
Pelham-Clinton. Henry Pelham Fiennes (5th Duke of Newcastle-under-Lyme), 34, 99,126,146
Pelham-Clinton. Lord Arthur, 177
Pelham-Clinton. Lord Albert., 8, 11
Pelham-Clinton. Lord Edward., 8, 12, 18, 24, 29, 32, 98, 114

Pelham-Clinton. Lady Susan, (sister of the 6th duke), 24

Pelham-Clinton, Henry Pelham Alexander (**6th Duke** of Newcastle-under-Lyme); financial problems, 2; death, 7; funeral, 8; shares in '*Ascot Hotel and Stable Co*' 175
Pelham-Clinton-Hope (née Hope). Henrietta Adele, duchess (wife of the 6th Duke of Newcastle-under-
    Lyme) 2, 9, 29, 73, 86 142
Pelham-Clinton Lady Florence., 31, 142, 177, 198

Pelham-Clinton, Henry Pelham Archibald Douglas
(**7th Duke** of Newcastle-under-Lyme), 8, 135, 159; aspects of his early years, 2, 13; letter to Mr Gladstone (1879), 12; leg amputation, 13; education, 24, 29; coming of age, 29, 31; presentation of loyal addresses, 33, Colour Plate 4; photographer, 38; marriage, 42; honeymoon at Pau, 44; purchase of the '*Bohemia*' caravan, 50; titles and appointments, 76; President of the English Church Union, 77; affairs of various parishes, 77; visits to USA and Canada, 77, 92, 112; robbed by his solicitor, 103; purchase of Forest Farm, 103; motor cars, 117; Silver Wedding (1914), 144, Colour Plate 6; death, burial and tributes, 178, 179; probate, 183;

Pelham-Clinton (née Candy). Kathleen, Duchess (wife of the 7th Duke of Newcastle-under-Lyme), 38, 48, 157, 168, 172, 195

Pelham-Clinton. Edward 'Ted' Charles (**10th Duke** of Newcastle-under-Lyme), 229, 242

Pelham-Clinton-Hope. Henry Francis Hope (**8th Duke** of Newcastle-under-Lyme), 31, 43, 135, 177, 181; financial problems, 73, 102, 175; first marriage (1894), 73; divorce (1902), 73, 114; shooting accident (1901), 74; foot amputation, 74; sale of heirlooms, 134, 157; death, 228; burial in Surrey, 228
Pelham-Clinton-Hope (née Yohé), Mary Augustus
    (1st wife of the 8th duke), 73, 182
Pelham-Clinton-Hope (née Owen). Olive Muriel,
    (2nd wife of the 8th duke),, 114, 134, 182
Pelham-Clinton-Hope. Lady Doria, Lots., 114, 135, 168,
    177, 189,228,229
Pelham-Clinton-Hope. Lady Mary Hope, 114, 135, 168,
    177, 190

Pelham-Clinton-Hope. Henry Edward Hugh (**9th Duke** of Newcastle-under-Lyme), 135, 177; birth, 114; education, 188; Clumber Cottage modernised for his use, 189; first marriage, 190; made his home in the Parsonage at Clumber, 191; cricketing interests, 191; travelled to America, 194; breakdown of first marriage, 205; attended the 1937 Coronation, 205; a s musician at the coronation festivities in Clumber Park, 206; preparations for war (1938), 211; divorce proceedings (1939), 221; inherited ducal title whilst on RAF duties

in the Middle East, 228; other wartime postings, 234; D. Day activities, 235; awarded O.B.E., 235; move to Wiltshire, 241; second marriage, 241; return visit to Clumber Park, 252; moved to Rhodesia, 241; second divorce, 242; third marriage and move to Jamaica, 242; third divorce, 242; death, 242
Pelham-Clinton-Hope. Jean Banks, Countess of Lincoln (1st wife of the 9th duke), 190, 201, 205, 221
Pelham-Clinton-Hope. Mary Diana, duchess, (2nd wife of the 9th Duke of Newcastle-under-Lyme), 234, 241, 252
Pelham-Clinton-Hope. Lady Patricia, 241
Pelham-Clinton-Hope. Lady Kathleen, 241
Pelham-Clinton-Hope. Sally, duchess (3rd wife of the 9th duke), 242
Philips. George (landlord), 104
Pike. Jack (choir boy), 187
Pike. Leslie Rupert (organist and choirmaster), 152, 197, 244
Pilgrim Trust, 239
Pioneer Corps., 225
Pointer. Harry of Norwich (demolition firm), 213
Pole. Reginald (estate worker), 230
Portland. Duke of, 6, 16, 46, 63, 93, 108, 121, 149, 179
Posting Proprietors Association, 58, 59, 144
Poussin (artist), 11
Pratchett. Billy (chauffeur), 184
Prentice Mr (house steward), 8
Pressley. Henry, (band leader) 29
Primrose League, 123
Pringle. William (farmer), 200, 212
Prisoner of War Camps (Second World War), 225
Pugh. Bruce (gardener), 247
Rainbow. Miss E. (organist), 152
Ranby, Notts., 4, 6, 8, 32, 36, 56, 71, 79, 87, 101, 104, 113, 135, 156,167
Read. Arthur (steamroller driver), 64
Read. Charles (chauffeur), 191, 201
Read. George (estate worker), 230
Read. John (estate worker), 108, 155
Rembrandt (artist), 138
Retford, 11, 16, 24, 32, 36, 42, 58, 79, 88, 89, 103, 104, 113,123, 126, 135, 138, 148
'*Retford, Worksop and Gainsborough Times*', 8, 9, 93
Reynolds (artist), 11
Ricketts. Kathleen Beatrice, 74
Rigby. T. (under gardener), 118
Roberts Doctor (organist ofMagdalen College, Oxford), 45
Robertson. Margaret Miss (housekeeper), 191
Robinson. Sir John Daniel, 56, 134
Roseveare. Canon. *See* Society of the Sacred Mission
Rosse. Earl of, 139,244,251
Rossmore Park, Co. Monaghan, 38, 172
Rossmore. Baron, 42
Rossmore. Lady, 104, 135
Rothschild. Baron Alfred, 86

'*Round the Horne*' radio programme, 190
Royal Army Ordnance Corps., 224
Royal Artillery Band, 63, 89
Royal Automobile Club, 124
Royal Engineers, 226
Royal Flying Corps., 156
Royal Horticultural Society, 198
Royal Scottish Arboricultural Society, 70, 73, 95, 124
Rubens (artist), 11
Rufford, Notts., 68, 105, 123, 125, 207
Rungay. J.W. (electrician), 113
Ruston Bucyrus of Lincoln, 226
Rutland. Duke of, 5
Rutlandshire, 42
Ruysdael (artist), 11
Salisbury Plain, 66, 126
Salmon. Elizabeth (head teacher), 39
Salmon. George (blacksmith), 70
Sandbeck Park, Yorkshire, 6, 123
Sault Ste. Michigan, 86
Saville. Lord, 105
Scarbrough. Lord, 6
Schmidt. Anna Karolina, 65
Schmidt. Rudolph, 65, 67, 128, 150, 161
Serlby, Notts.32,41, 126
Shafton (north of Barnsley), 16
Shakespeare (manuscripts), 19
Shaw. Reuben and Sons., Worksop, 29
Sheffield, 11, 16, 23, 93, 138, 157, 184, 221; trams, 104; Inland Revenue Office, 118; John Brown and Thomas Firth steelworks, 128; Grand Hotel, 128; Hippodrome, 128; Norfolk and Atlas cricketers, 133; Osterley Park, 188; Parson Cross, 219
Sherwood Forest, Notts. 86, 155
Sherwood Foresters Regiment, 66, 121, 143
Sherwood Rangers Yeomanry, 6, 42, 66, 70, 101, 125, 126
Shireoaks, 6, 8, 30, 56, 77, 87, 144, 162, 196, 244
Shireoaks Hall Farm.
    See Clumber Park - Normanton Gates
Shockerwick, Somerset, 242
Shrewsbury. Earl of, 100
Simpson. Arthur (estate worker), 230
Sissons. Frank and Ralph (estate resident), 231, 244
Sissons. George Pagdin (carter), 169
Sissons. Ron and Veronica, 231
Skinner. W. (under gardener), 118
Slade. Charles (head gardener), 89, 92
Slodden. Rev. Henry T., 25, 46, 129
Smith Richard. See Schmidt. Rudolph
Smith. Major Frank R. M.B.E., 67
Smith. T. (under gardener), 118
Smithsonian Museum, Washington, 103
Society of the Sacred Mission, 220
Society for the Maintenance of the Faith, 182
Somerby, Leicestershire, 42, 65
South Clifton, Notts., 87

South Scarle, Notts., 87
Southampton. Earl of, 203
Southwell Diocesan Rescue & Preventative Work, 174
Southwell. Bishop (and Minster) of, 35, 44, 75, 123, 244,251
Spencer's. Henry of Retford (auctioneers), 218
St. Cuthbert's College, Worksop. *See* Worksop College
Stableforth. Charles John, (personal agent), 252
Stanhope. Ada (laundry maid), 226
Stanhope. Barratt (joiner), 164, 212, 228, 241, 244
Stanhope. William (clerk of works), 29, 70, 71, 134, 164
Stanhope Sydney, 164, 166
Steetley, nr. Worksop, 6, 18, 44
Stewart. Marquis of, 79
Stokes. Fred (farm bailiff), 29
Storr. John (of Upper Morton Grange), 158
Storrs. Harold (Leading Fireman), 212
Storrs. Janet (nurserymaid), 211, 232
Straw. Willam (grocer), 32, 33, 106
Sutherland. Duke of, 124
Sutton-on-Trent, Notts., 41
Sweeting. Isaac (clerk of works), 5, 8
Swinderby, Lincolnshire, 236
Sysonby Lodge, nr. Melton Mowbray, Leics., 112
Tarr's House. *See* Clumber Park - South Lodge
Taylor. William (head gardener), 199
Teck. Duke and Duchess of, 69
Teniers (artist), 11
Thomas Barlow and Co. Nottingham (builders), 141
Thompson J.M. (of Kirton Hall), 113
Thompson. Cornelius (Rev), 4
Thompson. George (estate worker), 8, 145, 212
Thompson. John (of Tank Cottage, Clumber), 4
Thoresby, Notts., 6, 11, 32, 63, 67, 125, 143, 151, 155, 225
Thornbridge Hall, Ashford-in-the-Water, Derbyshire, 215
Tideswell. Cyril and Norman (estate workers), 230, 231
Titian (artist), 11
'*Toad of Toad Hall*', 51, 94
Tomlinson and Smith's (timber merchants), 238
Tomlinson. Wilson (Head Forester) 69, 123, 134; birth and baptism, 4; arrival at Clumber, 1,16; family events 16, 69, 108, 123; leisuretime activities, 23, 36; holiday in Germany (1895), 73; holiday in Ireland (1900), 95; holiday in Scotland (1913), 124; retirement and death 158,161
Tomlinsons of West Stockwith (boat builders), 130
Tranker Wood, nr. Shireoaks, 16
Trayner. John, (National Trust Agent), 244
Tredaway. George J. (headmaster, organist and choirmaster), 40, 68, 78, 128, 134, 140, 151
Trinity Hall, Cambridge, 182
Turfit. Winifred Miss (teacher), 197
Tuxford, Notts., 5, 9, 33, 41, 79, 87, 113, 123, 149, 161
Tweesdale. Marquis of, 199

University of Nottingham, 38
Van der Elst. Violet. Mrs, 207
Van Dyck (artist), 11, 19
Van Dyk. Peter, J. (gardener), 247
Vandermeulen (artist), 11
Van-Vos (artist), 11
Victoria. Queen, 3, 24, 32, 78, 98
Wade-Palmer. Lieutenant, 126
Waifs and Strays Society, 46, 144, 182
Wales. Prince of, 16, 24, 43, 125
Walesby, Notts., 68, 107, 113
Walkeringham, Notts., 219
Ward. Walter F.B. (kev), 46
Warwick and Richardson (brewers), 131
Wath-on-Dearne, Yorkshire, 188
Watson. Sir Henry (solicitor), 56
Weeks. Reginald (chauffeur), 211
Welbeck, Notts., 6, 11, 16, 24, 46, 63, 67, 89, 93, 101, 104, 105, 108, 111,112, 119, 121,124,125,138, 143, 148, 151, 174, 179
Welfit. Colonel, 126
Wellow, Notts., 154
Welsh Ponies, 112, 152, 153
Wentworth House, Yorkshire, 123
West Drayton, Notts., 77
West Markham, Notts., 8, 250
Westenra. Major and the Hon. Mrs, 156
Westenra. Hon. Peter Craven., 135
Westmacott (sculptor), 207, 250, 251
Wharncliffe. Earl of, 234
Whatley Hill and Co. (advisors to the 'L.F.G.'), 239
Wheatley, Notts., 68
Wheeler. Calvert (architect), 119
Whitaker. Benjamin Ingham, 56
'*White Rabbit No. 6*'
    See '*Nellie*' - trench-digging tank
Whitehead. Miss (Choir School matron), 141
Whitehouse. Major T., 226
Whitwell, Derbyshire, 18, 68, 117, 224
Wigan Coal and Iron Company, 85, 116
Wilde. Oscar (author), 43
Wilkinson. William (farm bailiff), 5
Williams. Mr, A.G. (Agent), 11
Williams. Lieutenant A.G., 101
'*Wind in the Willows*' 51
Windsor, Berkshire, 70, 98
Wingell. William (estate worker), 64

Winkfield, nr. Windsor, 42, 51
Winks. David (butcher), 32, 33
Winks. Florence, 33
Winthorpe, Notts., 87, 154
Woburn, Bedfordshire, 123, 165
Wollaton Hall, Nottingham, 148
Women, land workers, 151
Womersley, Yorkshire, 108
Woodard Foundation, 75
Woodhouse Rev. G.L., 196
Woolley, Derbyshire, 92

Worksop, 11, 32, 36, 42, 44, 58, 62, 67, 69, 87, 89, 105, 107, 115, 126, 138, 144, 174, 175, 176, 212, 237, 244, 247: Ashley House School, 67; Beard's Dam, 23; Biyth Grove, 33; Brass Band, 29, 33; Buslings, 29; Carlton House, 16; Clam Cat Farm, 116; Cattle Market Hotel, 126; Claylands, Worksop, 56; Cooperative Stores, 223; County Ball, 23; Court, 16; Forest, 113: Gaiety Picturedrome, 132; Gateford, 56, 249; Gateford Villa, 93; Greyhound Hotel, 59; Golf Club, 162, 175; Haggonfields, 56; King William public house, 223; Labour Exchange, 215; Lion Hotel, 79, 104, 123; Lord of the Manor title, 71, 100, 206, 249; Manor Park Lodge 56; Manton, 4, 9, 79, 249; Manton Colliery, 85, 104, 116, 134, 154, 204, 205; Manton Forest, 123; Manton Wood, 23, 113, 225; Park Cottage, 56; Park House, 78; Park Street, 107, 238; Plain Piece, 6, 126; Police, 68; Priors Well Brewery, 16; Priory, 4, 8, 23, 25, 30, 46, 68, 76, 101, 108, 121, 141, 144, 162, 179, 195, 196, 197, 223; Priory Gatehouse, 71; RAF Station, 236; Regal Cinema, 212; Royal Hotel, 23, 30; Silver Band, 174; Slack Walk, 56; Sparken, 4, 5, 85, 93, ll6, 189; St. Anne's Church, 134, 197, 223; St. Cuthbert's College: *See* '*Worksop College*': St. Mary's Church 179; Windmill Lane, 124; '*Worksop Glove*' 100, 133, 206
Worksop College, 120, 140, 141, 167, 188, 191, 220, 239,246
'*Worksop Guardian*' 67, 93, 212
Worksop Manor, 5, 6, 16, 23, 35, 56, 87, 100, 119, 124, 134, 138, 143, 179
Wortley Hall, South Yorkshire, 234
Yohé. Mary Augustus
    See Pelham-Clinton-Hope, Mary Augustus